Note

THE chapters in this book are essays rather than theses, and they are intended therefore rather to stimulate thought than to satisfy a quest for complete information. Everything almost in its subject matter is controversial and the authorities rarely agree with one another. The reader will therefore not expect to find more than a point of view and will need to go to other writers for confirmation or disagreement on many matters. The author would have preferred to spend ten years upon a longer History in many volumes, but as that does not seem possible a shorter work may have at least a temporary value.

Among books which can be mentioned as illustrating special points are Westermarck's *History of Human Marriage,* Crawley's *The Mystic Rose,* Lowie's *Primitive Society,* and a host of other anthropological text books, for the life of primitive women. For the effect of Christianity upon women as well as for a great deal of interesting matter on women in Greece and Rome, James Donaldson's *Woman, Her Position and Influence in Ancient Greece and Rome and among the Early Christians,* is invaluable and has been used constantly by the author. *Taboo and Genetics* by Knight, Peters and Blanchard is excellent for a general survey of women throughout the ages and for its treatment of the problems of human relations from the point of view of biology, ethnology and psychology. The Ancren Riule which has been used to illustrate mediæval Christianity and the ideal of virginity has been modernized beautifully by James Morton and published in the Mediæval Library. The best book, though it does not convince everybody, on witchcraft is undoubtedly Margaret Alice Murray's *The Witch-Cult in Western Europe*. Useful information for a later period will be found in W. Lyon Blease's *Emancipation of English Women* and a host of other books. Since the present work was written Briffault's important and erudite *The Mothers* has appeared and can be consulted with advantage; it puts the case for the matriarchy, in a sane sense of the word, with great force, and should therefore be read to supplement what is said on the subject in Chapter II.

Beyond the works mentioned here the author is indebted to various friends for help and criticisms, and to his wife for much cooperation.

JOHN LANGDON-DAVIES

San Feliu de Guixols,
Provincia de Gerona,
Spain. JULY, 1927.

Contents

II. Women in Primitive Society: The Birth of Fear and Contempt

treatment. § 5. The two periods when a woman is most likely to be dangerous to a man are, according to savage belief, at menstruation and on her marriage day: examples of this fear. § 6. Why does the history of mankind begin with strained sex relations? We must remember that even with these facts the life of a primitive woman had its advantages: she had interesting work to do and—§ 7.—she was always certain of marriage and maternity, that is of exercising her natural functions. § 8. But superstitious dread destroyed part of these advantages by imposing on women restraints and a division of labour which became unfair and burdensome. § 9. Women were excluded from religion in early savage society and this degraded and stunted them. § 10. Can we explain this terror of women which led to these important effects on their history? The fear of blood is largely the cause of the fear of women. § 11. But women are not only dangerous, they have a valuable monopoly, that of fertility: when men prized fertility more than they feared contact with women, they began to exalt and worship them. § 12. Especially in certain agricultural communities women, as the owners of the *mana* which makes all nature fertile, were able to rise above the primitive fear and to attain to power. § 13. It is quite false to suppose that polygamy necessarily debases women. § 14. Stendhal's classification of love and the facts of primitive existence: and a pleasant digression.

§ 1. Out of primitive communities such as those studied here came the first great empires of the east, of Asia Minor, of Egypt, of Babylon: here we find great mothergods implying a worship of fertility and a high position of women. § 2. In these circumstances there grew up such legal codes, as that of Hammurabi, in which women were very well treated, and similarly in ancient Egypt there are indications of an exalted status for women. § 3. Out of these came ancient Greece, where once more women were degraded. In Athens women were slaves in a slave state, and

Athenian drama, especially that of Euripides, proves this.
§ 4. This was largely due to the birth of reason and the rise
of philosophy as a characteristically male interest. Women
were no longer the only repositories of fertility, for men
transferred their reverence to the creations of their own
minds. § 5. In Sparta women were subjected to a eugenic
ideal and to the reproduction of soldiers and servants of the
state. The speech of Medea summarizes the position of
women in Greece. §. 6. In Roman history, on the other
hand, we see women gradually rising to great freedom
through the evolution of their legal position. § 7. The Roman matron was often able to develop great character—
Cornelia, the mother of the Gracchi; the women around
Julius Cæsar; the two Agrippinas. § 8. Was the freedom of
women in any way responsible for the alleged licentiousness
of the Roman empire? Was the Roman empire really so
licentious as we think? The stoics and Musonius. § 9. Some
conclusions.

IV.   WOMEN AND THE EARLY CHRISTIAN CHURCH   196

§ 1. Pan, the genial god, and how he is said to have died at
the moment when our era began. § 2. How Christianity accepted from the desert the primitive fear and contempt for
women. The Old Testament codified these and determined
thereby the degradation of women. § 3. St. Paul's spirit was
the same. § 4. At first a struggle took place between the existing religions and the new Pauline Christianity and on the
one side there were the ascetics pouring contempt on marriage and all sexual life. § 5. On the other side were the degenerate survivals of fertility religions, and especially the
Gnostics. These preached varying doctrines, all of them
tending to debauchery. § 6. The opinions of the church fathers as to women, love, marriage, maternity and the life of
the body. § 7. What was the effect of these stern doctrines
on women? A contrast between pagan Roman Law and
Canon Law.

V.   THE MIDDLE AGES: THE WITCH, THE VIRGIN
AND THE CHATELAINE   240

§ 1. We must now watch the effect of Romano-Christian
civilization and its outlook on women when it mingled with

A SHORT HISTORY OF WOMEN

Introduction

§ 1. THIS short study of a great subject should have been called "an analysis of the 'Female Character,'" but that title would have risked the very misconception which above all others a writer about women desires to avoid. Many readers would have suspected that it introduced yet another of those impertinent subjective books in which a W. L. George, or a Ludovici, or an Otto Weininger attempts to show his personal insight into the monstrosity he calls "Woman" or his personal success with the second-rate individuals he seems to regard as typical women.

In this literature of impertinence we find more knowingness than knowledge and more egoism and vanity than reason and thoughtfulness: for its writers see themselves as the norm of intelligent humanity, free from the vagaries of irrational conduct and needing no explanation; capable then of interpreting the contradictions and inconsequences of the other sex. We do not, however, find much help in their accounts of their own emotional experiences and we find less knowledge still of biology or history.

But there is a strict sense in which this little book can claim to be an objective analysis of the "Female Character." It tries to explain the forces and the elements which combined to produce the myth of a Female Character which so obsessed our immediate ancestors that even in our own day it is still hard for the average man, and woman also, to see the flesh and blood real individuals, who happen to be women, free from all preconceptions as to what they ought to be as feminine females.

The Female Character reached its maturity as a concept or a category by the end of the eighteenth century; and it is our object to trace it from its beginnings to the moment of that maturity, and then to leave it to the withering blast of Mary Wollstonecraft and the movement of emancipation which she founded. The book will end almost where most studies of women begin; where women, educated, thoughtful and indignant, revolted and tore in shreds the absurd myth which had hitherto disguised their humanity: but that story has been told so well and so often that there is nothing new about it.

What then is this Female Character? Let the reader turn to the last pages of the sixth chapter and read the extracts from Dr. Gregory's manual and consider the character of that great woman, Hannah More; he will be able to answer this question. Let him then consider the hairy ape, or even any other mammalian, dumb and deliberate in its loves and maternities, created male and female, marrying and taking in marriage, begetting and conceiving, requiring neither advice nor instruction in the treatment of its spouse or its children; understanding and accepting the opposite sex without hallucination or obsession or emotional conflict. By what succession of maladies of the mind did one animal, man, proceed from this to the pathology of Dr. Gregory and of Hannah More? How did the female animal dwindle and deviate into the female character? If this question seems important or interesting to him, he may find some little entertainment in the chapters of this book.

Further than this the reader may have suffered at the hands of certain apostles of the "new women," who try to prove that the new woman is a very old woman indeed, who gave them a bad time and played the tyrant in the good old days of the matriarchat. No more stupid and inconsequent theory has ever been poured into the vacant minds of an avid public than this. The mythical matriarchy must be consigned to oblivion before any woman can hope to think intelligently of her past or her future. It is indeed too true that the propagandists of progress, seduced by the badness of their opponents' arguments, have often been unscientific, devoid of historical sense, and, in short, grossly ignorant in their judgments of the past or of the facts of nature. Now, since no woman can understand the movement of emancipation of which she is a part without discarding the rubbish from the literature of feminism, this book may claim another interest beyond that of ancient history, if it can help to focus current feminist thought by giving a historic perspective to the living present.

Moreover, a history of women, however short, must begin by interpreting, not women to men, nor men to women, but the difference between them: it must be rooted in biology. We expect from history a light upon our own problems;

dead men and dead women are chiefly of interest in so far as they are able to enlighten the living ones; and in order that they may do this we must view them with a reasonable knowledge of the extent to which their mistakes were due to ignorance about themselves as living animals. In order to know what a man or a woman is in reality, it is not sufficient to be one or other of them.

This then is the justification of our starting our analysis with biology, although with the close of the chapter, it is true, these facts disappear, never again to return amid the mass of chaotic prejudice, humbug and compromise which is history. Not once in the whole vast pageant is mankind burdened with a scientific fact; not once is the reign of mythology effectively challenged by women or on their behalf; nevertheless these partial explanations, these guesses at the mechanics of existence, may be held in the mind's eye as a gauge of the ignorance and an indication of the perversity with which humanity has crowned its progress from the ape to the goose; and a possible guide to the further progress, of which some think it capable, from the goose to the wise old owl.

§ 2. THAT in brief is the scope of our study; we shall see that the history of women is built upon a series of fictions, polite and otherwise, invented to explain differences between men and women which were as mysterious as they were obvious; and it is not so much the real differences which have shaped that history as the ideas which have been held about them. To understand the past, we must know our biology and then we must know the false ideas which have taken the place of the true facts and forced us from the female animal to the female character.

As to these false ideas, here is a brief catalogue of them: Sex is a pervading force, dividing the universe into two parts, mysterious, dangerous, powerful. Women are physically weaker, mentally less active than men; they are more wayward and more changeable in temperament; nor can anyone hope to understand them nor please them for long. As they are infinitely desirable to man, so they are infinitely dangerous to him. Made for maternity, they are by nature unsuited to work save in the home and the nursery. They have different mental processes; incapable of reasoning, they make up the deficiency by a special intuitiveness. Man is man, but woman god or devil.—Out of these bricks has been built the history of women, and particularly out of two contradictions, one physical and the other psychological: women are weak, but they have the supreme strength of being the unique producers of children; women are dangerous and therefore to be avoided, segregated, caged and ill-used, but they are powerful because desirable beyond all else to every man. According as these two contradictions have been resolved in one way or another, so women have been exalted or depressed in social life.

From time to time, as we shall see, men have associated two or more of these ideas together in their minds, and the combination has dictated for a period their outlook on

women. For example, there is the idea of women as being
infinitely desirable and of their being the fertile means of
producing offspring: in certain periods of history we find
these ideas absolutely associated in such a way that it is
impossible to think of them apart. To the early Christian,
to Catholics today, to many others, physical sexual pleasure
and reproduction are indissoluble; one without the other is
at least wicked, if not impossible. To the Australian native
there is no connection whatever between the two; the sexual
act is not associated with conception and child-birth. Again,
in all civilized countries today the natural association between the two has been entirely obviated by knowledge of
neo-Malthusian practices and devices. It is obvious that
these three periods will each have its different morals, its
different idea of the relationship between the sexes, its different social outlook on women as a sex.

It would be possible, as Remy de Gourmont suggested, to
write a history of women, or any other history, based upon
the association or disassociation of ideas; to watch how
these changes changed history, and to enquire the cause also
of the changes themselves. History is the evolution of ideas
and of new combinations of ideas. The key to the history of
women, as we have said, is to be found along these lines; if
we want to know why a Greek woman had a different life
from an English woman of this century, we shall find the
solution in the fact that the Greeks tended to combine in-
dissolubly the idea of a woman with the idea of reproduction
and also to separate absolutely the idea of reproduction and

that of physical pleasure. Again, the idea of love and the idea of physical pleasure are sometimes combined, sometimes separated, and in either case the history of women is changed.

For ourselves, the children of one age, and often of one social milieu, it is difficult to appreciate that ages have rolled by, during which what seems entirely obvious and necessary and true to us has not so seemed; yet, until we acknowledge this, we are not able to tell what can be changed and what cannot, of all the many things which are not altogether satisfactory about us.

To study the past history of women is the best way to avoid taking for necessary what merely happens to be for the moment, and to label as unnatural what merely happens to run counter to the accepted ideas of our limited time and place. Moreover, from these changing ideas arise certain general principles which will be seen to govern the happiness and unhappiness of every age: the happiness of women in historical periods is dependent not in the least upon what king was on the throne, or what commercial prosperity produced, but upon what interests and ideals occupied men's minds.

§ 3. CERTAIN ideas have always been present in men's minds, but at one time or another have shown an increased or decreased activity, fluctuating from the point of being dormant to the point of being obsessions. And of these ideas some are always destructive of women's happiness, even though, as is often the case, women have done their best to encourage them.

Perhaps no human idea has destroyed the happiness of so many women as that of military glory. We can lay it down as an almost universal rule that the more warfare has been regarded in any society as the highest form of male activity, the more the position of women has been degraded in that society. It has, indeed, been well said that the degradation of women has been the enslavement of the forces of life by the forces of death: and yet woman, the life-giver, has invariably been willing to assist and encourage that which destroys her fruit; woman, the fertile field, has smiled while watching her own crops laid waste by the flail of destruction.

The author remembers a conversation which happened to him during the first weeks he spent upon American soil; a woman was talking of war and said: "That is what comes of a man-made world, women would have altered that." To which he replied that war fever and recent experiences in Europe hardly suggested that there was much to choose between the sexes; that behind most young men whose bones were now rotting in France was the finger of some young thoughtless woman pointing to the recruiting station or the mobilization centre with the light of battle in her eyes. The reply was startling: "You have come to a country now where women are respected and you had best not speak in that way here in America."

History shows without any possibility of contradiction,

however, that war is a woman's curse and yet invariably receives her blessing. In primitive society the warlike peoples ill-treat or degrade their women, who do not see that the iron chains which bind them are not wreaths of roses. "As the women have so decided a preference for the men whose bravery and deeds of arms are notorious, it readily accounts for the mass of the populace being addicted to war," writes an authority on the head-hunting natives of Borneo, adding: "It may even be doubted whether Europeans might not be found who would take the heads of their dead enemies to gain the smiles and embraces of beauty." The price paid for the savage equivalent of a uniform is hard labour for life, which is "always the case where the men spend so much time on the war path, and as the women keep the men up to the mark in this respect, they are scarcely to be pitied if extra work falls to their lot."

War destroys women in four ways; first, it makes them likely to be starved or killed by the ill-success of their men; second, it increases the chances of slavery a hundred-fold; third, it makes women industrial drudges by withdrawing the men from productive labour; fourth, and more subtle than all the others, it glorifies death as an end in itself and robs life-giving genius, that is woman's natural genius, of its legitimate appreciation.

But if war and military glory have lent a hand to the enslaving of women, there is another idea which has done even worse things to them, when it has been allowed to become an obsession—the idea of immortality.

Once man retires into the darkness beyond the grave and occupies himself with the future needs of his groping soul, the position of women is debased; this world becomes a Vale of Tears, the saltness of which sterilizes and kills the fields and vineyards which would otherwise have made it so green. Immortality and sterility go hand in hand; what use in a multitude of unprofitable children if the soul gives permanence to the doomed individual? What use in a name kept green if the soul will be green for ever?

And if children cease to be altogether desirable, women cease to be altogether necessary: instead of the fertile mother, they become the weaker vessel. Moreover, the works which are best suited to their genius are despised: they are the practical people, in primitive societies they foster the industries, while men foster the arts; they influence the crops and make the very ground productive. All this counts for nothing in the passage to the stars: all that women do best is a waste of time.

Once reproduction and fertility are despised, women are degraded; men wrapt up in their own souls see in them merely a temptation to linger from the really important aim in life. Women can make men desire life; what more wicked, since death is the gateway to perfection? Immortality, life in death, cannot become the constant mistress of men's thoughts unless on equal terms with sterility, death in life.

In our history of ideas we shall see that in primitive society women have many difficulties and dangers against which they have to contend. Ideas of physical sex made them despised and feared, but so long as men worshipped fertility these difficulties and dangers could always be surmounted. Women as the only givers of life were worshipped and revered. When men gave up the worship of fertility, the one anchor against the storm of sex antagonism was gone: in the first thousand years of Christianity women drifted hopelessly in a storm of horror and despair. Not until the Renaissance, the rebirth, the new discovery of the Divinity of fertility, did they begin once more to raise their head. Immortality ceased to be an obsession and old age, its stepping-stone, was discredited; youth triumphed and with it women, through whom alone can the world renew its youth.

The reader must not suppose however that it would be possible to make a neat diagram in which it could be shown that wherever there were fertility rites practised, wherever the increase of the earth seemed desirable, there women were always highly favoured: nothing in history works out so simply as this. But when we take a sweeping view of vast tracts of human history we do see that reverence for the forces of life exalts the woman who is their priestess, unless other things stand in the way. There is for example a world of difference between the attitude of the savage quoted in a later chapter, who explained that women must plant and attend to the crops since "it is only women who can cause the seed to bear fruit"; and that of St. Jerome who spoke of motherhood as "the tumefaction of the uterus, the care of yelling infants, all those fond feelings which death at last cuts short." And though all savages did not treat the women the better for their power over the crops, nor of course even believe in such a power, we cannot but see that women have more to gain in dignity and happiness from the crude ideas of the savage, than from the crude ideas of the saint. "Every woman," said Clement of Alexandria, "ought to be filled with shame at the thought that she is a woman"; if he had been filled with mistaken notions about Demeter and Persephone, about spring flowers and waving corn, about flower goddesses and corn goddesses, and women as their priestesses, he could not have felt like that about one-half of humanity.

§ 4. BUT if the worship of fertility is the outward condition of women's happiness, what is the inward condition? For happiness, as we all know from copybooks, comes from within. Let us consider for a moment Stendhal's division of love into four different types. First, there is Physical Love: "Out hunting a fresh, pretty country girl crosses your path and escapes into the woods. Everyone knows the love founded on this kind of pleasure: and all begin that way at sixteen, however parched and unhappy the character." In fact, this kind of love is the reaction upon one another of two healthy, beautiful bodies, in a state of nature. It is the attraction of "male and female created he them"; and in modern communities rare except in a debased and prostituted form, sicklied o'er with the pale cast of social convention.

Second, there is Passion Love: the opposite of the last

in that the woman for whom it is felt is not merely female, but an individual around whom in the eyes of the lover have crystallized innumerable phantasies and unconscious desires. This is the artist among lovers and of small social importance except in so far as all artists tend to claim exemption from social limits and convention.

Third, there is Gallant Love: "a picture in which everything, to the very shadows, should be rose-colour, into which may enter nothing disagreeable under any pretext whatsoever at the cost of a lapse of etiquette, of good taste, of refinement, et cetera. True love is often less refined; for that in which there is no passion and nothing unforeseen has always a store of ready wit. Passion Love carries us away in defiance of all our interests, Gallant Love manages always to respect them. True, if we take from this poor love its vanity, there is very little left: once stripped, it is like a tottering convalescent, scarcely able to drag himself along,"— in short, the love of courtiers and leisured classes in general.

Fourth, there is Vanity Love: "The vast majority of men desire and have a fashionable woman in the same way as a man gets a fine horse, as something which the luxury of a young man demands. Their vanity, more or less flattered, and more or less piqued, gives birth to transports of feelings. The happiest case of this uninspiring relationship is that in which to physical pleasure is added habit. In that case store of memories makes it resemble love a little; there is the pique of self-esteem and the sadness of being left. . . ."

To these four attitudes as described by Stendhal we must

add a fifth, Philoprogenitive Love; where a man wants a wife so as to have children and a home, to build round himself an extension as it were of his own personality, to assure for himself company in the evenings and in old age; for we can say without exaggeration that many men marry through fear of being alone in the dark, either of the night or of old age, and for the continuity of children. This kind of love is doubtless usually blended with one or other of the others—except "gallant love," which avoids the inconveniences of a household and the obligations of a family.

Now it is of great interest to consider how these five attitudes have affected the history of women by giving them or taking away from them, as the case may be, any reason for existence apart from their relationship with men. That history will also reveal the advent of each point of view, the causes of its flourishing and of its decline. For example, in primitive society Passion Love cannot exist because individualism does not exist. In Greek society the very idea of a woman "in love," that is of Passion Love between men and women, seemed disgusting; in the Middle Ages and eighteenth-century France, Gallant Love was very common, and in the earlier period fought almost single-handed, as we shall see, against the universal contempt into which women fell. Philoprogenitive Love exists of necessity everywhere, but wherever there is a leisured class Vanity Love is mixed in equal proportion with it.

If we examine history we shall find that Physical, Passion and Philoprogenitive Love tend to exalt women and increase their general chances of happiness, while Gallant Love and Vanity Love tend always in the end to destroy it. The reason is clear: these two demand idleness and leisure for their perfection and, however much women may be sought after by them, the first is too insincere and too unreal to make for happiness, while the second in the end overwhelms her with the fate of every other parasite. For work is the inward cause of happiness in women as in everyone and only when the prevailing attitude towards them deprives them of work do they become unhappy. It was not when women began to desire men's work, but when men began to usurp women's work, that feminism was born. The position of women in a modern industrial community is as pitiable in some respects as it was in the Middle Ages, and, especially in America, the danger of degeneracy from parasitism is as great as it has ever been.

Worship of fertility, then, and the right to work are the two safeguards of women's happiness: the first was temporarily destroyed by early Christianity, the second by the Industrial Revolution. Women's history is not one of steady improvement but of risings and fallings, and the highest rise comes when the two conditions we have outlined are both fulfilled.

§ 5. WORSHIP of fertility and the right to work: and to these must be added also a third necessity for women's happiness, namely, the acknowledgment that she is a rational being to precisely the same extent as a man is.

"It is no use arguing with a woman"; there does not exist a man who has not on more than one occasion said this at least to himself; and feminists would do well to recognize the essential truth of the statement while insisting upon the equal veracity of the twin-statement: "It is no use arguing with a man." It is essential to admit both that human beings are not rational and that irrationality is not a sex distinction. Yet it was not until the eighteenth century that anyone had the courage to·claim that the feminine mind is at basis the same in quality as the masculine.

"I will allow," wrote Mary Wollstonecraft, "that bodily strength seems to give a man a natural superiority over woman; and this is the only solid basis on which the superiority of the sex can be built. But I still insist, that not only the virtue but the *knowledge* of the sexes should be the same in nature, if not in degree, and that women, considered not only as moral, but *rational* creatures, ought to endeavour to acquire human virtues or perfections by the same means as men, instead of being educated like a fanciful kind of half being—one of Rousseau's wild chimeras."

Such a claim was regarded with horror by a world of men *and women* whose outlook coincided with that of Milton, when he wrote in *Paradise Lost:*

> To whom thus Eve with perfect beauty adorn'd:
> "My author and Disposer, what thou bidst
> Unargued I obey; so God ordains;
> God is thy law, thou mine: to know no more
> Is woman's happiest knowledge, and her praise."

And the claim has not been altogether accepted by all men today. Based upon primitive superstition, early Christian teaching and certain misinterpretations of natural biological differences, the belief in women's emotionality in contrast to men's rationality dies hard. Moreover, it has such obvious advantage for the lazy woman, the brainless woman, the uneducated woman,—that is, inevitably, for most women, since few of either sex escape these three categories,—that women themselves encourage and condone it. The fool likes to believe that he is a born fool, for predestination excuses what is really one's own fault.

Nevertheless, it is clear that to the worship of fertility and the right to work must be added the respect proper to a reasonable being, or else the happiness of woman remains the happiness of an animal.

§6. To trace the fluctuations which have been experienced by these three ideas will be the chief object of this brief History of Women: and therefore it will appear to lack many of the essential characters of a history, an omission which can perhaps be justified briefly.

A History of Women should consist, some readers will say, of a chronicle of important events in their emancipation. Such an event, for example, as Lady Astor's taking her seat in the British House of Commons should rank large in it; and changes in the law affecting the property of married women or the rights of motherhood are the bricks and straw of which it should be built. This is true no doubt;

but it is also true that the actual fact of Lady Astor having become a Member of Parliament is not particularly important in the history of the average woman: very few women indeed are the least likely to want the right to sit in the House of Commons; even fewer can ever hope to exercise it. The story is told, however, that when Lady Astor was seen walking in the Lobbies without a hat on her head, an indignant Conservative member approached her and begged her never to do such a thing again, as it was most unsuitable that a woman should have her head uncovered in such a place. Now, whether or not the story is true, it is far more important in the History of Women than Lady Astor's membership of the House, because it is an example of an idea which affects every woman's life daily, and has done so from the most primitive times of which we have knowledge. To trace the idea of woman's uncleanness and inferiority and its effects upon social life is the real aim of a History of Women and not the mere chronicling of exceptional and spectacular events.

Again, the history of women is a tangled skein of wool and yet many people think of it as an ordered process, which can be wound up into a ball by putting the skein over the back of a chair and keeping patient. History is never evolution; it is never tidy; it is never continuous nor unbroken. Yet many people expect it to be; in childhood they have been shown the development of an egg from the day of fertilization through all its complicated, yet orderly, unfolding until the chicken chips the shell and flutters its downy wings; and, with vague memories of this, they expect to find the history of women beginning with the primitive degradation of an Australian aborigine, evolving into higher and higher stages, until the American woman, in all her glory, breaks the shell in which all her sisters had been confined in the dark ages of the world. We shall try to destroy this fiction once and for all, and to illustrate the fluctuations, which, as we have said, have been the features of women's history in all ages.

The worship of fertility, the right to work, and respect as for a rational being: these ideas are influenced and conditioned by many factors, the past history of a given society, its economic structure, religious ideas, climate, contact with alien cultures; all of these and others like them can change and modify the position, the influence, the history, of women so that no rules or simplifications can be found to explain satisfactorily what has occurred in any particular place at any given moment. We cannot offer an evolutionary diagram, only a suggestive freehand drawing.

§ 7. Our analysis must begin with an account of primitive man; and here again we find a need for a preliminary note of explanation. To the average man a savage is just a savage and there is no distinction between one and another; in our study of the lower civilizations this attitude would tend to obscure the facts. We must realize that our higher culture is not a culmination of the evolutionary process of which primitive societies are earlier stages. By turning our eye over the peoples of the world, we are able to see a hundred different experiments in living, each one revealing a new idea of women and of their social position, and from this we are able to get some appreciation of the relativity of human nature even where we had been accustomed to expect the most absolute values.

But when we warn ourselves not to underestimate the difference between one savage and another, we must also warn ourselves not to overestimate the difference between all savages and ourselves. The importance of superstition in the dead past is that it often remains to distort reason in the living present. The position of women in America and England is not so far removed from their position in Polynesia or Madagascar as we sometimes imagine. A little allegory may assist us in recognizing this.

Some months ago a modern Gulliver, who had accumulated a small fortune as a worker in Mr. Henry Ford's factories at Detroit, set out to see the world. In the course of his travels, an account of which has never before been published, he came to a country the habits of which interested him much and surprised him not a little.

At first glance he noted with a certain natural pride that there were, in the streets and city squares, several of a type of vehicle which he knew well enough, having assisted at the birth of about two million of them; but he was immediately perturbed to see that these cars seemed in lamentable condition and that those of the inhabitants whose faces were not entirely covered with bandages wore a dejected and discouraged expression. Loyalty prevented him, of course, from attributing either the features or the bandages to his own mechanical children.

What then was his surprise when a few days of observation taught him that these people were convinced that, except when the moon was not full, the cars would not go well; that if a driver saw a magpie on the left of the road he must put oil in the gasoline tank, and gasoline in the oil tank; that a yellow dress on the footpath ahead obliged him to use only the lowest gear; that without first going through magical ceremonies, it would be impossible to crank a car; that the accelerator was a perpetual source of spiritual danger from which the driver must be insulated with still other magical ceremonies; and, finally, that a puncture was likely to be caused by a cloud in the sky above rather than by a nail in the road, and that a leaking carburetor float must be mended by reciting the seven penitential psalms.

The simple Detroiter was no longer surprised that the usual tranquil relationship between man and car was here but partial, intermittent and precarious; but since he was only a simple Detroiter he did not notice that this relationship between man and car approximated closely to that which exists in ordinary everyday life between man and woman.

Further inquiry revealed to the new Gulliver that these men among whom he found himself knew nothing at all about the mechanical nature of a car, being quite content in this respect with what they could learn from their fathers, who in their turn knew even less since they had derived their knowledge from grandfathers, whose cars were ox-wagons. The simple Detroiter did not reflect that this was precisely in accord with most men's knowledge about their wives and with most women's about their husbands: a fact which has reserved for man the doubtful dignity of being the only animal who does not get on, as a matter of course, with his mate, and, largely in consequence of this, who does not know instinctively the best way to behave towards his own offspring; who has, indeed, to be taught and coerced into a passably tolerable domesticity.

For a man who thinks, it is laughable, for one who feels, tragical, to compare the relationship of a man with his wife and that of a man with his motor car. In the second, things usually go exceedingly well: the mistakes are few; the car does what is expected of it; it arrives and departs according to known rules of conduct; and it is happy in the only sense in which an inanimate object can be happy; it is not tem-peramental and shows no sign of dissatisfaction so long as it is well and rationally treated.

Not one of these things is always true when we consider the relationship between a man and his wife. Nor is this simply because both parties have separate wills and sep-arate desires; for though the car is helped to content by its voiceless servility and would, perhaps, be fractious with a will of its own, we may suppose that in a rationally con-ceived universe the man's will and the woman's, though separate and unlike, would be two in one and one in two, complementary not contrary, and fashioned to find a different satisfaction in a single end.

No. It is because the relationship between men and women is upon lines similar to that between man and car in the country visited by this simple Detroiter. The past History of Women proves this to be so, and is explained by it.

The reader will protest that this allegory is absurd: let him read the second chapter and he will admit its relevance to savage life at least. And if he watch his neighbour in the daily course of life, perhaps he will feel that the time has not yet come when the last lowly trace of our savage origin has been erased from the concept of women in our own sophisticated community.

Chapter I

THE BIOLOGICAL BACKGROUND TO WOMEN'S HISTORY

§ 1. *What Is Sex?* A STORY is told of a little boy and a little girl looking at a picture of Adam and Eve at the London National Gallery. "Which is Adam and which Eve?" asked the boy. "I don't know," replied his sister, "but I could tell you if they had their clothes on." It is a curious fact, but true, that most people, when they think of sex differences, think of a race of beings who wear skirts, living on moderately good terms with a race of beings who wear trousers, and of a natural state of affairs wherein the former exist to solace the latter, and the latter to work for the former.

It is, however, clear that to understand the history of women we must first understand as much as possible about the meaning and use in nature of sex; we must realize that sex existed not only before trousers and skirts, but before men and women; that it is one of the most widespread phenomena in nature, complicated and infinitely variable. For we shall find that our history is based largely upon one misconception about sex after another, beginning with ideas about ribs and ending with the strange pseudoscientific aberrations of extreme feminist propagandists to-day; and, moreover, if we have imaginations and a taste for useless speculation, we may consider what sort of society it would be that began with biological fact and modelled its institutions upon chromosomes, endocrines and whatever else science could tell it instead of upon legends and emotional misinterpretations. But at least a foundation of biology will serve as a useful support to the dreams and ravings of our forefathers and of ourselves, the sum total of which make up history.

What is sex? And why is sex? We do not as yet know one-tenth the necessary facts to make more than hesitating guesses in answer to these questions. We know enough to realize that the difference between a man and a woman is by no means what one might suppose from being one or other of them; and indeed the scientific research of the last twenty years has thrown much light upon practical matters which will in time entirely alter our point of view about these differences.

In order to prepare ourselves for such a change, we must first try to see the word and the thing "sex" from the standpoint of a biologist: to think of them in a way which makes them applicable not only to men and women, but to animals, to flowers, to insects and even invisible living things, fulfilling their instincts and passions in every cubic inch of air and water: we must discover a common measure for all these manifestations which is true not only for ourselves but for everything; and it will be a useful rule to assume that the reason for two sexes in man is the same as the reason for two sexes elsewhere in nature, and that any reason suggested by man which is not the same is probably false. Thus, if we find that a female's place is always to have children, whether she be a human being, a bird, a fish, or a flea, we may assume that that is a universal tenet of femaleness. If someone says a woman should always darn a man's socks and we find in other animals that often the male darns the female's socks, metaphorically speaking at least, then we cannot agree, on these facts alone, with the universality of female darning of socks. If, as so many of the early Christian fathers seemed to think, women were "meant" to be a danger and a temptation to all godly men, we shall ask if the female spider, rabbit, butterfly, elephant, was also intended to interfere with her spouse's salvation, and, if we do not so find, we shall not admit spiritual dangerousness as an inalienable female characteristic.

Clearly, then, we need not apologize for beginning history with biology, and in so doing we shall find that the questions we wish to ask the biologist lead finally to this most important question of all: "In the world of everyday things," we shall say to him, "we find that men and women are different; their bodies are different and their minds are different; most men are physically stronger than most women; women have produced fewer writers, poets, musical composers; they are emotionally likely to react in another direction from the average man; they can almost be said to have another set of virtues and vices; *now of all*

*these differences, which are ordained in the biological na-
ture of things, and which, using the word in its widest sense,
are the result of education?"*

An answer to this problem is essential to the right interpretation of women's history; but before we are in a position to answer it we have a long way to go, for we must ask
first for a little information on the nature and meaning of
sex and of the existence of two sexes in the world of men
and women.

§ 2. *Primitive* IN the first place we may notice that sex is not
Reproduction. by any means universal; there are many animals which dispense with it altogether. To divide a species
up into male and female is not necessary for life; it is only
one of many ways by which life succeeds in continuing to
exist.

It is important to appreciate this fact, because to many
generations of human beings the existence of two sexes has
seemed an inevitable and universal law of creation: to early
man, not only were all animals created male and female, but
everything else in nature had sex, earth and heaven, sun and
moon, sea and sky, every star and stone, hill and valley. To
many people today there are two "principles" in the universe, the male and the female, and innumerable philoso-
phies and mysticisms, all with their repercussions on
women's history, have been built up around this idea.

The simplest and earliest animals, however, were neither
male nor female; they were sexless; and when they were

ready to fulfil the law of life which we call reproduction, they did so in the simplest possible manner: they split in two and each half went its own way. Now if we want to find out the use in nature of sex we can very well begin by asking ourselves why life did not go on forever forming and reforming by such a simple and adequate means as this. Can we see anything which life gained by dividing into male and female?

The answer to this question can be suggested by the behaviour of a minute animal called Copromonas, which can be found in any pond where frogs live. Copromonas is a small mass of protoplasm with a whip-like tail with which it propels itself through the water: it has a mouth with which it absorbs frogs' dung and when food is plentiful it increases in size for a time and then splits in two and becomes two separate living beings. These two old-new individuals repeat the process several times until hundreds of Copromonas exist instead of the original one animal.

But this does not go on forever: after a time the Copromonas seem to get exhausted and languid; they no longer split up, life is at a standstill, a sort of impotent old age attacks the whole colony. Now there occurs a very curious thing: instead of splitting up forever, two individuals come together and mix themselves with one another until they have become a single individual by complete union. After an interval, during which the new individual may be swallowed by a frog and brought once more into close contact with an ample food supply, it once more resumes the process of splitting up; it has become rejuvenated.

This is a most interesting fact, for it seems to show that there is a limit to the amount of splitting power such an animal can possess and when this limit is reached two individuals must unite and revivify their bodily powers by such union. The union is not a sexual union; both individuals are exactly the same as one another and they mix as completely as two drops of water on a window-pane: but it is clearly a step away from the first simple process of reproduction towards something far more complicated, and all that is needed for it to become truly sexual is for the two individuals to be unlike one another in bodily form.

When we realize that the animals of which we are speaking are formed of one single cell of protoplasm, it will be clear that such sexual differences will be very minute indeed; nevertheless, we can trace their early beginnings in one or two forms of life only a little different from Copromonas.

If you steep a cod's head in water for a very long time there will appear a miscroscopic animal called a Bodo, which behaves exactly as Copromonas, first splitting up for several generations, then growing tired or age-worn and rejuvenating itself by joining up with another individual. The two Bodos look exactly alike still, but it is noteworthy that one of them remains anchored to a piece of solid matter while the other swims about until it finds the first. Thus the behaviour of the two is different although no microscope has been able to detect any difference in form: one is quiescent and waits to be found, the other goes a-courting.

The next step is to be seen in a microscopic animal with an immense name which lives in the digestive system of a centipede. Like Bodo and Copromonas it consists of one cell; like them it can increase in numbers for a long time simply by splitting in two; but sooner or later, again like them, it needs to mingle with another individual in order to rejuvenate its failing powers. To accomplish this end it adopts a more complicated method. Some individuals grow into larger egg cells; others split into smaller sperm cells: the egg cells do not move, but have a great deal of nourishing food stored up in them; the sperm cells move about rapidly and are shaped for motion rather than for food storage. The sperm cell moves about incessantly until it finds an egg cell, when it bores its way into it. After several more steps the result of this union is a number of individuals like the earlier ones, which split and re-split until their vital force is tired, when once more they change into two different forms and repeat the process ad infinitum.

There in brief is the way in which sex seems to have come into the world: how are we to account for the facts, and what light do they throw on the meaning of sex?

First we can assume that after a time the protoplasm of one individual becomes tired and ceases to grow bigger, so that there is a limit to the number of times it can split up into new beings. Second, by some virtue, chemical or otherwise, the mingling of two individuals with one another

rejuvenates the protoplasm and enables it to grow and sub-
divide for a time at least with its original vigour. Third, we
see that quite soon in the history of such unions there appears a difference of behaviour and form between the two
uniting individuals, and that one moves about vigorously
and the other waits quietly to be found.

This last point is the most important for us because to
a large extent it explains the origin of sex differences in
early forms of life. Motion and nourishing food storage are
the two necessities for successful union; they are incompatible, just as the heaviness of a cart horse is incompatible
with the swiftness of a racehorse, and so the two animals
divide the labour between them,—one moves, the other
stores.

The different forms which this division of labour imposes
are what we call sex differences: the moving individual we
call the male, the larger, richer individual the female.

In one sentence, let us remember that division of labour
is the cause of different sex forms; the male does one thing
and is by definition therefore male; the female another and
is by definition therefore female. So long as all animals combined in themselves the ability needed to carry on and propagate life, sex did not exist: only in so far as animals
specialized, did they become male and female.

If then life had never evolved into any higher form than
these microscopical animals infesting the inside of centipedes, the answer to the question, *what is sex?* would be:
"First, it seems a rule of living matter that it cannot go on

forever growing and splitting up without becoming vitally exhausted, and this exhaustion is counteracted by the physical mingling of two individuals and the mixing of their protoplasm; and second, it is easier to bring about the satisfactory mingling of individuals if one devotes itself to storing up rich protoplasm and the other to keeping thin and moving rapidly in every direction in search of its mate."

§ 3. *Sex-cells and Other Cells.* LIFE, however, did not stop short at the microscopical animal infesting the inside of centipedes: it went further and produced incidentally the centipede itself, and after it many other forms, including man. We must therefore at this point digress from the history of that division of labour which we call sex, and consider another division of labour between living cells, the result of which has been even more important.

The animals we have considered so far are all of them single-celled animals; in them one small piece of protoplasm does all the work for each individual,—motion, digestion, sensation, reproduction, all are accomplished by one and the same cell, by the same implement which is the complete individual. Such a state of affairs did not last long.

It seems to be an invariable rule of life that living matter becomes more and more efficient exactly in so far as it specializes in the work it does. When two lowly cells happened to divide the work of food storage and motion between them, instead of both trying to move and to grow fat at once, they gave themselves a start over their competitors in the struggle for life, which carried them far. In exactly the same way the peasant craftsman who sits in his shop making the whole of a few beautiful earthenware pots is not so efficient in the modern struggle for survival as the factory where each worker concentrates on one out of twenty or thirty processes; although the latter loses all sense of the beauty of the whole through concentrating on the part. So, too, early in the history of life two and more single cells, instead of leading separate existences, remained or became joined together and existed as parts of a many-celled animal. We can guess what happened and see some of the steps still going on in nature. For example, a group of cells combined together to form a tube of living matter, in which some cells pointed outwards to the world at large, others inwards to the bore of the tube. Automatically these two groups found themselves confronted with different problems and forced to perform different labours: the outside cells protected the whole from attacks from without, and they moved the animal from one spot to another; the inside cells accepted the food which floated in through the tube,—they digested it and absorbed it. Thus, in place of a single cell occupying itself with all the processes necessary to life, we have a division of labour, a factory of specialized processes; and life became more efficient than before in the struggle to survive.

In these many-celled animals some of the cells take upon themselves the single process of reproduction: instead of the whole animal being concerned in propagating life, only a part of it is so concerned, and we have indeed animals with organs of sex, just as they have also organs of motion and organs of digestion; sex has become a part only of the living form and we have clearly advanced a step nearer to what the plain man or woman understands by sex.

We have moreover complicated our understanding of sex enormously by bringing in a new problem: in all these animals where only some of the cells, only part of the body, performs any sexual function, we ask ourselves what is the relationship between the sex cells and the rest of the body? Is the whole of the animal male or female, or is only that part of it which is sexual male or female, and the rest neutral or neuter? Before attempting to answer these new questions, we must safeguard ourselves from any too narrow an idea of what a living being with many cells and two sexes must be like. It is good to see how many schemes Nature has up her sleeve, and how different the sex relationship and life may be from that which we know to exist between men and women.

It will be valuable to see how different the method of reproduction can be from the human method, by studying for a moment the history of the Hydra. The Hydra is a very small water animal, just visible to the naked eye, and living in every ditch and pond. By one end it is anchored to a piece of plant matter and it looks like a branched tree itself. It is really a tube, the walls of which are lined with two thicknesses of cells, and there is an opening at the end opposite to the one by which it is attached. From the main tube or trunk sprout branches, and tentacles surround the mouth opening, waving in the water and forming little currents down which float particles of food. The inner lining of cells digests this food, while the outer lining protects the animal from being hurt by hard things grazing against it.

The Hydra takes no chances in its effort to reproduce itself; each branch can in time detach itself from the parent stem and float off, a complete animal, to become attached to some straw or weed on its own; and besides this a-sexual way of reproduction there is also a true sexual way. Just below the mouth and its bodyguard of tentacles a small swelling appears in the outer layer; these cells split up into smaller ones, each with a whip-like tail. They are male sperm cells and can move about to find the female egg cells. In shape and function they are just like the same sperm cells in higher animals and in man himself. On the same individual, near the attached end, another lump appears formed of a colony of cells in the outer wall; but instead of these cells splitting up and becoming sperm cells, they eat one another until only one large well-nourished egg cell is left. When this egg cell is fully grown, it breaks the wall which has hitherto guarded it, and becomes exposed to the surface. Sooner or later a sperm cell, attracted in some way or other towards it, finds it out, bores its way to the centre and thereby fertilizes it. After a short period of growth, the new individual breaks away from its parent, falls to the bottom of the pond and becomes in course of time a full-grown Hydra.

This short description will help us to see how sex as we

know it is only one of many ways of performing the same
need of living matter. The Hydra reproduces both with and
without sex, but we must note carefully that even when it
uses sex there is only one individual concerned, that the
parent Hydra is both father and mother of its offspring.
Clearly we need to widen our ideas of the universe by the
inclusion of this experience of life, and to realize that not
only is there reproduction without sex at all, but also sex
which does not include the participation of two individuals.

§ 4. *How Na-* AT first sight perhaps the Hydra does not
ture Ensures
Variety. throw much light on the question which
ultimately we hope to answer, namely, what is
the relationship between the sex-cells and the rest of the
body of a many-celled animal? Clearly as the same individual Hydra has both egg cells and sperm cells, it is
hermaphrodite and the rest of its body must either be both
male and female, or neither male nor female; and we shall
learn little about the difference, let us say, between a man's
body and a woman's in either case. But the Hydra has suggested another question which will lead up to what we are
trying to discover. The very fact of the Hydra's being hermaphrodite, that is, having both sexes in one individual,
and of its being able to fertilize its eggs with its own sperm,
without the help of another individual, leads us to ask this
question: "Why does life prefer that the sex cells in a many-
celled animal should be divided between two individuals, so
that the sperm cells of one individual fertilize the egg cells

of the other?" That life does prefer this is perfectly plain from the facts; it is only low forms of life like the Hydra which are hermaphrodite and all the higher forms are bisexual.

That it is an advantage for the living being to have separate individuals for its father and mother, is nowhere more clearly suggested than by the efforts and stratagems adopted by flowers which have both seed and pollen in one individual to bring about what is called cross-fertilization and to prevent its opposite—self-fertilization. An excellent example of this can be seen in the common primrose.

Every primrose flower has both male and female germ cells, that is, both pollen and seed; and so each flower could perfectly well fertilize itself, but in actual fact the fertilizing is accomplished by insects attracted by honey, and carrying the pollen of one flower to the seed of another.

Now in order to avoid the quite simple way of each flower fertilizing itself and to substitute for it the fertilizing of one flower by another, the primrose has developed an amazingly complicated machinery. In the first place, it cannot move about in order to find another flower, and so it has to employ an insect as a carrier; and since insects, like all other carriers, require payment for service rendered, it has had to secrete honey from itself in order to attract insects. But it has done more than this; it has developed a means whereby an insect cannot fertilize the seed of any flower with pollen taken from any other flower on the same plant.

If you will look at a bed of primroses, you will find that

half the plants bear flowers of a shape different from the others: the two shapes are known to gardeners as pin-eyed and thrum-eyed; and if you pick specimens and tear them open, you will find that in the pin-eyed flower the pollen is low down the tube and the seed, or rather the organ by which the pollen is conveyed to the seed in order to fertilize it, is high up. In the thrum-eyed flower, the positions are exactly reversed.

Now consider what happens to a bee which explores flower after flower for honey: he must thrust his proboscis deep down into the tube past seed and pollen in his search. If the flower is pin-eyed, some pollen will stick to the higher part of his proboscis; if it is thrum-eyed, to the lower, and he flies about with two different kinds of pollen on two different parts of his proboscis. When he visits a pin-eyed flower the pollen from a thrum-eyed flower will come in contact with the seed—the other pollen will be in the wrong position; and the same will be true when he visits a thrum-eyed flower—only the pin-eyed pollen will reach the seed, Thus as all the flowers on one plant are of the same sort, no flowers will be fertilized except by pollen from a different plant.

What do we learn from this? It confirms our suspicion that, for some reason, it is so much better that separate plants should fertilize one another, that even when a plant could quite easily fertilize itself, the most complicated machinery is evolved in order to secure cross-fertilization, and to avoid self-fertilization; and that in the same way with animals, a very definite value results from the separation of male and female germ cells in different bodies, since even when they are not separated the greatest pains are taken to avoid one and the same being, animal or plant, becoming both father and mother of the new generation.

§ 5. *Advantages of Sex.* WHAT is this hardly-won advantage which the primrose has gained over the Hydra? We can easily answer the question now.

It is a law of life that all offspring take after their parent or parents, but that within limits offspring vary from their parents. All children have some features like their fathers or mothers, but no child is exactly like them. The little Hydras will be Hydras as their parents were, but within limits they will be different: they will have fewer or more tentacles, longer or shorter stems, quicker or slower movements, stronger or weaker powers of anchoring themselves to the weeds of their ocean pool or stagnant pond.

Now out of this tendency to vary has come, we believe, the whole evolution of animal and vegetable life into higher forms; for some of the variations will be valuable to the individual,—will give it a start in the struggle for existence against all those individuals which do not possess that particular variation. In short, ability to vary is of the utmost value to life and rewards its possessor with the prizes of vital development into higher forms.

Since then offspring vary only within limits and take

after their parents, it is an enormous advantage to have two parents from whom to acquire one's characteristics, for it increases the possibility of variation.

Let us imagine, for the sake of example, that there are two plants of the same kind of flower; one with white petals, the other with red; one with a hairy stem, the other smooth; one ripening in May, the other in June; one requiring a great deal of water, the other less. Suppose also that these plants, as is the case with so many others, could fertilize either themselves or one another. Plainly, in the first case, each plant would have offspring only like itself, with slight variations; but in the second case, since there are two parents from each of which characters can be inherited, any one of the four characters could be inherited along with any of the other three, so that there would be the possibility of sixteen major variations, out of which several might be more fitted to survive than either of the parents.

In short, the existence of two sexes enriches the inheritance, increases the chance of survival and improves the race; so that those species which like the primrose succeeded in evolving complicated safeguards to ensure cross-fertilization, or those species which avoided the danger of self-fertilization altogether by having only one sex in one individual, were best fitted to survive and have done so, leaving the rest at the bottom of the evolutionary scale. The primrose plants, though not so different as the hypothetical plants we have invented, differ among themselves to a less degree; each of them contains in itself the experience and variations of a long line of ancestors which are shared by their joint offspring.

Hence we can now give several partial answers to the questions with which we began, namely, what is sex and why is sex?

I. Sex is rejuvenation; whereby the senility of the individual protoplasmic cell is made young again and capable of growth and renewal.

II. Sex is division of labour, whereby two individuals by sharing the labours of life are better able to perform them than either would be alone.

III. Sex is increased ability for variation, whereby the offspring has a greater reservoir of characteristics upon which to draw, and in consequence an exalted chance of success in the struggle for existence.

§ 6. *The Story of Phylloxera.* WE have now cleared the way for a full consideration of the vital question suggested as long ago as the third section, namely, what is the relationship between the sex cells and the rest of the body in a many-celled animal? Is the whole of the animal male or female, or is only that part of it which is sexual male or female, and the rest neutral or neuter? On how we answer this depends the whole interpretation which we shall put upon the history of women, and it is therefore of the utmost importance to try and find a clear answer. Let us proceed by way of a concrete object lesson, and see how bodily sex

forms may vary in order to fulfil varying needs—which
is excellently shown in the life history of the Phylloxera.

This insect is found in its natural home in Colorado, but
it migrated in imported vines to Europe about 1863, and by
1888 it had caused four hundred million pounds' worth of
damage to vineyards in France alone. In one single com-
mune it so destroyed the wine manufacture that output
dropped in six seasons from over two hundred thousand
gallons to eleven hundred. Five years after its first European appearance it reached Austria, next it attacked
Italy, then Russia, Germany, Switzerland, Spain and Portu-
gal in turn. Clearly such progress is proof of very ingenious
adaptation to the problems of life, and, as we shall see, it is
largely due to a remarkable complicated sex life.

If a vine is attacked by Phylloxera, a number of the insects will be found on the roots; less than a millimetre in
length, they are attached to the root by a long sucking
mouth, with which they drink the sap. All of these individuals are females, capable of producing about forty eggs,
without any fertilizing by a male. Every one of these eggs
hatches out rapidly, grows to maturity and lays more
eggs in a very short period, so that it has been estimated
that one Phylloxera dying in March may have twenty-five
million descendants by October. All these would be produced by a succession of virgin births, without a father,
and all would be females.

In this way, the Phylloxera increases and multiplies; but
it is obvious that its very success endangers its existence;

for in a state of nature there are no vineyards with miles of vines neatly placed at a distance of a few feet, so that when one vine has been sucked dry by the millions of parasites, it can be left for another.

Towards the end of summer, and in response to a stimulus which cannot be discovered, some of the eggs, exactly like all the rest though they are, produce quite a different form. This is a winged female which can fly about from vine to vine and so spread destruction far and wide. How this happens it is hard to see, but the fact is clear—just when the food supply is in danger of being exhausted, the means appears of flying to a fresh world. It is just as if the human race, upon the approaching and inevitable exhaustion of our planet, put on wings and flew to Jupiter or some other less moribund home beyond our atmosphere. In this latter case, which in the dim future may happen in fact, the change would be due to conscious intelligence, but though we may rule out the same cause with the Phylloxera, it is hard to find another to put in its place.

This is, however, only the beginning of Phylloxera's story: the new female with wings flies off to conquer new worlds, and when autumn is just beginning, she lays her eggs, still by virgin birth, upon some vine, and dies. Her eggs, however, are not the same as the earlier eggs; they are, to begin with, of two different sizes; out of the larger are hatched more females—and out of the smaller, for the first time, males. These females are quite unlike both the other kinds of female; they have no wings and are therefore fixed for life to their birthplace; and they have no digestive system; they are, indeed, nothing but a machine for producing eggs. The males also are wingless and digestionless, and these abominable, degenerate objects mate, live a few days and die, after leaving behind them one fertilized egg only.

Once more sex has conformed to the needs of a new situation, for, as we have said, autumn is already with the Phylloxera and winter is near at hand: how could the tender little insects, hatching out and themselves laying eggs at intervals of a few days, survive the cold winds and sapless rigour of winter? The new egg, produced by ordinary sexual function between father and mother, is totally different from everything yet seen; instead of hatching out in a few days, it remains dormant throughout the winter until the spring comes back.

So far the danger of an exhausted food supply and of a rigorous winter have both been surmounted by means involving revolutions in sex form and function, and the rejuvenating of the stock has also been accomplished by the sexual conjugation; but even this is not all. The period of sappy green leaves has come, the winter eggs hatch out, again into females only, who by virgin birth can reproduce without males, but these females once more are quite different in body and behaviour from their predecessors. They are adapted to lay toll on the leaves of the vine, to utilize to the full the green youth of spring. They crawl into the buds and bore a hole into the new leaf; with some chemical substance they create a gall or wart-like swelling, inside which they take up their abode and lay a great many eggs, all of them apparently alike.

Again, however, similar eggs produce dissimilar insects: again we can see that the sex changes are such as to use the resources of nature to the full. On the one hand, for several weeks the leaves will still be young, and therefore some of the offspring when hatched creep into new buds and make fresh galls, where they reproduce in turn. But, on the other hand, summer will follow spring, the hot sun will dry up the leaves, the roots will be cooler and fuller of sap, so some of the young insects creep down from the leaves to the roots, where they begin once more this incredible cycle of changing habit and form.

Here we see complicated changes of sex form and habit, each one of which is obviously of value to the animal as a means of avoiding some natural difficulty or danger. How are we to interpret these changes?

§ 7. *"An Egg's* A CONSIDERATION of this complicated life
Way . . ." history forces us to the feeling that the body which grows from the egg is no more than a tool or factory built by the egg to secure the laying of another egg. The imperative law of living matter is to ensure that life shall continue, and in this particular instance this law can be fulfilled only by definite and complete changes of tactics on the part of the egg, leading to new designs for its tool and factory. It is as if a sort of unconscious will to live existed in

the egg and fostered in it a knowledge equally unconscious that when perhaps the warm sun of summer had stimulated it to a definite degree, it was a signal for giving wings to the machine in order that the failing food supply should be replenished elsewhere; that when chilly evenings warned of coming winter, the egg knew that it must remodel its machine once more in order to produce the dormant winter egg, which needed no food through the barren months of the dying year.

The difficulties of putting such an idea into scientific form have puzzled scientists for generations, and we are no further towards a solution at the present day; but fortunately our present purpose need not wait upon the revealing of these riddles of existence; for us Phylloxera is important chiefly because it gives us a brilliant example of the truth that, as Samuel Butler put it, "A hen is merely an egg's way of producing another egg"; it brings us therefore to the beginning of an answer to our question: "What is the relation between the sex cells and the rest of an animal's body?"

We saw how the lowest many-celled animals are nothing but a loose colony of individual cells, each doing some special task for the whole community. They have no central authority, but live in a state bordering upon anarchy, in the sense not of "chaos" of course, but of "no government." As life evolved into more complicated forms, this anarchy, which served well enough in very simple communities, gave place to an ever-stronger system of government, which directed and subordinated every cell within the body: in short, animals developed central nervous systems and became individuals and personalities, one and undivided, under the leadership of the brain. These personalities are influenced by all the varieties of body and limb and organ, according as they differ from individual to individual; they are not altogether despotic governments, for, although they use freely all their subject cells, they are in their turn influenced by the nature of those cells: a strong muscular man uses his muscles, but the fact that he has more muscles than another man will give him a different outlook on muscles and on life in general from the other man's. How then does the basic fact that one individual has sperm cells and another has egg cells, influence the whole of the rest of their body and with it their actions, their thoughts and their desires? To the questions, what is sex? and why is sex? partially but sufficiently answered before, succeed the questions: what is the difference between a boy and a girl? and why is one a boy and the other a girl? and the clue to their solution, as exemplified by Phylloxera, is that a hen is merely an egg's way of producing another egg.

A boy and a girl, a man and a woman, differ first of all in three manifest ways:

I. By definition, the first produces sperm cells and the second egg cells.

II. In consequence, the first has organs modified and fashioned to produce sperm cells and the other has organs modified and fashioned to produce egg cells.

III. The first has organs still further modified and fashioned to help the sperm cells in their task of finding
the egg cells; the other has organs still further modified and fashioned to help the egg cells to receive the
sperm cells, and to permit, in the most favourable
circumstances, of these two joining as a complete
fertilized individual.

But Phylloxera has taught us to expect another and more
universal difference affecting perhaps the whole body: for
since a hen is merely an egg's way of producing another egg,
then the egg which fashioned the hen will have a different
end in view, throughout the whole of its task, from that
which another egg will have in view when it sets about to
fashion a cock. In other words, all the differences between a
cock and a hen are subservient to the fact that one is to
contain an ovum, the other a sperm, out of the junction of
which will come a fertile egg.

Or if we consider our real subject, man and woman: are
we not led to expect that every cell in each is modified by
their sex,—that sex is of the whole body, that no amount of
similar education, opportunity, habit, will eradicate the basic
fact that the whole of a woman's body is female and the
whole of a man's is male? Need we underline the importance
of the question for our understanding of history? Is it not
the central question which governs the life and hopes of all
men and all women? Does not the wiseness or foolishness
of every social habit affecting the relationship of the sexes
depend upon how it is answered?

And yet the answer is very difficult to find. At first sight perhaps it seems simple enough, for if the facts are as we have stated them, then we are forced to assume that the man and the woman are utterly different, as indeed we know them to be from personal experience. But man is not Phylloxera; he has ideas, he dominates physiology with psychology, he makes things good and bad, right and wrong, fated or capable of change, by thinking them so. He interferes with the egg's unconscious will; he decrees that a woman shall not merely be a human egg's way of making another egg, but a man's way of increasing his own comfort, and a woman decrees that a man shall not merely be an egg's way of getting another egg fertilized, but a woman's way of adding to her comfort. In short, we must distinguish carefully, as we have already said, between sex differences which are natural, that is, implicit in the needs and nature of sex, and sex differences which are artificial, that is, having nothing to do with sex, but merely with the transient and mortal individual, made indeed for the egg, but living for itself as well.

§ 8. *Early Mistakes About Sex.*   So far we have attacked our various questions by looking for the beginning of sex far down the chain of living beings and at its earliest appearance as part of life's mechanism. We must now seek fresh light in a new direction, and find out what happens when a new individual begins life in the body of its mother; for hidden in the womb is the secret of why one individual is a man and another a woman, of how the egg cell or sperm cell, as the case may be, contrives to fashion the rest of the body to its will, of how far the he and the she are of the .whole body and personality.

It is extraordinary how late in the history of mankind has any knowledge of this moment, when the new being starts its career, been discovered; and even today countless thousands have not the slightest idea of "how babies are born" or at least of how babies are conceived. It has been very important to the history of women how this question has been envisaged at different times, for false ideas of conception have influenced the position of women in society in a way scarcely to be realized without detailed knowledge of primitive people.

There was a time when no human being knew that children were the result of intercourse between the sexes, and today tribes still exist in this state of primordial ignorance. Nor is this as remarkable as it may at first appear, when we consider how little the primitive human being understands the laws of cause and effect. The Australian savage woman begins her married life directly she has reached the age of puberty. Every day almost she has intercourse with her husband or other lawful mates; this intercourse is not followed immediately by any visible sign of pregnancy; weeks or months after, as she is passing some tree or rock, the child quickens within her; is it surprising that she should believe that it is at that moment that the new life has entered her, and that it has come from the rock or tree where in spirit form it had hitherto been waiting?

An Australian woman who had spent much time at the white man's camp gave birth to a child which betrayed its half-caste parentage; her husband explained the child's colour and features satisfactorily to himself, by saying that his wife had eaten too much of the white bread which she was given at the white man's camp.

Among the Australians, intercourse is considered at most as a preparation for the reception and birth of an already formed spirit child, who inhabits a local sacred spot. In one tribe there is a special stone through a hole in which the spirit child looks out and awaits a mother: any woman who approaches the stone will conceive forthwith, and any woman who wishes to avoid having a child and yet has to pass by the stone, disguises her youth carefully, distorts her face and hobbles by with a stick. She bends herself double and in a cracked old voice cries: "Don't come to me, I am an old woman."

Out of such complete ignorance come the innumerable beliefs about the power of inanimate and animate objects to make a woman conceive: in order to become pregnant she eats, under ceremonial conditions, all sorts of substances, she wears amulets and charms, she takes curious medicines and performs mysterious rites; all testifying to the same universal ignorance of physiological functions. From this stage to modern half-enlightenment the road leads through many erroneous theories, some having so deep an influence on women's history as to need our attention.

We will quote at length, therefore, a passage from Addison's *Familiar Introduction to the Study of Natural History,* written in 1763 and summing up the attitude of that time to the problem, as well as that of past episodes in its history:

"The generation of animals has excited curiosity in all ages, and the philosophers of every age have undertaken to explain the difficulty. Hippocrates has supposed fecundity to proceed from the mixture of the seminal liquor of both sexes, each of which equally contributes to the formation of the incipient animal. Aristotle, on the other hand, would have the seminal liquor in the male alone to contribute to this grand effect, while the female only supplied the proper nourishment for its support. Such were the opinions of these two great men, and they continued to be adopted by physicians or schoolmen for a long succession of ages, with blind veneration, till Steno and Hervey, guided by anatomical inspection, perceived" the ovaries and Fallopian tubes in the female body. "This discovery soon altered the opinion of the philosophers; and as the followers of Aristotle ascribed the rudiments of the fœtus to the male, the followers of Hervey gave it entirely to the female. This last opinion, therefore, was established in the schools for a long time without much controversy, till Leeuwenhoek discovered that the seminal liquor in the male had numberless living creatures, each of which might be considered as a miniature of the future animal. The business of generation was now, therefore, given back to the male a second time, though not without long controversy and some abuse. Succeeding speculators, willing to compound the matter, were of opinion that the seminal animal might enter the egg predisposed for its reception: and thus both sexes might conspire in the formation. . . . This hypothesis [a new one of Buffon's] as well as all the rest, is embarrassed with unsurmountable objections, and only serves to show that too minute a pursuit of nature leads to uncertainty; . . . modest nature has concealed her secret operations from such presumption . . . we cannot discover how animals are generated."

We see from these paragraphs that some people have ascribed the child entirely to the man, others to the woman: both theories, ridiculously false as they seem to us now, have had profound effect upon the history of women, for they have had very important social implication. Thus Gibbon writing in 1790 argues from the theory that the woman is the sole active parent: "According to the philosophers, who can discern an endless involution of germs or organized bodies, the future animal exists in the female parent; and the male is no more than an accidental cause which stimulates the first motion and energy of life. The genealogist who embraces this system should confine his researches to the female line,—the series of mothers; and scandal may whisper that this mode of proceeding will be always the safest and most assured. But the moral connexion of a pedigree is differently marked by the influence of law and customs: the male sex is deemed more noble than the female; the association of our idea pursues the regular descent of honour and estates from father to son; and their wives, howsoever essential, were considered only in the light of foreign auxiliaries." (*Antiquities of the House of Brunswick.*)

James Boswell writing at precisely the same date argues from the opposite theory as follows: "I, on the other hand, had a zealous partiality for heirs male, however remote, which I maintained by argument which appeared to me to have considerable weight; as first, the opinion of some distinguished naturalists, that our species is transmitted through males, only, the female being all along no more than a nidus or nurse, as Mother Earth is to plants of every sort; which notion seems to be confirmed by that text of Scripture: 'He was yet in the lion of his *Father* when Melchisedec met him.' Heb. VII, 10; and consequently that a man's grandson by a daughter, instead of his surest descendant, as is vulgarly said, has, in reality, no connection whatever with his blood."

Students of history of women will do well to consider these three quotations, for they have many points of interest. We note that both Gibbon and Boswell were wrong; that though Gibbon's biological theory would be favourable to women in society, nevertheless it is overruled in his mind by legal theories and by the fact that "the male sex is deemed more noble"; and that Boswell's theory would be even more unfavourable to women than current legal theory, and that it is supported biologically by the authority of St. Paul, whose biological knowledge and ideas came entirely from Genesis, and similar sources. It is then "heads" men win and "tails" women lose with the whole question.

Of the two theories in their extreme form, the one accepted gratefully by Boswell that a woman is just a fertile field into which the seed is poured has been the most commonly held by early civilizations. To the social and historical interests of the question we shall return, but we must continue the purely biological aspect a little further.

So recent is any basis of exact knowledge on the nature of conception that it was actually not until 1854 that researches finally revealed the fertilization of the egg cell by the sperm cell, thus setting at rest forever the rival claims of man and woman in the matter, by giving to each an equal share in the work of conception.

§ 9. *The Chro-* WHEN first sex appeared in the world of liv-
mosomes.   ing forms, one cell, as we have seen, went courting and the other waited at home to be courted. In human beings, precisely the same is true: every individual starts life by the intermingling of two single-celled beings; one of them is produced by a mother and remains quiet waiting to be found, the other, produced by the father, is in every way fitted to move and find its mate. As far as sex is concerned, the whole of the rest of the human body is nothing but a complicated arrangement to assure these single cells meeting and to nourish them when they have met.

If we could find a way of inducing a human sperm cell and a human egg cell to meet and mingle and then to develop like an egg in an incubator, we could produce a child outside its mother's body. The first task is comparatively easy,—the second infinitely harder, though still possible, since all that is necessary is to get the right chemical foods and to invent a way of inducing the fertilized egg to absorb them.

Now what is it which decides that out of these two single cells shall come something so utterly different as a man or a woman? A minute speck of protoplasm with a whip-like tail with which it can move rapidly about, plunges its head into a much larger, richer, though still minute piece of protoplasm and a human individual begins to form, sometimes a male, almost exactly as often a female; what determines which it shall be? If we examine the sperm cell and the egg cell under the microscope, we find within a circle a transparent fluid matter, a darker mass, the nucleus. At certain periods of the cell's life, if we stain it with a special chemical, we can see within this nucleus a group of rod-like objects, which are called chromosomes, simply because staining with a chemical enables them to be seen. These chromosomes vary from animal to animal, but are nearly always the same in every particular kind of animal, and in every cell in its body.

Only in the ripe sperm cells and the ripe egg cells will the number be less by half than in the other cells of the body. This reduction of chromosomes in the sperm and egg cells is brought about by a complicated way of maturing, which results in every one of these cells splitting into two before they are ready to meet one another in the act of fertilization, and half the chromosomes going into each half. When the sperm and the egg cells mingle together, they regain the right number again, whereas if there was not a process of reduction to half the number first, they would contain twice as many. When the fertilized ovum spilts into two and then four and then eight cells, and so on to form the full-grown individual, each chromosome splits in two and half of each goes into each new daughter cell, so that every cell in the grown body contains the same number of chromosomes, made out of the original ones, half of which were contributed by the sperm cell from the father, and half by the egg cell from the mother.

Now, although we know nothing at all about the nature of these chromosomes except that they can be seen by staining with a special chemical and that they behave according to constant rules, we know a great deal about their effect. We know that when half of them go into one mature sperm cell and the other half into another, it matters a great deal which of these two cells fertilizes an egg cell, for the grown individual will be totally different in either case. In other words, these little rod-like objects contain in them the physical basis of heredity. What is of importance to us here is that in mankind a distinct difference can be seen between the chromosomes in one daughter cell and those in the other; for, whereas all the other chromosomes have an identical pair which goes off into the other daughter cell, one which is called x has a differently shaped companion called y, so that x goes into one cell and y into the other. In short, half the mature sperm cells have an x chromosome and the other half have a y. If the sperm cell with an x fertilizes the egg cell, a male individual results; if one with a y, a female. Thus all the differences between man and woman, down to the wearing of trousers and skirts, begin because a rod-like object capable of being seen when stained, called x, existed in the single cell from the male parent rather than another called y.

It should be added that the egg-cell does not have any

unequal pair of chromosomes: so that all the mature egg-cells in a woman have an x chromosome. It follows therefore that an individual is a man or a woman because of some chance circumstance to do with the cell that comes from his father, and not because of anything at all that he inherits from his mother.

§ 10. *Bonellia and Sex-Transference.* WE have reached a point now when we begin to see at last how the difference arises between man and woman and we know quite definitely *when* this difference begins. It begins at the very beginning of the individual's life, and it is carried into every cell of its body.

But we run a grave risk of thinking the problem less complicated than it really is. We know that a variation in the chromosomes goes with the sex of a person; but we cannot say that this chromosome variation determines the sex for the following very good reasons:

There is a worm-like animal called Bonellia, which might well be taken as a badge by any club of Amazons, who hold males in complete contempt. The female is about two inches long, exclusive of an enormous proboscis, which is often more than eight inches in length. She lies in a crevice of a rock or in a tunnel dug out of the sea bed, and waves her proboscis about in search of food; sometimes she swims about at night time, using her proboscis as a sort of revolving propeller. Her young, after growing for a while inside her body, pass out into the water; they swim about and look for another female Bonellia, and if they fail to find one, they gradually sink to the bottom, there to grow up to be females themselves. If they are successful, however, they attach themselves to the female proboscis and thence pass within the body to the sexual organs: there they remain, minute little threads, a millimetre and a half in length. And this is the extraordinary fact, that these young Bonellias who have succeeded in becoming parasites are the males, who remain forever utterly degenerate in the female's body, fertilizing her eggs and dying.

For a long time it was thought that it was the males which sought the female proboscis, while the females went about their business and grew up; but experiments have now shown that any young larva, which succeeds in becoming attached, becomes male, and that if one is prevented from remaining fastened on, it will become a female. Stranger still, if a young Bonellia is allowed to remain on the female for a time and then is taken away, it will show signs when growing up of being hermaphrodite; that is, half male and half female.

We must assume therefore that in Bonellia, to be a male is part of the reward of successful parasitism, a reward purchased at the price which has always to be paid by parasites—beastly degeneracy.

Bonellia therefore thoroughly complicates the question of sex determinism; we cannot believe that it is simply a question predestined in the ovum and spermatozoon, for clearly what happens at a later stage of growth is seen to reverse any effect that the chromosomes may have.

If the individual succeeds in attaching itself to the female proboscis, it does away with any need to develop the means of locomotion; this satisfactorily accomplished, it passes to a spot where the duties of self-preservation and food quest are also excused it; and nothing at all is left except a petty life in a degenerate form fertilizing the eggs of the female. If it fails to become a parasite, it has to develop its powers of locomotion, to feed itself, to protect itself, and it becomes a female. To be a member of the male sex is not the gift of a chromosome, but the reward of successful parasitism.

What happens to Bonellia happens also to a much better known animal, the barnacle. The young of these animals swim freely about and when they find a suitable rock or log of wood, they settle down and become the familiar sedentary barnacle in its shell; and in this case the individual is always either a female or a hermaphrodite. If however the young swimming barnacle alights on an adult individual in its shell, it fixes itself in its host, never grows up and remains in its infantile form; and, moreover, this form is a male.

Here again, it is not the question of the male sex being the gift of a chromosome, but rather of its being the reward of parasitism.

Remembering these animals as a warning against too

easy solution of our problem, let us return again to higher forms of life. If we think of the human body, we realize that the sex distinctions as we know them are not caused by a man and a woman having any part of their body absolutely different from the other: the sex organs of a man and a woman are at basis precisely the same, but they have been modified to perform the different functions peculiar to either sex. The physiologist can draw a diagram which represents the organs of both sexes indiscriminately, and all that is necessary to make them male or female is to enlarge some, diminish others, alter the positions of others. What the scientist does with his drawing is precisely what nature does with the organs themselves: at an early stage of growth in the mother's womb, the organs of the unborn individual are neither male nor female; they are like the generalized neutral diagram; then, as growth continues, an invisible force from within the growing body modifies and alters them one way or the other and the child becomes a boy or girl as the case may be.

We can assume that, other things being equal, given the natural conditions of growth, the sex chromosomes contain the force, probably chemical, which performs this task of modifying the organs one way or the other; and in this way the sperm cell or the egg cell is finally produced by the organs which can perform the task.

The way is now clear to consider closely our most important question of how the egg cell and the sperm cell get the body they require.

§ 11. *The Ductless Glands.* WHAT is the machinery whereby the sperm cell secures the 'sort of body form which is most suitable for its growth and success in the struggle for existence? How does the egg cell see to it that it owns the vast army of servant cells, which we call a hen, rather than the, for it, useless army called a cock? That may sound a very far-fetched way of putting it, yet it is substantially true as we shall see.

First, what is the difference between a cock and a hen? One is male and produces sperm cells, the other is female and produces egg cells; each has the sexual organs suitable in shape and function for producing and protecting these; each has, besides, certain characters in which they differ from one another. The cock has a gay plumage, which seems to be his way of attracting his wife, he has a cock's-comb and spurs, the latter for fighting rivals. It is perhaps not surprising that the sperm cell has suitable organs for its production and storage, but if these other features are a means to attract the female, then they are the sperm cell's method of securing that it will one day meet an egg cell. Have we any evidence that the sperm cell controls these features in any way?

The organ which produces a sperm cell is called a testis, and that which produces an egg cell is called an ovary: if the testis of a cock is removed by an operation at an early age, the animal never develops a true cock's-comb and its spurs are weak or absent altogether; its features are not much altered, so that we can say that the cock which has been castrated still looks like a cock, but is of a very poor, unvirile type. If the ovaries are taken from a hen, a far more astonishing result is seen: the hen develops a cock's-comb, and takes on the male plumage. In both cases it is clear that there is some relationship between the sexual organs and the general make-up of the body; for, although the hen was born with the chromosomes which would make it develop into a hen, this natural development can be upset by a later factor.

More remarkable still are the experiments which have been carried out by Steinach on guinea pigs. When the testes or ovaries were removed from these, the individuals grew up obvious males and females, but less masculine and feminine in their general appearance. When Steinach grafted an ovary into a male guinea pig whose testes had been removed, the animal grew up to resemble a female in every way, it developed perfect milk glands and suckled young ones and behaved like a female guinea pig. Similarly a female into which a male testis was grafted grew large and powerful, and pugnaciously attacked males and courted females. In short these experiments show that it is possible to change the sex of an animal, and with it its whole body, its habits, its instincts, its nature.

The result of all these and many other practical experiments may be expressed as follows. The sex organs, testis in the male, ovary in the female, each produce two quite different products: one is the purely sexual product, sperm and egg cell respectively, the other is a secretion which is poured into the blood stream and carried into every part of the body, and has different effects according as it comes from a testis or an ovary. This secretion influences all the cells in the body and induces them to develop into male or female characteristic shapes, sizes, colours, functions, as the case may be. Thus a man is a human individual who produces sperm cells and who is influenced throughout his physical being by a secretion which induces all the cells of his body to become suitable servants to those sperm cells: a woman is a human being who produces egg cells and who is influenced throughout her physical being by a secretion which induces all the cells of her body to become suitable servants to those egg cells.

Moreover, many of the innumerable differences between men and women are due to the functions of their sex organs: a fact which is of great importance because there has been more than one attempt to show that most of the physical differences between the sexes are due to habits of living: a great many of them are, but even if a girl and a boy were brought up in precisely the same way they would constantly have their bodies influenced from within by two widely different secretions, shaping and modifying the utmost cell to answer the demands of sperm cell and egg cell respectively.

In short, the secondary sexual differences between man and woman—that is, the bodily difference of height, weight, muscular development, shape, blood pressure, temperature and so forth—are not altogether due to different social habits, as some feminists would like us to believe, but also to deep-rooted biological causes arising out of the very nature of male and female.

Indeed we can see evidence of this fact which helps us to realize its significance: not only do the feathers of birds change when a scientific experiment upsets the chemical balance of the ductless glands, but in normal life changes in the sexual organs produce changes elsewhere in the body. When a woman conceives, changes take place in her breasts to prepare them for their use in due course; when she gives birth to the child, the breasts at once begin to flow with milk. So used are we to this fact that it hardly seems to us very surprising. Yet a change in one part of the body has produced the most elaborate changes in other remote parts, and the necessary provision over against a future date when a new human being shall want food has been accomplished. How is this done? Our ancestors would have said, "The Lord will provide," but we ask how He succeeds in doing so.

It is accomplished by the action of the secretion from the ovary which penetrates through the blood stream and stimulates the breasts to develop and to function. In the same way other necessary changes take place in remote parts of the body; the egg is in the very act of producing the right sort of hen for its purpose of producing another egg.

Now such facts as these would lead us to say that the whole body is controlled by sex, that a man is not a neuter being with some male sex cells added and a woman is not a neuter being with some female sex cells added, but that a

man is masculine and a woman feminine "to their finger
tips." We have to add another statement to this one, namely
that the cause of as well as the effect of sex is not confined
to the sexual organs but is distributed throughout the body;
it is not merely the secretion of the ovaries which gives a
woman a womanly body, but that secretion mixed with several other secretions coming from a group of little organs
called the ductless glands. These glands together pour into
the blood stream a special mixture, a mass of chemicals,
which varies in every individual. It is the sum total of all
these chemicals which determines the sexual make-up of the
body; the most important of them, the ones which actually
make a person male or female, are the ones from the sexual
organs, but the others are able to modify their effect and
to reduce the maleness or the femaleness to less than a
hundred per cent.

For the sake of clarity we may put it like this: the en-
docrine system of ductless glands produces a mixture of
chemicals which varies from person to person; an ideal mixture can be imagined which could be called 100% male, a
second ideal mixture can be imagined which could be called
a 100% female; but in actual life no man or woman is
ever the result of exactly these mixtures, they are blends
which are nearer one of these than the other, and except in
very rare cases the body which has a chemical balance to
which a testis contributes a part is a man, and the body
which has a chemical balance to which an ovary contributes
a part is a woman.

This accounts for the gradations in physical and mental types to be seen everywhere: the "he man with hair on his chest" is perhaps a 100% male person and the American ideal of a man, but there are other sorts of men and other sorts of ideals. Thus the Greek statue, the Apollo or the Hermes, is a hermaphrodite type; that is, it is an ideal of masculine beauty in which there is a mixture of certain feminine traits. The Greek god is only 80% male in physique and with his muscular strength combines a softness of skin and a chest form which show an admixture of ductless glands which would be despised by the American he-man.

In short, the human body contains in every cell the potentiality of being modified into a male or female pattern and the extent and direction of this change are brought about entirely by the chemical balance of the secretions from the ductless glands. This balance always varies, and what we call a man is an individual containing more that is·masculine and less that is feminine and at the same time having sperm cells and the potentiality of using them to reproduce the species.

§ 12. *Sex Throughout the Body.* WE are now approaching the point when we can consider how far there is any biological justification for certain theories about the difference between men and women held instinctively by uneducated men or put forward rationally by educated ones.

In the first place, we know that women are commonly

called "the weaker sex," and a great many feminists suggest that this weakness, in so far as it exists, is the product of education and environment and in no way part of their nature. As we have seen, natural history gives these writers plenty of justification, and the size and strength of female spiders, for example, show that as far as the whole animal kingdom is concerned femaleness is not always synonymous with weakness. We may observe, however, that there probably never has been a feminist movement among spiders, and that in women relative physical weakness is obvious; the real question to be answered is: "How far is this physical inferiority due to habits of human social life and how far due to the feminine chemical balance?"

Before we consider the question when phrased in this way, we must add that it is worth while doing so only in so far as an answer has social significance. It does not matter in the least if certain individual women would like to be as powerful as a docker or a coalheaver, or think that their sisters could or ought to be as strong; but it is important to find out whether or not all women on an average are naturally handicapped in their competition with men economically by their physical sex-disabilities. A great deal of the feminism which advocates everything as equally possible for both sexes is clearly a recrudescence in a less engaging form of that "wishing I were a boy" habit of the average young girl: perhaps owing to a feeling of "organ inferiority," or merely because she finds that custom restricts her more than her brothers, most girl children want to be men, and a certain type in later life substitute for it a wish, more logical in form only, to do as a man. Discounting this we are bound to weigh the pros and cons of the same wish when it is thrust upon women by social and economic pressure.

We can certainly state that the modern woman is less powerful than she need be owing to social habit and convention: in savage communities where women do a great deal of manual work their physical condition is much better than among civilized peoples, in spite of the absence of doctors, hygiene and dietetics. But then so is that of the men, and most observers agree that there is as great a difference between primitive man and woman as between civilized man and woman.

For example, Dr. Ales Hrdlicka has made a detailed study of American Indians from the physical and medical standpoint and he has tabulated his results in a form which throws interesting light on our question. Indian women all work hard; not only do they look after the children, but they make pottery, repair even stone houses, help with the ploughing, grind corn laboriously by hand, tend sheep; in fact they do their share of the hard work and have every opportunity of developing muscle and strength. Moreover, the average number of children to each woman is, or used to be, about seven. In these circumstances where work and social custom plainly do not militate against a fine female physique, we do not find that women have the same development as men, but that

I. Men are almost exactly as much taller than women among Indians as among Whites.

II. All Indians have on the average a slower heart beat than Whites, but among them the women's hearts beat almost exactly as much faster than the men's as among Whites. Respiration and temperature vary between the sexes as in Whites.

III. In muscular force, measured by the ability to grasp and to pull weights, the Indian men are less powerful than White men and the Indian women are about as powerful as White women; but the men are much more powerful than the women. Thus the same difference between the sexes is found where the women work hard and live healthily, although the difference is exaggerated among Whites by the debility of our women. Even an average Indian woman is only two-thirds as powerful as an average Indian man.

IV. Although women work hard all their lives among the Indians, they are more likely to become stout than the men.

Such facts as these help us to answer the question: "How far is the physical inferiority of women due to social habits and work and how far to differences in chemical balance?" A man has more muscular force in his right than in his left hand; that is due to habits of work. An Indian woman is not so much weaker than a White woman as an Indian man is than a White man; that also is due to habits of work. An

Indian woman and a White woman are both respectively less strong than an Indian man and a White man; that is clearly due to the difference in chemical balance between male and female. In short, when we eliminate the effects of social habit, in so far as they tend to produce or increase differences in muscular strength and physical stamina between the sexes, we still have a very large margin left which must be put down to the female physical balance. This is the answer which must be made to the ridiculous assertions of a certain type of extreme feminist who would have us believe that women, educated and trained like men, would have the muscles and stamina of men. Women are by nature the weaker sex, though this difference is often exaggerated by foolish habits and education. All the evidence goes to support this assertion and to prove that there are physical differences between the sexes—apart from primary sexual differences—which are not the result of social habits.

Now alongside this idea that women are the weaker sex is the idea that they are emotionally less stable, less reliable, more changeable, more unaccountable. We shall meet with many examples of this permanent generalization and shall consider later the psychological causes both of the belief in this fact, and of the fact itself, if it be shown to be true. But first we must look at some biological characteristics of women, which have a bearing on this later study.

The ductless glands control the chemistry of the body, and we should expect that this control would be different in the two sexes. Now the way in which a living thing lives is summed up in the term "metabolism"; metabolism is, briefly, the taking in by living matter of outside material, and the changing of it into energy. Every single cell in the body is engaged in this task almost unceasingly: chemical substances are absorbed and changed into useful energy and the waste products are thrown out and carried out of the system along special channels. We can measure the rate of metabolism in various ways and such things as the heart beat, respiration and temperature are all gauges of how the process is being carried on; from them we find that there is a constant sex distinction in metabolism.

The sex difference in metabolism can be summed up by saying that the female stores up energy longer than the male; that is, the period between taking in the outside matter and giving out the energy produced from it is longer; and hence women tend to store fat rather than muscle. Muscle is always the result largely of use and of action; a man who exercises his arms, for instance, will be more muscular than the other man; but apart from the effects of work and education, there is a sex difference due to different rates of metabolism; no amount of gymnastics will make women on an average as muscular as men.

So much we have already seen in the previous section, but there is a more important result of sex difference in metabolism, which we shall now proceed to describe.

One of the functions of the human body is to extract from food a chemical, calcium salts with which to build up tissues; and to allow the unused residue to pass out of the body.

During childhood in both sexes these salts are extracted and used to make bone; at puberty they begin to be needed for the reproductive system; and since puberty begins at an earlier age with girls, girls have less calcium to use for making bones than boys, and are lighter in consequence. But women need far more calcium than men, and especially when they are pregnant, for they need a great deal to build up the skeleton of the unborn child. And again, when the child is born, the calcium is used to help the breasts produce milk.

Two interesting results follow these facts: first women need to have more calcium salts than men; second they sometimes require far more calcium than at other times. The latter result brings about a periodical unevenness in a woman's metabolism: she is sometimes producing more calcium and at other times less. The extra calcium which cannot normally be used by a woman is passed out of her body every month, but even then she is by nature forced to be less steady, more changeable, than a man.

Now metabolism affects one's outlook on life. If a man is suffering from defective metabolism, he tends to have a jaundiced outlook on life: the very words we use in common speech reflect our unconscious knowledge that body influences mind and makes it jaundiced, or splenetic, or phlegmatic, or bilious. It has been said that a young man who is a conservative must have something wrong with his heart, while an old man who is not a conservative must have something wrong with his head: it can be said with biological truth that the change of opinions which comes with age is largely influenced by the increasing calcium salts in the old man's or woman's body. "Senex, the old man, often says to younger people, 'These things you pursue are valueless—I too have sought them, later abandoned the search and now see my folly'; not realizing that if his blood were to resume its former chemical character he would return to the quest."

If, therefore, we can show good reason for attributing in part the change in a person's outlook on life as he grows older to the changes in the chemicals his body secretes, excretes or stores, and if further we know that men and women differ largely on account of their chemical differences, then we are at liberty to assume that a part of the difference of outlook which we observe between men and women is due not to social habits and conventions, but to the physiological sex differences. Give a man and a woman the same life and the same habits, they will still differ widely in the use they make of that life and the value they put on its various details because of their innate chemical differences.

Moreover, a woman, we have seen, is more erratic in her metabolism, she is periodical in her use of calcium salts, for example, and if one of the differences between a radical youth and conservative age is nothing more than calcium, then we may expect that women are, not only because of social habits, but also because of chemical instability, less likely to be even, uncontradictory, reliable mortals. There is, in short, some little biological ground for the theory of the relative instability of women, as women; but we shall assume that this innate tendency is exaggerated by education and suggestion; women are born with a tendency to greater instability, but it is their environment which insists upon that tendency seizing them by the throat.

§ 13. *Conclusion.*   WHAT do we learn from such a brief exposition of the biology of sex? Why is it a necessary beginning to the briefest history of women in history?

In the first place nine human beings out of ten are obsessed by what they would call the "mystery of sex." So long as sex remains a mystery, the history of women remains a mystery: there is no point in trying to understand what has happened, unless we know a little about the thing to which it has happened. If Adam and Eve had known some things, it would have altered their children's whole history; if St. Paul, Tertullian, Milton, Hannah More, had known some things, they would not have made the appalling mistakes with regard to women which have made them ridiculous in the eyes of all honest and just people. The less mystery there is about sex the better for society, and that does not mean that there need be less reverence for the relationship between man and woman; it is surely not essential that one should be ignorant or have hallucinations about a thing in order to be reverent about it.

In the second place, since history is the record of human

imbecilities and errors, especially when it is the history of women, we need to know what is fact and what is error in order to appreciate what has been happening during the last few thousand years. Gibbon and Addison, to say nothing of Tertullian or Dr. Johnson, made idiots of themselves almost every time they mentioned the social relations of the sexes, simply because they did not know a line of sound biology. It was hardly their fault, since nobody knew anything about the nature of sex until this century in which we are living, but if these great men could make such fools of themselves, surely we also are not altogether free from a like danger, with less of an excuse!

But most important of all is it to know what factors in a woman as she exists are the result of her biological nature and what factors are the result of the false ideas, the artificialities, the habits, with which she has been successively distorted throughout the ages. It is hoped that the reader will have been given the data which will enable him to clear his mind in this matter. Not least is this important because in recent times feminist propagandists, righteously indignant about the futilities of human thought and action, have made themselves ridiculous in their turn by claiming every sex difference as the effect of social habits. There is very little of which we can be quite certain, but we do know that that at least is wrong, and just as the history of women in the past has been made painful by one set of errors, so its future might be made painful by the opposite errors.

But we must turn now from scientific fact to the highly entertaining though often very depressing quicksands of women's history, not as it ought to have been, or might have been, with a little more understanding of nature, but as it actually was.

Chapter II

WOMEN IN PRIMITIVE SOCIETY: THE
BIRTH OF FEAR AND CONTEMPT

§ 1. *The Rule of Magic.* OUR journey begins in the midnight forest inhabited by the primitive mind: there we see a handful of men and women groping their way through life and slowly accumulating the discoveries which have so far ended in our present-day civilization.

We must not imagine them as hesitating and simple philosophers, seeking the why and wherefore of existence, digging beneath the effects and discovering the causes, and often the wrong causes, of what they experienced. They did not face life with questions, they fought it with desires. For them the world outside was not littered with facts, which they could bind together with theories; it was part of their own personality, subservient to their will, chained by their thought, conditioned by their needs.

There were no natural laws making the sun rise and set, storms gather and rain fall, the trees to give fruit in due season. It was the human will which bound the sun to his path; it was the human will which gave and withheld the rain; it was the human will which ripened both seed and harvest.

Usually society as a whole by carrying out the requisite ceremonies brought about the state of affairs desired; sometimes individuals worked particular magics for their own end. In either case mystical means were employed for producing practical results and even when failure was frequent the unyielding cement of custom supported habit against every attack from disintegrating personal experience: though practice seemed to deny the truth of theory, no one could feel it so; though no rain came to the rainmaker, that was not his fault but the working of another and hostile human will.

But even so men were aware of certain limits to their desires: a crocodile might eat them, a tree fall upon them, a stone bruise their feet, an illness waste them; did not this give them the first glimpse of the universal subservience to natural law? No, it was but the expression of other wills opposing their own; something else besides man, everything else, indeed, had such a will, such a power, such a force; and man could control his surroundings only by setting up his own will against the capricious wills about him. Did a bough of a tree fall upon him and break his back? It was clearly the will of that bough to do so. There was no difference in kind between the two events, nor between them and the stone which bruised a man's foot. Everything around him was clearly the possessor of power, of *mana,* by which it thwarted or assisted humanity.

This mysterious *mana*—so called by anthropologists from the word used by certain primitive peoples in this connection—pervaded nature and man alike; and belief in it is a clue to the whole history of women, as we shall see. Sometimes an accident was caused by an enemy using his *mana* to control that of a tree, or a stone, or a crocodile: all trees do not fall, all stones do not bruise, whenever a man bathes he is not eaten by a crocodile; clearly, there is something special about this tree or stone or crocodile; an enemy is using it, and one's own *mana* must be exerted against it.

In short, when man found that his thought, his desire, was not omnipotent, he explained it by assuming other opposing thoughts around him; indeed, we can hardly say that he *explained* it as if he had reasoned about it; to him *it was so,* and needed nothing by way of explanation. With no clear sense of cause and effect, with absolute ignorance of mechanical and physical laws, man had to admit that *his* thought was not omnipotent; but in so doing he retained to the full his faith in the omnipotence of Thought. Wherever we see in nature the working of natural law, he saw the working of thought.

Primitive man elaborated complicated systems to deal with the *mana* of surrounding things, to enlist on his side that which was useful, to insulate himself from the effects of that which was evil: and to understand what follows we must observe some of his methods.

§ 2. Mana *at Work.* WHEN we hear of a man who has tuberculosis, we know that he harbours within him a parasite, a bacillus, which is gradually destroying the tissue of his lungs, and that his body must be made, by healthy surroundings and sound living, strong enough to resist the very practical and material enemy within. We know this because scientists have succeeded in proving it by experiment, in tracing the logical.sequence of cause and effect, in demonstrating to human eyes what is happening.

Not long since, such an outlook would have been quite impossible, for in place of the scientific point of view another existed. Moreover, only this morning my Spanish servant showed us a small bottle which contained the sweat of a miraculously perspiring figure of the Virgin from the next village; she used it externally as a prophylactic against various diseases and told us that some people advised its internal use also; but so far she would not go; though, she saw clearly enough, "it couldn't possibly do anybody any harm."

The Spanish servant is, in this particular, a savage, although she wields the electric iron with expedition; she has a belief in *mana*, a belief that mystical causes are more powerful than material. She is spiritually the sister of the Congo savage, who was advised by the missionary not to sit in a cold wind on a rainy day but to go home and change his wet loin cloth. "It does not matter," he replied. "People do not die of a cold wind; people get ill and die only by means of witchcraft."

In Australia diseases are cured by a medicine man who sucks out of the invalid's body a quartz crystal which someone else, by magic, has put there: the crystal is not imagined as doing any harm by physiological means, but as having a *magical* power to harm the sufferer. To produce such crystals is the proof of a medicine man's power; they have a virtue which enables him to perform miracles as well as to hypnotize people. They are, in fact, reservoirs of *mana*, dangerous to the ordinary man and valuable and powerful in the hands of the doctor.

If we turn to the great repository of mediæval learning and science, the works of Bartholomew Anglicus, we find the following passage about the sapphire: "The Sapphire hath a virtue to rule and accord them that be in strife, and helpeth much to make peace and accord. Also it hath virtue to comfort and glad the heart. His virtue is contrary to venom, and quencheth it every deal. And if thou put an attercop (spider) in a box, and hold a very Sapphire of Ind at the mouth of the box anywhile, by virtue thereof the attercop is overcome and dieth, as it were suddenly. And this same I have seen proved often in many and diverse places. And they that use nigromancy mean that they have answer of god more thereby than by other precious stones. Also witches love well this stone, for they ween that they may work certain wonders by virtue of this stone. This stone bringeth men out of prison bonds, and undoeth gates and bonds that it toucheth. The Sapphire loveth Chastity, and therefore lest the effect thereof be let in any wise by his uncleanness that him beareth, it needeth him that beareth it to live chaste."

If now we compare the Spanish servant, the Australian

aborigine, and the learned mediæval scholar, they clearly believe in the same non-natural powers working without material means; and moreover they all believe in *mana,* the *mana* of the quartz crystal, the *mana* of the sapphire, the *mana* of the sweat of the Virgin's statue. It is well thus early to emphasize the continuity of beliefs among the three, for our history will show that the study of primitive belief is not a mere academic study; it is essential for understanding our own twentieth-century selves, for *especially with regard to women we are savages yet.*

To return, however, to our savage and his belief in *mana,* in a mysterious power pervading nature and opposing a will to his own will. If any mysterious thing happens, that too is due to some manifestation of *mana* and anything out of the normal is mysterious. All accidents are due to somebody using the *mana* of an object against an enemy: for example, the Australians insisted upon killing a man because he had thrown his spear high up into a tree, whence it had glanced downwards and killed an old man. The owner of the spear happened to be a medicine man and what was clearly an accident was assumed to be the result of his magic. "In this typical case," comments Levy-Bruhl, "it was difficult and, indeed, practically impossible for the natives to listen to reason. First of all they had to satisfy the dead man, whom there would have been good reason to fear had he not been avenged; in any case, therefore, they were obliged to put someone to death, and nobody could have been more suitable than the one who (whether voluntarily or involuntarily mattered little) had been the cause of the misfortune. Moreover, the missionary would never have succeeded in making them understand that it was simply a case of accident. They would inevitably have asked, why, when the spear rebounded, did it fall exactly on the old man's neck, and not just in front or just behind him? Why should it happen to belong to a medicine man? And as for the absence of any deadly intention on the part of the culprit, how was that to be proved? It could only be presumed, and a presumption cannot weigh against a fact. Besides, it might have been intentional on his part without his even knowing it."

Plainly, then, as every action is attributed to somebody's *mana,* every kind of precaution must be taken against allowing another to get power over one. The ways in which such power can be gained are innumerable; some are material, others spiritual. Of the first we may mention such things as the getting of some portion of a person's body, a hair, nail parings, his saliva; with these magic can be worked; if you burn a hair of a man's body, you destroy the whole with the part; he too will die. The spiritual ways are of equal importance; anybody who produces a feeling in you has a power over you, can control your *mana,* can bend it to his purpose. A strong feeling is, after all, a disturbance; a disturbance is something out of the ordinary; anything "out of the ordinary" is dangerous, witchcraft, *mana.*

Some people are more likely than others to practise witchcraft; they are those who have a peculiarity: twins; strangers; anyone who behaves differently; anyone who does not react in the same way at all times; anyone who is variable, unreliable; anyone who has physical peculiarities. And among things, that which stands out is full of *mana:* a rock of peculiar shape, a prominent tree, a cave, a spear with a peculiar handle. Each and all in varying degrees are the possessors of *mana;* but one thing especially is its possessor.

§ 3. *Women's Place and Mana.* IF everything in the universe possesses *mana,* one thing above all else is invested with a double dose of it: and that is a woman.

In her is the quintessence of the unexpected and the misunderstood; the very fact that she is eminently desirable for all men makes her mistrusted; that she has palpable effects upon them renders her suspect to every man, whether husband, brother, father or son. A permanent source of danger, she is to be kept always insulated; a permanent source of pleasure, she can only thus be enjoyed without hurt. She and all that she does, all that she touches, all that she has, must be made innocuous, must be exorcized, must be freed of dangerous and excessive *mana,* lest the electric current of maleficence strike her husband like a thunderbolt and shrivel him up.

It is, however, a curious fact that, whereas most things which to the savage mind are fuller than usual of *mana* are regarded as reservoirs of supernatural power which can be used by him for valuable purposes, the *mana* in a woman is more often a reservoir of supernatural power which is dangerous and to be carefully avoided and guarded against. Magic formulæ, dances, stones, pieces of wood over which spells have been said, a hundred such *mana*-laden matters are dynamos which produce power, but women are bottles of poison which need antidotes. The reason and import of this will become clearer as our story proceeds.

In this chapter we are to consider the history of primitive women, for in it is rooted all her further history, and the manners and modes of the present also; but before we proceed there are several misapprehensions which must be removed from the average reader's mind, for no part of history has been more severely mishandled by propagandists than the dim dark ages before history proper can rightly be said to have been born.

There are primitive women and primitive women: in some communities their lot was totally different from what it was in others, and, just as it would be ridiculous to talk of contemporary women in a way which did not distinguish among the habits of Spanish, American and German women, so we must avoid over-simplifying the picture we are about to draw.

But first of all, what is meant by "the position of women?" Many people would like a neat diagram showing an evolution from low to high of women's legal position, her personal happiness, her morals, her social functions, her power, and, of course, they would like these to be shown marching hand in hand with the rise of general culture and enlightenment of social customs as a whole. These probably begin with a picture of a savage woman, insulted and injured, degraded by polygamy, overworked, the slave of foul passions, defective moralities, and corrupt ideas. A disappointment awaits these.

Others have heard of a golden age of feminism when women ruled and were in consequence superlatively happy, perfectly efficient, and elevated beyond their almost parasitical mates. This matriarchy has been made an excuse for all sorts of whimsical claims, some of which were noticed in the preceding chapter. Believers in the matriarchy have been duped by the false interpretations of partial knowledge; for the matriarchy has never existed in any form which justifies the enthusiasm of its modern adherents.

It will clear the air if we lay down, by way of preface to the description of facts which is to follow, a few general truths, not all recognized by the general public which has interested itself in these matters.

1. The status of women cannot be successfully correlated with the stage of general cultural advance in any given society. We can find a great many examples of very backward peoples where women occupy a fortunate position compared with that of women in the higher civilizations. In the Andaman Islands, which are inhabited by tribes of hunting pygmies devoid of all the higher attributes of social life, women may occupy a position of influence similar to that of the men. The wife of a leading man generally exercises the same sort of influence over the women as her husband does over the men, and they exercise a good deal of influence in

connection with quarrels, either of individuals or of local groups. Moreover, a man is not free to dispose of his wife's personal property, which is everything she herself makes, without her permission. The older women share with the older men the regulation of tribal affairs.

If we compare this state of things with the position of women as we know it in modern Egypt, or even in modern Spain, we shall find that the Andamans are better off in several respects. Many other examples of this general statement will be given later.

ii. Legal status cannot be taken as proving that women have a higher social position. Thus, the Andamanese woman is better off with regard to her ownership of property after marriage than a nineteenth-century Englishwoman. Moreover, among the Iroquois Indians a position has been attained by women wherein they are actually the legal rulers of the people and, as Professor Lowie points out, George Eliot and Madame Récamier, in spite of their social positions, did not even remotely approach this legal position of the average Iroquois woman.

iii. The recognized customs and codified law of a community do not always tally with the practical social habits as far as women's position is concerned. Oliver Goldsmith in *The Citizen of the World* makes his Chinese traveller observe: "Their laws and religion forbid the English to keep more than one woman; I therefore concluded that prostitutes were banished from society. I was deceived; every man here keeps as many wives as he can maintain; the laws are cemented with blood, praised, and disregarded. Their laws may be compared to the books of the Sybils; they are held in great veneration but seldom read, or seldomer understood." If we compare the position of women in some primitive communities with that under the codified social laws of England or the United States, doubtless the comparison will usually be in favour of the latter; but it is an obvious fact that whereas the savage obeys his code to the letter, even though it is not perhaps very high, the civilized man falls below his and in so doing sometimes falls beneath the savage's practice and precept as well.

iv. The habit of naming the child and reckoning descent after the mother does not necessarily prove that the mother has more power. This habit began for the simple reason that the facts of procreation were, as we have seen, for long not understood and that it was often quite impossible in any case to tell who the father was: a difficulty which, as Gibbon cynically remarks, argues for a continuance of the custom long past savage times. This statement need not be taken as a suggestion that a stage of sexual communism everywhere preceded individual marriage,—a point which is very much disputed and cannot be adequately discussed here; but in all early societies we find a degree of extramarital sexual intercourse which is certainly sufficient to prevent any child being wise enough to know its own father. Since so many writers mislead the public into a belief that this custom involved a state of society in which women were rulers—the *matriarchy* itself—it is of the utmost importance to remember that the evidence is wholly against any such state of affairs. "Probably," writes Professor Lowie, "there is not a single theoretical problem on which modern anthropologists are so thoroughly in accord as with respect to the utter worthlessness of that inference. The testimony of the ethnographic data is too clear to be swept aside by *a priori* speculation. Of the Australians some tribes are matrilineal, others patrilineal, but the lot of woman is not one jot better or more dignified among the former. The same holds for the Melanesians. In British Columbia the Tlingit and their neighbours trace descent through the mother, but such authority as her side exerts over the children is wielded not by her but by her brothers. Here property of certain types is highly prized; however, it is not held by women but transmitted with automatic regularity from maternal uncle to nephew. In Africa we hear of female rulers, but their occurrence seems independent of the rule of descent and no more affects the status of the average Negress than the reign of Catherine the Great affected the position of Russian peasant women."

v. We must always remember that in our judgments of the position of primitive women we are very liable to be influenced by our own personal feelings and ideas. For example, nothing seems more obvious to some people than that the Christian religion has exalted women, and among much that is more true these will instance the, to them, appalling degradation of primitive orgiastic religion. Missionaries will usually believe that to save a savage from her participation in a fertility rite is a paramount duty of all decent men. If it is possible to provide a comprehensible and acceptable alternative this is certainly so, but it is as well to recognize the crude good even in what to us is repulsive. If we realize that a belief that sexual love makes the whole world fertile exalts women, we shall be less willing to suppose that such an idea must be exchanged forcefully for one which cannot be understood at all by people of another and simpler culture.

VI. We must remember that among ourselves individualism is a very large part of life, to the savage it is practically non-existent. To us therefore there can be no social habit to which all women can conform with equal happiness. Some women will always have a "fish-out-of-water" feeling, but the savage can never have this feeling, since she is dominated by "sheep-through-the-gappishness," and therefore her happiness comes from conformity with the crowd, ours largely from a position of advantage above the crowd.

VII. Finally we should not forget that a savage woman's lot, in so far as it is a hard one, is so not only because she is a woman, but because she is a savage, between whom and disaster there is nothing but hard work, much endurance and a ceaseless struggle to wrest from nature the means of subsistence.

Moreover, this idea of the savage's lot being infinitely harder than the lot of civilized human beings is very much exaggerated by most observers. Savages are rarely so near the danger line of starvation, rarely so legitimately filled with a concern for the morrow as the majority of our own citizens. The miner's wife and the agricultural labourer's know more of hardship than the average savage woman, faced as they are by an enemy quite as dangerous as the blind forces of nature; namely, the folly of other men.

Fully realizing that it is likely to be impossible to gauge the extent of woman's happiness from time to time in their history and that all generalizations are bound to be wrong and misleading, let us return to contemplate that dangerous, powerful, frightening, contemptible mystery, called woman.

§ 4. *A Wom-* IN order to get a first view of the primitive
an's Life in woman, we will follow the details in the life of
Madagascar. an average woman on the island of Madagascar. The picture will be typical of many which could be drawn from China to Peru, and will contain all the chief features of any savage woman's life.

The hour of birth has come and the mother has given birth to a child: it is a girl. For weeks and months she had tried to avoid this calamity and to secure that her child would be a boy. A girl is well enough for grafting a good stock on another tree, but it is a son that embellishes the family stem, says a Malagasy proverb.

To get a boy, she had assisted at a circumcision and eaten meat given her by the officiator; to avoid a miscarriage, she had carefully abstained from picking any green thing, and with the same object, she had not entered a room where there was a corpse, nor eaten anything alive, nor passed near a gourd-stem; to avoid having a child with twisted legs, she had not walked past a hatchet; to avoid the child's being marked with red birthmarks, she had not eaten mulberries; to avoid its being fat and ugly, she had carefully refrained from laughing at any fat or deformed creature.

Well, the child has been born and though it is but a girl it is alive and healthy; many possible dangers have been circumvented, things could be worse.

It is a girl, and the convalescent mother cannot but remember the proverb: "a son is born of you, they will bury you on a high rock; she who has only borne a daughter will remain laid in the tomb beneath a flagstone, on a slippery stone."

It is a girl, and so the father remains indoors, in no hurry to announce the fact. Had it been a boy, he would have taken his axe and, going out into the courtyard, chopped with all his might at the first piece of wood he met, making as much noise as possible to draw the notice of all his neighbours, and crying: "Look at me, I'm the father of a little boy."

During the pregnancy, social custom had regarded the mother as being dead, and now upon her delivery she has been congratulated on coming alive again. She has also been socially dangerous, and unclean, and she must undergo various ceremonies to make her clean again.

The life of the little girl is uneventful during childhood, save that every sort of game and occupation is hedged about with taboos and restrictions, mysterious dangers and obligations. The first hair-cutting is of great importance and takes place amid friends and relatives with much ceremony, the coming of the teeth is another critical period; but as we are chiefly concerned with sex distinctions we cannot consider them at length.

We pass over her puberty and her marriage, for these we will study elsewhere. As a married woman she will have her own special work and she must on no account interfere with her husband's occupations, nor touch anything which pertains to them. Any kind of stepping over the dividing line would cause quite irreparable ill; a woman's sphere and a man's sphere are strictly separated and must remain so.

The women cook and make clothes, the men hunt and fish; but often it is forbidden to men to fish with a net, or to mend the nets, or to carry water; for these again are women's tasks and would sap the man's virility. In other tribes fishing is practised by all alike, but within the art there are sex-differences; the men must catch only eels, the women must use the net only for catching small fish, while the children of either sex may fish with a line. When the men have caught an eel they must leave it upon the ground for the women to pick up and take home, for no man dare risk his virility by doing such labour.

Whatever else is to be done in the course of daily life has to be divided between the sexes with the same rigorous care: a house is to be built, the men must do the woodwork, while the women add the plaited sides; women make pottery; men get the firewood. In one tribe the men prepare the rice fields, procure game, build houses and discuss public affairs; the women gather vegetable food and fruit, weed the rice fields, dry the rice and make fibre mats. Details vary from tribe to tribe, but everywhere is the same principle, a woman's sphere and a man's sphere, and a partition between charged inches-thick with *mana*, no more to be touched with impunity than a high-tension cable.

Curious things happen when distant tribes chance to meet; thus among the Antimerina the woman must walk in front of her husband, while in south-east Madagascar she must always walk behind. This last rule is due to woman's dangerous character: her passage might provoke some malicious power and harm her husband as he passed; probably the other rule is due to precisely the same reason: women being dangerous had best be kept in sight. In both cases all goes well until culture contact takes place, and the strange customs of foreigners excite irritation in those who do not know them.

The dangerous character of the woman modifies even the least domestic detail; at the table, though the men may all dip their spoons into the common dish, the women must have two spoons, one with which to help themselves and the other to convey the food to their mouth; for eating together is the first rite of the human being and is a time of great danger for the unwary.

Thus work and manners, travelling and eating, are all conditioned by the primary dangerousness of women, but this same quality is even more apparent when man and woman partake of the most intimate of all physical unions. Then especially must evil results be avoided with every care.

When a whale fisher goes out upon a whaling expedition he is beholden for luck in the chase to the goodwill of the whales themselves. These will in no wise let themselves be caught against their will and they must be approached with offerings of grease and oil. "O Whale," the harpooner sings, "O Whale, give me thy child, give me thy child, and I will give thee a present of silver or a present of oil." When a whale is caught it is with humble apologies to its mother and a request that she should go elsewhere lest her maternal feelings be outraged. Now the whale, like the Grail, will grant success only to a pure hunter; to have had sexual contact with his wife makes a man impure and no harpoonist may touch his wife for days before any expedition. Moreover, not only is such contact dangerous, but the actions of his wife even in his absence are liable to affront the whale and stultify her husband's efforts. Throughout the time of the expedition she must remain at home behind locked doors, speaking to no one, least of all to a man.

In spite of all precautions, however, the successful harpooner is unclean and dangerous: and when the expedition returns to shore, he must on no account touch the ground; he must wait until the men on shore seize him, haul him out of the ship and carry him to the doors of his house. This period of uncleanness can come to an end in only one way, and that a way which will seem paradoxical after what has already been said; he must have intercourse with his wife and then only will the impurity fall from him. The very act which is dangerous and likely to make a man unclean and unsuccessful at one time, is his sole means of purification at another.

When the woman comes to die she is still inferior; her husband must mourn for her three weeks, whereas if he had died she would have had to mourn for him for six. In death too she must be divided from her husband, and no man and woman can be buried in the same grave. Such in brief is a typical savage woman's life; but it remains to fill in some very important details.

§ 5. *Menstrua-tion and Mar-riage.* THE life of a woman in Madagascar reveals to us several important facts: first, a woman is unclean and dangerous of her very nature; second, she must therefore not have anything to do with men's work, lest she stultify it with her malign influence; third, no man may defile himself by doing what is woman's work, lest he become unvirile; fourth, sexual intercourse is dangerous to a man and can spoil all his efforts as a hunter; fifth, in certain circumstances sexual intercourse acts as a purifier and is the only way to end a man's own uncleanness. In short, woman, endowed with a double dose of *mana*, is at every moment of her life a sleeping volcano ready to burst forth and do harm to its surroundings.

There are two occasions, however, when a woman is most

apt to be dangerous to man, when the sleeping volcano is most likely to awaken and destroy the happiness of all around.

The first of these is the recurring period of her menstruation. Throughout the primitive world this function, mysterious as it certainly is, was viewed with the utmost fear and suspicion. A perfectly authenticated case is known of an Australian aborigine who discovered that he had slept upon the blanket used by his wife at this period, and forthwith killed her and died of fright himself within a fortnight. "Among all the Déné and most other American tribes, hardly any other being was the object of so much dread as a menstruating woman. As soon as signs of that condition made themselves apparent in a young girl she was carefully segregated from all but female company, and had to live by herself in a small hut away from the gaze of the villagers or of the male members of the roving band. While in that awful state, she had to abstain from touching anything belonging to man, or the spoils of any venison, or other animal, lest she would thereby pollute the same, and condemn the hunters to failure owing to the anger of the game thus slighted. Dried fish formed her diet, and cold water, absorbed through a drinking tube, was her only beverage. Moreover, as the very sight of her was dangerous to society, a special skin bonnet, with fringes falling over her face down to her breast, hid her from the public gaze, even some time after she had recovered her normal state."

Examples of precisely the same nature could be given

from every portion of the globe. Fear of menstruating women is absolutely universal: indeed there can be little doubt that the whole outlook on women has been coloured by the fact, so strange and terrifying to the savage, of her recurring sickness. Instead of accumulating examples, however, we will give a summary of the sort of dangers expected from sexual uncleanness by the Moors.

It should first be noticed that sexual uncleanness is due to any kind of defilement of a sexual nature, whether from menstruation, from the sexual act itself, or otherwise.

Sexual intercourse, says Westermarck, is looked upon as defiling and in certain circumstances as a mysterious cause of evil. No sexual act must be committed in a holy place, a mosque or a shrine, nor is a person who has been polluted sexually allowed to enter such a place before he has washed himself. Should he do so he would suffer some misfortune; he would get blind, or lame, or mad, or he or some member of his family would become ill, or die, or he would lose some of his animals, or his corn crop would be bad. If a person who is not sexually clean visits the tomb of the Aglu saint, Sîdi Daud, which is situated on an island, he will find that the water in the sea has suddenly risen to such a height that he cannot go back to the mainland, but has to wait till it has gone down. A scribe is afraid of evil spirits only when he is sexually unclean, because then his reciting of passages of the Koran—the most powerful weapon against such spirits —would be of no avail. Sexual cleanness is required of those who have anything to do with the corn; for such persons are otherwise supposed to pollute its holiness, and also, in many cases, to do injury to themselves. The ploughman must be sexually clean; otherwise there will be no *baraka* in the seed, or there will grow mostly grass and weeds on the field. So also the reapers and anybody who comes to the threshing floor when the corn is there must be clean; and the same is true of the women who clear the crops of weeds in the spring, lest their work should be without result and they should become ill themselves. When a woman is grinding corn she must be clean or else the flour will be bad.

If then the first of these two periods in a woman's existence particularly dangerous from the point of view of men is her periodical sickness, the second, as might be expected, is her marriage day. Then indeed must a man run a risk which may prove fatal, and when we look at the vast mass of marriage rites and ceremonies devised by mankind in the course of history and bear in mind the *mana* of a woman we realize that most of the marriage services are nothing more nor less than devices to insulate and immunize men from the evil effects of a contact which is nevertheless so much desired. A summary of Moorish ceremonies, again condensed from Westermarck, will suffice to show this.

Amongst the ceremonies in the bridegroom's house before his marriage is the painting of the groom with henna; this is to protect him from bad influences such as evil spirits, magical tricks and the evil eye. For the same purpose he is washed and shaved; he is then beaten by his bachelor friends to rid him of evil influences and a bowl is broken

with the same object. Burning candles and a bottle of water
keep the evil spirits at bay; guns are fired off, loud music is
played, the women keep up a quivering noise, all to warn off
the forces of evil which are accumulating in the atmosphere;
he carries a sword or dagger, other swords are crossed over
his head; charms are worn and salt is sprinkled. Over his
face a hood is pulled and his mouth is covered up to prevent
the entry of any evil thing.

Meanwhile the dangers to which the bride is exposed and
those to which she exposes others lead to ceremonies of purification. She is taken three times across the river to and fro,
or round a shrine, or she is pelted with stones as she leaves
her home. This last custom is variously interpreted as freeing her from evil and as safeguarding her from divorce, or
as making her take with her the evil influence she might
exercise against her village.

When the bride reaches the bridegroom's house more ceremonies take place to prevent her having an evil effect upon
him: she is taken several times round the house; she throws
wheat over her head to rid herself of evil; more shots, more
loud music and more noise from the women warn off attendant spirits; she throws barley over the face of the animal on which she has ridden lest her contact make it barren;
she is carried to the nuptial bed behind a shelter of blankets
to protect people from her dangerous glance. When the two
are left alone together numerous further ceremonies of a
like nature are performed: so dangerous indeed is the consummation regarded that it is stated upon good authority

that sometimes the bridegroom is saved from the possible evils attendant on it by the good offices of a substitute. Even such an inadequate summary as this shows the lengths to which their fear of a woman's *mana* has forced men in their terror to go; yet it could be duplicated from any part of the world; man must protect himself from woman, the universal danger, even when she comes to him as a smiling and much-desired bride.

§ 6. *A Bantu* Two questions naturally arise out of a con-
Woman's templation of this strange picture: first, why
Work. does the history of mankind begin with such strained relations between the sexes, and, second, what practical effect, apart from those already mentioned, had these universal obsessions upon women's life? Before, however, we proceed to examine these questions, it is of importance to affirm once and for all that, in spite of taboo and the fear she aroused, the lot of primitive woman compared very favourably in certain respects with the lot of civilized woman today; and it will be best to proceed forthwith to justify such an assertion. In this night of superstitious terror, what elements were conducive to the happiness of women?

Undoubtedly the first redeeming feature for primitive women is the fact that she had plenty of hard work, though many women have regarded this as something for which she deserves much sympathy.

Indeed, nothing is easier than false sentiment about the

savage woman and her lot. "Don't cant in defence of savages," said Dr. Johnson, and the advice is excellent as far as it goes; but, since so many people deprecate the life and morals of primitive peoples simply to justify the abominations of civilized man in comparison, it is worth while asking how far a savage woman was necessarily more unhappy than any other, even though she had to work harder.

We can pity the wretched lot of the poor Australian mother, her maternal instinct lacerated, her son, flesh of her flesh, torn away from her at puberty forever: but she would not be in any way grateful for the kind sentiments. To her, happiness is to be measured by conformity to custom, as with all other human beings save for a very few intellectualized and individualized exceptions among ourselves. Since the customs are different the thing which produces happiness or unhappiness is different; and not all the taboo in the world can alter that.

The Australian woman at a funeral gashes her scalp horribly and covers herself with blood from self-inflicted wounds; stop her and she will be as grateful as an American negress whose mistress tries to save her the pain of going to a funeral.

Her lot is hard, undoubtedly, but that is not altogether a sex distinction: the savage lot is in many ways hard, though not so hard as it seems to the civilized observer, who is forever, in imagination, putting himself in the savage's place and finding the result distasteful.

Far from its being a burden, we repeat, it is the savage

woman's good fortune that she has plenty of work to do; and in spite of shallow traveller's tales her share is not so unfair as is often thought. Take, for example, the work of a husband and wife among the African Bantu. Here is a yearly schedule of work of a Bakaonde household:

September: The Man has an easy month of it: he helps his wife in the garden, hunts a little, gets honey and makes salt. The Woman hoes the low ground, gardens and sows early corn and beans.

October: The Man continues those occupations and collects five or six different kinds of wild fruit as they ripen. He hunts the cane rat, a great delicacy, and spears fish in the drying pools. The Woman goes on with her planting and sows more corn, beans and pumpkins; she also waters the seedlings.

November: The Man works as before and also collects three more kinds of wild fruit which have become ripe. He begins to hoe the high ground gardens farther away from the house and plants ground nuts and sets fish traps. The Woman sows corn on higher ground and weeds the early gardens where the grass grows rapidly and helps her husband sow ground nuts.

December: The Man collects more wild fruits and digs the sweet potato beds. He starts fencing the high gardens. The Woman plants sweet potato slips in the beds prepared by her husband and collects mushrooms. Both hoe and weed the kaffir corn beds.

January: Both Man and Woman hoe and weed every day this month and the unmarried women go to live in special shelters to look after the crops.

February: The Man stacks the corn cobs and cuts poles for house building. The Woman gathers the corn cobs, pumpkins, cucumbers, beans and stores them. She collects swamp grass for making mats.

March: The Man fences the sweet potato and nut fields and places the poles in position for hut building. The Woman pounds grain and muds the walls of the new huts.

April: The Man goes on building the huts and makes a scaffold for drying red millet. He cuts thatching grass and begins to thatch. The Woman reaps the red millet, digs sweet potatoes and nuts. Both man and woman trap fish.

May: The Man cuts down trees for next year's gardens. The Woman scares birds all day and takes out her grain-pounding apparatus into the garden so as not to be interrupted.

Road cleaning is done by both sexes for the Government; the Women weed and clean, the Men build bridges.

June: The Man continues clearing the ground for next year's cultivation and poisons fish. The Woman reaps kaffir corn.

July: The Man builds temporary grain stores for the kaffir corn and iron smelting is done. The Woman threshes the kaffir corn.

August: The Man builds the permanent grain stores and cuts trees in the swamp grove ready for early planting. The Woman stores the kaffir corn in its permanent store house.

Besides these, there are the daily tasks in which man and woman have an equal share; on the march the man will carry the elder child if necessary; otherwise he carries a spear and an axe to protect the party. As the women say: "What would I do if we met a lion and my husband were carrying a load?" The woman carries any load, such as cook pots and food, on her head and the younger baby on her hip.

In short, the amount of work a woman has to do in such a primitive community is not because she belongs to the weaker or oppressed sex, but because the savage has less leisure in his fight with nature for the means of living. To us the amount of manual labour may seem irksome to the last degree, but nobody has argued since Rousseau that he would like to be a savage. Moreover, just as it may be a law of human justice that he who does not work neither shall he eat, so it is certainly a law of nature that she who does not work neither shall she be happy: as we have already said, it was not when woman began to covet men's work that feminism arose, but when man took away from women their own work. We shall see ample reason later to commiserate not the savage woman on her hard labour, but the civilized woman on her parasitism.

§ 7. *Marriage as Natural Fulfillment.* A FIRST fountain of savage woman's happiness is, then, that she is able to work, without which no living being, male or female, man or animal, can ever be healthy or happy. A second is that she is always able to fulfil her biological functions, she is always a wife and a mother, unless by some rare ill-fate she is physically abnormal. It does not matter where we look amid the vivid kaleidoscope of custom, every woman, as soon as she is ripe for marriage, has a husband. Sometimes, as in Australia, she is the wife at least temporarily of a whole group of men, sometimes she is one of a numerous group of house slaves, sometimes she is a single partner in daily work; she is bought and sold, she is captured by violence, she is got by forced elopement, she is allotted without her will, or she is wooed and won; but always she is married.

A bachelor or an unmarried woman is regarded with suspicion and contempt as a thing most unnatural; and a

barren woman likewise. The fruition of the biological end
of the sexes is an unbroken and inviolable law of necessity
and custom. To have children is the wish of all individuals
from the moment that they themselves cease to be children.

Out of the innumerable accounts of marriage and preparations for marriage suitable for the purpose we will choose
the Ba-ila customs to illustrate how completely and
promptly biological needs are met. Directly an Ila girl is
found to have reached the age of puberty, the women of her
household take hold of her and dance; all her clansmen
join in crying, "Our child has grown up"; the father presents the men with a hoe and asks them to dance for his
daughter. Then the girl is secluded in a dark hut, playing
games and musical instruments; her betrothed husband—
who may have been chosen years before—brings her a
wooden doll decorated with strings of beads.

After two or three months the betrothed husband, becoming impatient, says: "I want my wife to come from under
the bed." At last preparations are made for a great feast
and an old woman gives her final instructions about wifely
behaviour. "You are to be married," she says. "Remember
that a man is to be obeyed, and his food cooked. And when
people come to pay a visit, do not hide your face, but receive
them warmly and hospitably. When you have people in the
house, treat them kindly. And if your mothers-in-law send
you on an errand be quick in starting; they are to be hon-
oured; food is to be ground for them, water drawn for them,

and they are always to be answered respectfully. And in
your house, things are to be done nicely; the pots are to be
kept clean and in good condition, and the house is to be
swept within. And your husband is to be obeyed implicitly
and not answered angrily. When you are married do not act
childishly; you are to provide food. O woman, cook well
and do not spoil the food; you are to be perfect in cooking."

Last counsels having thus been given, the final ceremony
of marriage takes place amid much ritual killing of oxen,
giving of presents, singing, dancing and feasting. Then the
girl is taken to her future husband's house; and on the way
her feet must not touch the ground, she must be carried even
though the husband's village is far away. When she arrives
the women of her party shout, and the bridegroom runs
away and hides: he is afraid of the unknown before him;
as in the tale told in the Apocryphal Book of Tobit there is
danger of disaster during the marriage night; the bridegroom may die of the strange *mana* of the woman he must
touch.

A cousin of the bridegroom, therefore, a young boy,
spends the first night innocently by the girl's side; he is said
to "eat the marriage"; in fact, he renders the bride innocuous in some mystical sense and paves the way for a safe
consummation of the marriage by the husband. The latter
comes next day and the couple eat together, as a symbol of
their equality in the new unity. The husband is instructed to
treat his wife properly: "That child of others," he is told,

"is to have fruit gathered for her and be anointed with fat and clothed with rugs. That is good husbandship, and if you do not anoint her they will take her away from you."

The significance of this is that such customs entirely do away with the ill-effects of enforced celibacy with which we have to reckon in all civilized communities. In England and Wales the percentage of women of marriageable age who are married is 49.2%, in Ireland 33%, in Sweden 44%, in Germany 52%, in Austria 51%, in France 57%, in Italy 56%. Thus in three of these countries more than half the women are unable to fulfil their biological functions in any way recognized by society and in none of the other countries does this proportion fall much below half. Since nature makes it a well-nigh universal law that when any part of our physical machinery is not used, it rusts and throws the rest of the machine out of gear, it is obvious that such a state of affairs is responsible to a large extent for the enormous mass of hysteria, neurosis and insanity which, unlike savages, our civilized communities have to bear. To the savage not only as individual but as a community, the proper ordering of the sexual life is the very basis of existence; and, even if we have ceased to regard it as the end, at least it is sheer hypocrisy to pretend that it is not largely the means of sane social habit and personal comfort. We must indeed assert emphatically that just as the life of a savage woman is on a firmer basis of happiness because she has plenty of work to do, so it is on a firmer basis of happiness because the sexual life is never neglected nor distorted into other and less satisfactory channels. To a "civilized" man, a celibate is often a logical necessity, to a savage he or she is always a pervert.

A very interesting example of the consequent difficulty of explaining the Christian ideas about celibacy and chastity to a savage who has his own ideas on the subject comes from East Africa. According to Dennett, "the great power Bunzi objects strongly to unmarried women; increase and multiply are his standing orders. Virginity, therefore, after one has come to the age of puberty is almost unknown, and is not a state that a woman can be proud of." When therefore the translator of the Gospels into Bavili looked about for a word for the Virgin Mary, and explained that the essential point to be understood was her virginity, he was provided with the word *Ndumba* as being the most suitable. In this version of the Gospels *Ndumba* to this day is the name used for the Virgin, but in reality the word means "fallen woman" or "woman who has lost her virtue," the native interpreters being quite incapable of imagining that "virgin" could be anything but an opprobious epithet; the great god Bunzi believes too strongly in the virtue of fruitfulness.

§ 8. *Superstition Imposed Restraints.* PLENTY of work and an ideally satisfactory sexual life are, as we have just seen, the lot of nearly all primitive women; so that they may be said to possess the principal requisites for biological health and happiness. But this satisfactory foundation is sicklied o'er with the pale cast of thought. It is not that they have hard work, nor even that there is a strict division of labour between the sexes, that depressed their lot, but the nature of some of the conventions which influence those factors.

Division of labour is a biological and economic necessity: to the advantages which it brings we owe the very existence of two sexes, and our distrust of a strictly limited "woman's sphere" must not be allowed to blind us to the fact that there is a sound basis of biological common sense beneath the laws and customs which decree what work men and women respectively shall do in primitive societies.

Husband and wife are partners with different gifts and powers: the former is more muscular and stronger in general; his share is the guarding of the family from enemies and wild animals; he leaves the carrying of burdens to his wife, and this for an excellent reason—his arms must be free to deal with a hidden enemy or a wild beast. The sentimentality of superficial travellers has often thought that this last habit proved a savage woman to be regarded merely as a beast of burden. It is true that these travellers come of a society where great courtesy is shown to women in such matters, where a man of manners "is upon all occasions to shew himself in very great pains for the ladies: if a lady drops even a pin, he is to fly in order to present it"; but the practical good sense of the Bakaonde lady quoted herein would appeal more to the African matron than the more refined and less useful manners that rule in London society.

The woman is peculiarly fitted, or perhaps finds her usefulness limited by nature, to certain other occupations; for periods of months, she is handicapped by pregnancy, and less able to move about efficiently at great distances from the house. Her occupations radiate out from the home, therefore, and are those which enable her to keep an eye on the children already born and to safeguard those yet to come.

So far the division of labour is reasonable and logical; it is what all animals other than man observe without consciousness of its good sense; the partnership between men and women is the same as that between tiger and tigress or between two swallows. It is possible to say that had men and women remained tigers and tigresses all would have been well; but instead of so doing primitive man dislocated the biological division of labour by his beliefs in *mana* and his distrust and terror of women. In consequence he grafted on to the natural and, indeed, admirable biological division of labour a quite different division based upon his thoughts and emotions.

This terror of women, as we have seen, extended to all her works and to all she used to do her work; for to the primitive man an implement or a tool was, as it were, a detachable limb, a physical part of the individual who used it; so that if a woman was full of dangerous *mana*, so too were the tools and the material she used. They were not to be touched or seen with impunity by any man and often they could deprive of his virility any man who was careless enough to touch them.

We have seen the practical effect of this already, but to show how far such ideas can go we may mention the strange belief of the Omaha Indians. When a young Omaha reached puberty he was obliged to fast and undergo a discipline which put him into an abnormal, hypnotic state; while he was in this condition there sometimes came to him in a dream a powerful supernatural Moon Being. In one hand the Moon Being held the symbol of male labour, a bow and arrows, in the other the symbol of feminine labour, a pack strap such as all Indian women use. The boy must take from the Moon Being's hand the bow and arrows; but he must be very careful indeed how he did this, for at the last moment the Being might cross his arms over and give him instead the pack strap. If this terrible misfortune happened, the boy upon waking was obliged to act for the rest of his life as a woman, to speak and dress and work as one and even to take men as husbands. It is extraordinary to think how powerful this feeling must be in the mind of a primitive man, for it is quite certain that the dream is sometimes dreamed and not concealed but acted upon by the unfortunate dreamer. Such is the fear of touching a woman's tools in certain cases that a man's life is ruined by it; and though such an example is rare, it illustrates what in less marked forms is an almost universal feeling.

We must, however, ask ourselves a question at this

point: does this mystical division of labour between the sexes really tend to depress the savage woman? Clearly, her dangerous *mana* has effects which, like the ripple from a splash, spread in ever-widening circles to the confines of the universe.

But, when all is said and done, what has all this to do with women's happiness? Her freedom of action is very much restricted, it is true, but only within the bounds of a rigid convention which she breathes and assimilates as easily as the air about her. It is, indeed, only at a later period, when these hard-dying conventions remain on though the conditions have changed completely, that they begin to handicap women severely; for in the progress of time and the growth of civilization the woman's sphere gradually decreases and the man's increases, until all that is attractive is to be found in the latter and women find their time hang heavy on their hands. But this history belongs to a later chapter; we need only repeat here that though the artificial division of labour did little or no harm to primitive women, the idea of a circumscribed sphere, carried over from primitive societies, was a main source of women's discontent in later days.

§ 9. *Exclusion from Religion.* IF we cannot be dogmatic about the evil effects of the savage dread of women as far as this leads to a sexual division of labour, however stupid it seems to us, we can, without any doubt, point to another practical effect of this dread which is undoubtedly evil in every way.

Since women were unclean they were, in the early stages of savage society, rigidly excluded from the religious life of the community; thus in Australia tribal ceremonies may be divided into major and minor, and at the latter only could women participate.

Both alike centred in the great moment when the boy, having reached the age of puberty, was to be received into full tribal membership, to leave the company of women and children and to become a man, with all the privileges of that state. As the moment when the central mysteries that were to be revealed was approaching, all the women had to leave the sacred ground and return to their own camp; for the ceremonies about to be held were those which no woman might see and live. At these Tundun, God himself, came down and made the boys into men, and though the roaring of his voice could be heard far and wide, no woman must see him. So strong was this feeling, Howitt tells us, that fifty years after the country was settled by the white man, a headman said: "If a woman were to see these things, or hear what we tell the boys, I would kill her."

The boys who are to be initiated are told that they are going to be "shown their grandfathers." They are placed in a row and covered with blankets so that they are unable to see anything which is going on about them. Shortly an appalling noise is heard, a roar like a ship's foghorn, rising and falling, wailing and groaning in the air about their heads. In spite of the frightful experiences already suffered by the unfortunate novices, sweat pours from them as they listen to the voice of God. Next they are bidden to stand up and look into the sky. "Look there! Look there! Look there!" cries the headman, pointing with his throwing stick first up- wards, then gradually lower till he reaches sixteen men who have been responsible for the noise. The terrified novices learn then the secret of Tundun's voice; it is made by whirl- ing a "bull-roarer," a flat piece of wood on the end of a string, like the civilized child's "buzzer," which howls loudly as it is whirled about their heads.

Next, two old men run to the novices and in a very earnest manner command them: "You must never tell this. You must not tell your mother, nor your sister, nor any one who is not initiated." After further explanations the boys take the bull-roarer in their hands and whirl it with some re- luctance for the first time.

Later in the day a great ceremony takes place with the name, significant for our history, of "Frightening the Women." Each novice, bull-roarer in hand, advances to- wards the camp where are the women and children; these have always been taught that the hideous noise heard in the distance is Tundun himself come to "make the boys into men," and they have been warned never to leave the camp while he is about, lest he kill them. Concealing themselves behind trees and bushes, the initiated youths walk round and round the camp, whirling their bull-roarers with gusto, thoroughly entering into the fun of frightening the women, who are terrified at the sound.

Here we have in a simple naïve form the early relationship between women and religion: they are excluded from the Holy of Holies, unfit for the crowning mysteries of life; they remain a child where social maturity is the sharing in just these ceremonies which are forbidden to them. Puerile as the imposture of Tundun may seem, such things are tolerated and encouraged throughout the lowest social organisms; moreover, the women themselves have the firmest belief in the wickedness of their seeing any of the mysteries. Thus Bishop Codrington tells how a woman in the New Hebrides accidentally saw a newly initiated youth during his purificatory washing, and fled to a neighbouring mission school in terror at her sin; when her people came after her, she voluntarily gave herself up, and returned, to be buried alive without a murmur.

Apart altogether from the loss of interest and self-respect caused to women by their exclusion from the mysteries of their tribe, they often suffered a great deal from being deprived of their share of everyday work by the same cause. Often religion centred in the main material interests of the community as with the Todas of India, a milk-drinking people, who developed an elaborate ritual around their dairies. In this dairy ritual women, being regarded as unclean, could take no part, they could not milk the buffalo nor churn the milk; they could enter only into the outer buildings of the dairy, and this only when they were being used as funeral huts and contained the bodies of dead men. Even then they could sit only along one side of the room and only when dairy operations were not in progress. Sometimes, if important dairy ceremonies were being performed, all the women had to leave the village altogether until they were over. The more important sacred dairymen might have very little to do with any woman; some might have intercourse with one on Sunday and Wednesday but lost their posts if they were so much as touched by one on any other day; others of a higher grade had to be totally celibate. One of the consequences of this exclusion was that Toda women had little work to do; they might take no part in the dairy work; they might do no cooking, at least if milk was an ingredient of the dish, as in most cases it was; they confined their efforts to pounding grain, cleaning the hut and decorating clothes. Their intelligence, left unstimulated by their lack of social importance or duties, was less than that of the men, and though some of the younger women were almost the intellectual equals of their men, all the older women were hopelessly stupid. When Dr. Rivers gave them psychological tests they did not apply themselves to them with anything like the interest shown by the men. Thus, as might have been expected, seclusion and exclusion from religious rites and social interests degrade and stunt the women who have to submit to them.

§ 10. *The Ter-* THE practical effects of the belief in women's
ror of
Women. uncleanness were a division of labour which,
though not strictly conforming to biological principles, did not usually depart from them too far; a rigorous conventional partition between the man's and the

woman's sphere; and the exclusion in the earlier communities from religious participation. Can we now give any suggestions as to the cause of such a universal idea?

The most superficial reason which suggests itself is that the superior physical strength of the man conquered the weaker woman and kept her as a slave. If the practical effects of this slavery had been all to his advantage, it might have been worth while following this idea further; but it is at once clear that the primitive man's outlook on women is in no sense dictated by self-interest, but by fear. To be in such a state of terror of a captive would indeed be paradoxical.

It is hard to estimate the effect of women's physical weakness upon their history; it certainly terrified men, more than men's strength terrified women; and where women enjoy a higher status they are not physically stronger, nor is brute strength less in evidence. In short, we must look elsewhere for an explanation of the belief in feminine uncleanness. To think it is merely a ruse of the brutal male in order to keep his wife in subjection is as stupid as the remark of a lady in Boston who objected to the author's using the phrase "maternal instinct" in a lecture, and said "maternal instinct was invented by men to keep women in subjection." Her position does not help our comprehension of the facts even if it gets some support from the doctrines of Professor J. B. Watson.

There is more reason to believe that behind man's attitude to women there lies the shadow of a physiological experience; the bitter experience which Shakespeare described in the hundred and twenty-ninth sonnet, the disappointment of possession:

> Enjoy'd no sooner but despised straight;
> Past reason hunted; and no sooner had,
> Past reason hated, as a swallowed bait,
> On purpose laid to make the taker mad:
> Mad in pursuit, and in possession so;
> Had, having, and in quest to have, extreme;
> A bliss in proof, and prov'd, a very woe;
> Before, a joy proposed; behind, a dream.
> All this the world well knows; yet none knows well
> To shun the heaven that leads men to this hell.

The same fact was put more tersely by the classical poet when he reminded us that "all animals are sad after the sexual act, except the cock who crows." It is quite possible that this psycho-physiological tiredness and distaste is responsible for the fear of women, especially since savages at an early stage can hardly have known how to be temperate, when their full strength was required for fighting or hunting; this would explain also the taboos upon sexual intercourse before these expeditions, for excesses might very well make a warrior feel "effeminate" and it would be only natural for him to blame the wife, who was the unconscious and perhaps unwilling cause. Thus, too, would be explained the fear of being made unvirile by a woman's touch, for nothing can in very fact so surely unman a man as sexual excess.

However, a place must be found for a third possible cause; namely, the fear which we have abundantly illustrated of contamination from any product of the human body, a fear which would naturally be oftenest stimulated by women. Especially would women come under the ban, by reason of their menstrual periods, when they lose that which is the very symbol of life. It is this which causes the rigid seclusion of girls at puberty all over the world and their periodical seclusion thereafter; it is this too which makes the marriage of a man with a virgin so dangerous that the most elaborate systems of insulation have grown up to save his life; it is this which makes childbirth a time of great spiritual uncleanness from which both mother and child must be purified with all formality.

Blood, symbol of life, is the substance which is most charged with *mana* and therefore most surrounded with taboo; the Creeks and Cherokee "through a strong principle of religion abstain in the strictest manner from eating the blood of any animal, as it contains the life and spirit of the beast." In East Africa animals are stoned or beaten to death so as not to shed their blood; throughout the world it is the same. In one direction such beliefs may have led to an increased respect for life and a general humanitarianism, but it is sad to think that in another they have led men astray in a bewitched forest of ignorance and stained their relations with women with a more indelible stain than any blood might leave.

§ 11. *The Worship of Fertility.* THE reader will not have failed to notice that many of the examples given show the beginning of a change from the condemnation of women to the praise of chastity. Both men and women must be chaste in time of war, before and during a hunting expedition; and upon innumerable other occasions, great virtue or *mana* appertains to those who do not diverge from perfect continence.

A woman's every action is bound to have an effect on the fortunes of the chase: In Indo-China if an elephant, once it is captured, breaks away, it is because the wife of a huntsman has been unfaithful; if a rope snaps, it is because she has cut her hair; if it slips, it is because she has anointed her body with oil. In all these cases the hunter has a right to divorce his wife on his return, while he on his side must carefully refrain from all sexual intercourse while the hunt is continuing.

In the same way with fishing; we have seen the care with which the Madagascar whaler avoided his wife. The custom is universal. Among the Tlingit of North America a man who is about to hunt sea otter fasts and avoids his wife for a whole month; otherwise, when he is about to aim, his arm will shake and cause him to miss. The Tlingit also believe that the pubescent girl can destroy at a glance the luck of a hunter, a fisher or a gambler, and turn things to stone, and so they shut her up in strict seclusion for two or three months.

There is nothing to be gained by accumulating examples

of how chastity is regarded as essential to success in hunting and fishing. Throughout the world it is the same story, some variation or other on the same interminable theme. In the Caroline Islands a fisherman must avoid women throughout the eight weeks of the season; if he goes ashore, he must go to the men's Club House; if he glances at his wife or any other woman, flying fish will bore out his eyes. If his wife, mother or daughter brings him a gift or wishes to talk to him, she must stand on the shore with her back to the men's Club House: not for an instant must she look in his direction, nor he in hers.

Sometimes the dangerous effect of a woman's presence or contact prevents the fermenting of beer; sometimes if the man and woman who brew honey-wine have not been chaste the wine is undrinkable and the bees fly away; sometimes the presence of a woman prevents poison being venomous; in order to protect themselves from demons the people of Bura anoint themselves with coconut oil, but this must have been prepared by virgins; elsewhere coconut oil is an antidote to poison, but only if the nuts have been gathered by virgin youths and the oil extracted from them by the maidens. In South Africa married people must be continent while a new village is being built, otherwise work is stopped and a new site chosen, since the chief would die and the village be unlucky for the old one. Finally, the continence of warriors is almost universally enjoined among all primitive peoples.

In some of these examples we seem to approach a point

of view which is to occupy much of our attention later; the condemnation of women, involved in a fear of them as dangerous, is commuted as we have said into a praise of chastity:

> She that hath that, is clad in compleat steel,
> And like a quiver'd Nymph with Arrows keen
> May trace huge forests, and unharbour'd Heaths,
> Infamous Hills, and sandy perilous wildes,
> Where through the sacred rayes of Chastity,
> No savage fierce, Bandite, or mountaineer
> Will dare to soyle her Virgin purity,
> Yes there, where very desolation dwels
> By grots, and caverns, shag'd with horrid shades,
> She may pass on with unblench't majesty,
> Be it not don in pride, or in presumption.
> Som say no evil thing that walks by night
> In fog or fire, by lake or moorish fen,
> Blew meager Hag, or stubborn unlaid ghost,
> That breaks his magick chains at curfew time,
> No goblin, or swart faery of the mine
> Hath hurtfull power o'er true virginity.
>
> —*Comus.*

We must, however, distinguish carefully between the primitive outlook upon chastity and the Christian outlook of a later date: as we have already seen the primitive did not regard chastity as good in itself, nor yet as a special virtue in women. To him it was sometimes necessary for a man or for a woman as a precaution against the mysterious dangers of sexual contact; it was merely the state of avoiding the possibility of contracting a mystical contagion, a purely negative precaution. As a rule of life chastity seemed unnatural, ludicrous, wicked, and for a very important reason, which we must now explain, prefacing such explanation by suggesting to the reader that we are about to study one of the three most crucial points in the whole history of women.

We have seen women excluded from all religion and all the mysterious ceremonial side of Australian savage life; and although it would be wrong to infer that women were in consequence less happy, they are certainly debarred by such a system from any advancement, spiritual or mental, and from any power: they may be happy, but at best theirs is the happiness of a cow.

Yet even here there is a glimmering of what will later carry them to a great height: for when an important council or meeting is being held by the men of the tribe, women are kept upon the meeting-ground and with them the debaters have intercourse from time to time. The reason given for this is that it prevents anything from going wrong with the ceremonies, for example the decoration of down and feathers will not fall off the men. In another tribe a woman performs a singing ceremony in order to make a lizard, which is an article of food, grow fat. In some tribes headache can be cured by putting a woman's head ring to the spot: the pain will pass into the ring and can be thrown away with it into the bush.

In these rude ideas we see the beginning of a reverence of women because of their fertility: and it was this idea which blossomed out and became their greatest defence against the fear and abhorrence which they inspired; it grew and expanded until at the opposite end to this simple, uncouth feeling we find the gorgeous and full-hearted cult of the great goddess of fertility: Isis. Let us look for a moment at what lies between.

Not only was woman the giver of children, but by her power she could also give or withhold fertility from the fields, the woods, and all the children of nature. Without her life-giving power the crops would fail and the cattle grow fewer, and in order to ensure rich increase of the earth in due season her constant presence and attention were needed.

It is for this reason that the women work in the fields so hard and are little helped by the men, as the missioner, Father Gumilla, found, when he tried to interfere on humanitarian grounds with the natives of the Orinoco. "My brothers," he asked, "why do you not help your poor wives in the labour of sowing the fields, for they work hard in the heat of the sun, with their infants at their breasts? Do you not realize that they may fall ill and your children likewise? Come now, come and help them!" "Father," they would answer, "you do not understand these things, and that is why you are troubled about it. You must remember that our women know how to bring forth and we do not. If they sow the seed, the maize stalk yields two or three corn-cobs; the yucca stem bears a triple yield, and thus everything is increased. Why is this? Because women are able to bring forth, and are able to command the seed they sow to be productive. Let them do the work of sowing, for we do not know so much about it."

Just as the hunter, the fisher, the warrior, all those who destroy life, must keep away from their wives when about to become the ministers of death, so the moment when the seed is about to be sown, when increase and fertility are to be sought, is the moment when men must seek women and celebrate the rites which seem most obviously to symbolize and to invoke the end in view. Among the Pipiles of Central America it was a sin to sow the seed unless at the same moment men and women were consummating in their own persons the worship of fertility. In Java, when the broom is appearing upon the rice, the husbandman and his wife repair to the fields at night to perform the same ceremony.

So too in other parts of the world when the rainy season is beginning, the populace proceeds to help nature in her task of making the world young again: the sun, the male-principle, represented as a lamp of coconut leaves, is hung in the fig trees, whence he descends to fertilize the earth: men and women dramatically represent this mystical union in the most realistic manner, while all around the rest sing an epithalamium. Prayer is offered to the sun that every she-goat may have two or three young, the people multiply, the rice baskets be filled, and pigs come to replace those which have been killed.

Nor are these beliefs and practices confined to isolated and remote quarters of the earth. Sir James Frazer tells us

of customs in various parts of Europe which are clearly
based upon this same belief, that intercourse between the
sexes is valuable for increasing the crops and the harvest.
Thus in Ukraine, on St. George's Day, the 23rd of April,
the priest in his robes, attended by his acolytes, goes out to
the fields of the village, where the crops are beginning to
show green above the ground, and blesses them. Then the
young married people lie down in couples on the sown fields
and roll several times over on them, in the belief that this
will promote the growth of the crops. In England, it seems,
says Sir James Frazer, to have been the custom for young
couples to roll down slopes together on May Day and the
same was to be seen until lately near Dublin on Whit
Monday. "When we consider how closely these seasons,
especially May Day and Whitsuntide, are associated with
ceremonies for the revival of plant life in spring, we shall
scarcely doubt that the custom of rolling in couples at such
times had originally the same significance which it still has
in Russia; and when further we compare this particular
custom with the practise of representing the vernal sowers
of vegetation by a bridal pair, we shall probably do no injustice to our forefathers if we conclude that they once celebrated the return of spring with grosser rites, of which the
customs I have referred to are only a stunted survival."

§ 12. *Exam-*
ples of Matri-
archy.
WHY is this? "Because women are able to
bring forth, and are able to command the seed
they sow to be productive. Let them do the

work of sowing, for we do not know so much about it."
The rebuke of the Indians to Father Gumilla contains the
explanation of women's rise to power and respect in spite
of all fear of their *mana*, and all disgust at their uncleanness.

It is abundantly clear, therefore, that such a state of exalted social esteem will be associated with agriculture most
often; for esteem in primitive communities is granted to
those individuals who deserve most of their companions, because they are most valuable to the whole group. Women are
clearly most valuable where the group depends for its very
subsistence upon the fertility of mother earth and the increase of cultivated crops, since in the opinion of primitive
man by virtue of their sex they are indispensable to their
fertility. If the group depends upon its hunters only, and
upon the power of dealing death to the creatures of the
earth, then women are degraded, since their touch may take
away the strength which the men need in order to kill; if the
group depends upon the gift of life, all the strength of men
is of no avail without the *mana* of women.

In order to understand the history of women we must
realize the absolute universality of this rule: women are
respected and exalted in the long run not because of any
idealism or high code of social morality, which may be
preached, but in so far as they are valuable members of the
community; and their value to the community depends upon
the economic structure at any time of a given community.
Thus women are always fertile beings, and givers of fer-

tility in a far wider sense than a merely physical one; but because the gift of fertility is sometimes more appreciated and sometimes less, the status of women varies.

But having made such a generalization it is necessary to hedge it round with certain limiting provisos: if we look at all the primitive communities today we do not find any hard and fast rule that women are *always* more fortunate in agricultural than in hunting or pastoral communities. Thus in Africa it would be very hard to prove that the women of the Herero, who are a purely stock-raising people, are de- graded as compared with other Bantu people, who practise agriculture. This does not, however, deprive our general statement of any force; at a given moment the social customs and with them the position of women are conditioned not merely by the actual economic structure, but by the whole past economic history of the group. If, for example, we imagine that of two agricultural tribes one gave up agricul- ture for pure stock-breeding and the other did not, it would take many generations for the social conventions to alter sufficiently to degrade the women in the former; but in the end the tendency would lie that way. We know from biology that the parasite loses its bodily independence and becomes hopelessly degenerate in form and function, but it takes time for this to happen. Thus though the application of the law is difficult, the law of itself is unshaken.

It should perhaps be explained that it is not so much that fertility rites in themselves exalt women as that in the realization of their necessity lies the germ of a feeling which promises advancement to all women. Thus if a community thought that the crops would grow better if the blood of a woman was poured over them and if for this purpose many women were killed, it would be hard to say that the fertility rite added to the actual happiness of women. But it is true to say that the mysterious connection felt by some savages to exist between women and fertility has in it the basis of what may grow into a just appraisal and valuation of women as a sex. We may perhaps make this clearer by an analogy from modern life: it would be absurd to suggest that it exalts women or increases their happiness to employ them as stenographers rather than to leave them sitting about at home; but the economic freedom which may come and the realization of their usefulness will probably have an excellent effect upon the male outlook on women as a sex.

Let us see further to what length this worship and need for fertility in nature has exalted women in certain exceptional cases, such as the Khasis of India and the natives of the Pelew Islands.

The Khasis are a tribe of rice cultivators in the hills of Assam: among them the position of women is exceedingly interesting. Upon marriage the husband goes to live in his wife's mother's house and remains there at least until several children have been born. While they are in the mother-in-law's house the wife's earnings go to her and are spent by her for the family expenses; the husband does not contribute: later, if the couple have a house of their own the wife pools her earnings with the husband's. The wife is the

owner of the ancestral property and through her it is inherited. If there is a divorce the wife has the custody of the
child, but she cannot be divorced during pregnancy nor
without her desire. Descent is reckoned from the mother
only; the man is of little importance since he will be lost to
the clan when he marries, and as a husband he is regarded
merely as a begetter; sometimes indeed his wife's family
merely call him "someone else's son," yet the wife calls her
husband "lord."

Religion is completely in the hands of the women; they
perform the family ceremonies and propitiate the family
ancestors. The youngest daughter owns the house, but she
must consult her sisters before she disposes of it. Even
before marriage a man does not himself own the property
he may acquire; it belongs to his mother.

In short, the social organization of the Khasis is one of
the most perfect examples of a "matriarchal" institution in
existence; the mother is not only the head of the family but
the only owner of real property and only through her is
inheritance transmitted. The father has no kinship with his
children, since they belong to their mother's clan. Most of
the spirits propitiated by sacrifice and libation are female,
the demons of sickness and death are female, the guardian
spirits of the house are female, priestesses assist at all sacrifices and the priests are subordinate to them. In one case
the head of the state, a royal priestess, is a woman.

We can pass all the way from India to Micronesia and
find much the same state of affairs among the Pelew Island-

ers. Here descent is female and a man's heirs are not his own children but those of his sister or of his maternal aunt. The members of the clan worship a goddess and not a god, every village-state has its own deities, a goddess as well as a god, but the goddess is the older and the god has been added later.

In such a system the life of a woman is more important than that of a man, since the most important thing is the continuity of the clan. Even if every man perished the clan would still go on, for the women would marry men of another clan, as usual, and their children would inherit their mother's clan. But the death of the women would be the death of the clan; hence the women are treated with equal or greater respect in social life and are called "mothers of the land." It is even stated upon good authority that they are politically and socially superior to the men and that feminine influence is predominant.

Why is it that the natives of the Pelew Islands who are not distinguished by any high culture or civilization in other ways have thus elevated women to so high a position? Fortunately a clear answer can be given: it is because the Pelew Islanders are cultivators who conceive of women as the possessors of a special gift of fertility and leave the cultivating of the staple crop, taro, entirely in their hands. "This cardinal branch of Pelew agriculture, which is of paramount importance for the subsistence of the people, is left entirely in the hands of the women. . . . The women

do not merely bestow life on the people, they also do what
is most essential for the preservation of life, and therefore
they are called 'Mothers of the Land,' and are politically
and socially superior to men. . . . No chief would ever
come to a decision without first consulting with the 'Mothers
of the Family.' From this point of view it is impossible to
regard the assignment of the taro cultivation to women as
a consequence of their subordinate position in society: the
women themselves do not so regard it. The richest woman
of the village looks with pride on her taro patch, and although she has female followers enough to allow her merely
to superintend the work without taking part in it, she nevertheless prefers to lay aside her fine apron and to betake
herself to the deep mire, clad in a small apron that hardly
hides her nakedness, with a little mat on her back to protect her from the burning heat of the sun, and with a shade
of banana leaves for her eyes. There, dripping with sweat
in the burning sun and coated with mud to the hips and
over the elbows, she toils to set the younger women a good
example."

In the same way the Khasis are agriculturists first and
last and although customs with regard to women and the
crops have not been recorded, we may be sure that the position of women is directly to be traced to the same ideas as
those which produced the matriarchy of the Pelew Islanders,
and all the other examples of women's power and exaltation
we have been examining.

§ 13. *Polyg-*
amy Not De-
basing.

I⊤ is precisely the handful of cases like the Khasis, the Pelew Islanders and, perhaps the best known of all, the Iroquois Indians, that has led to the mass of false doctrine and propaganda nonsense of the matriarchy. They have been taken as survivals of a golden age of women's emancipation and domination, and by some of male ruination and damnation. As we have seen, this idea has been bolstered up by the undoubted fact that throughout a large part of the world descent was traced on the mother's side, before it was traced on the father's side; but this was an effect not of a reverence of women nor of their importance, but of the ignorance of fatherhood, as a natural function, or of the actual father of a given child.

But the institutions of the Khasis, for example, are not primitive at all, except by a common abuse of the term; they are not examples of an early stage of human evolution, but the latest outcome of precisely the same period of history as the women's suffrage acts in America and England. The period from the beginning of the human family to the year 1927 is the same for a Khasi as it is for ourselves and in that time they have produced a "matriarchy" just as England has produced women's suffrage.

The idea of an ordered evolution of human institutions must be given up by all who would study successfully the history of women; otherwise all sorts of misunderstandings creep in. Thus it is quite commonly believed by a great many people that the scale of women's ascent is marked by the sexual institutions of promiscuity, group marriage, polygamy and monogamy. Nothing is farther from the facts: to begin with, there is no good evidence to believe that promiscuity, as a legalized social custom, has ever existed widely; group marriage, whereby a group of women are married to a group of men, is found only rarely; while polygamy and monogamy certainly do not follow one another regularly in every society. Moreover, missionaries and sentimentalists have deliberately misstated the facts of polygamy in order to suit their own theories of life.

Polygamy—that is the possession of more than one legal wife by a single man—is a widespread phenomenon; that is, there are innumerable societies in which it is practised; and yet it is perfectly well known that throughout the world the proportions of men and women are almost equal. Clearly then, it is possible to *practise* polygamy only in a few limited cases. Thus an African tribe, the Bakaonde, are polygamous, but the proportions of the sexes are as thirty-seven women to thirty-one men. There are, therefore, only six women in every thirty-seven who are left over by a system of monogamy. It is not surprising, then, that only two men have six wives, four men have five, fifteen have four, one hundred have three, one thousand one hundred and ten have two, while four thousand seven hundred and seventy-eight have one only; the rest are unmarried, so that what injustice there is in polygamy is largely borne by the men who are deprived of a wife by the greediness of other men.

Moreover, even this exaggerates the practice of polygamy, for by a wise rule the widow of a dead man becomes the wife of his brother, who is bound to protect her; so that quite a large proportion of the plurality of wives is due to inheritance rather than the free choice of the men.

A most important point follows from this: polygamy is a class distinction, it is an example of the break-down of the equality of all individuals within the group, which distinguishes many primitive societies. The rich man or the powerful man has several wives, the poor one at most one: it is a different thing to be the wife of a poor man, and the wife of a rich: a new element has entered into the question of a woman's happiness, that of envy of others within the group; and also it is a different thing to be the first and favoured wife and to be a subsidiary one; there is also envy within the family.

Out of this last fact many people have built a wretched picture of a woman's lot in a polygamous household: but close observers do not always agree that this is so. Among the Bakaonde, for example, "on the whole things go quite smoothly"—and what more could be said of an average monogamous family?

The same deductions can be made from another African tribe, the Ba-ila, so brilliantly studied by the Reverend Edwin Smith and Captain Dale; the excess of women over men is as 110 to 100, therefore only ten men in a hundred could be polygamists, and these ten will very often, it appears, have as much trouble as solace from their extra wives. "The life of a polygamist," writes Mr. Smith, "is not always a rosy one; if he wishes to preserve domestic peace he has to exercise considerable tact. While he must be careful to show no marked favour to one wife at the expense of another, there is a recognized scale of dignity in the family. The chief wife, e. g., may, if the man is rich in cattle, have thirty cows allotted to her household to milk, the second wife fifteen, and the third ten. While they fight among themselves, they will in case of necessity unite against the husband. Cases are not unknown where the husband is chastised by his wives when they consider themselves slighted collectively by his attentions to other women. A friend of ours once witnessed such a scene in a village. The four wives of a man were giving him a thrashing and talking something like this: 'Why did you marry us? You spend your strength on other women and we have no children. Are we not women also? If we cannot have children by you, what is the use of you? We will all leave you.' On the other hand, many polygamists are very devoted to their wives and live happily. We know of one such man, who, in his anxiety to satisfy his eleven wives, sought a strong aphrodisiac from a missionary that would enable him to visit them all each night."

The authors quote Westermarck with approval that "polygamy implies a violation of woman's feelings"; but they point out that Ba-ila women's jealousy is compensated by the fact that many hands make light work, and that it is dignified to be the wife, however inferior, of a rich man. And here we meet with a point which has escaped the notice of many critics of polygamy: often polygamy is a positive and very practical benefit to even the women themselves.

If we turn to Northern Nigeria, we find this even more clearly: there we are told that it is commonly the wife who incites the husband to add to the number of his wives, no doubt with a view to lightening her domestic burdens. In short, where marriage means, for the woman, chiefly doing her husband's work, she desires to share her husband with other women; where, as with ourselves, it means chiefly spending her husband's income, her feelings are violated by the thought of it. There are psychological ramifications of the question, but the difference of views suggested is in itself very real. The point of view of both man and woman is admirably summed up by R. E. Dennett in *At the Back of the Black Man's Mind*, thus: "With regard to polygamy and its effect upon the condition of the women, it is true that, apparently, certain women have always existed in this country who object very strongly to sharing their husband with others, and such are said to be 'bad women' or 'women of spirit.' But as a rule the first wife asks her husband for women to help her in her work, and such a woman is called a good woman or creature."

In parts of the world where polygamy has been thought to degrade women, it will generally be found that such degradation is at least equally caused by other factors, such as easy divorce and the outlook we have so often discussed here. But enough has been said for our purpose, which is to discredit the facile supposition that marriage has always

evolved through lower forms to higher, ending in monogamy, and that polygamy is in itself symbolic of the degradation of women. In so doing we have been discussing
legalized polygamy and not the practical polygamy of our
own community, which, by fostering deceit, disease and vul-
garity, degrades all human beings.

§ 14. *Stend-hal and a Di-gression.* ALTHOUGH with the present section this chapter must be brought to a close, we cannot as
yet indicate adequately how important the
study of primitive women is for the understanding of
women's history as a whole. Much that is of interest will
be seen in its true colours only as the rest of the story un-
winds.

We can, however, ask ourselves a few general questions.
In the first place why, in primitive societies, did men want
women, and why did women want men?

Turning to Stendhal's four categories and the fifth which
was added to them, we see that philoprogenitive love was
the chief bond between them: their union implied a family
and a home and, indeed, so natural and powerful was this
desire that men and women might be said to approximate in
practice to the theory developed in Plato's *Symposium;* that
originally each complete individual was both a man and a
woman, but was sliced in half by Zeus and that ever after
the two halves have rushed about seeking to combine again
into one. In short, the human unit among savages is not a

man or a woman, but a pair living united in marriage. The desire to have children overpowers all other motives, but second to it is the economic dependence of one individual upon the other.

Of passion love there are no traces, except very rarely: that is, the preference of one individual for another for irrational motives unconnected with usefulness or wealth is the product of civilized sophistication. Of physical love there is less than is often imagined: that is, very few savages are interested in women sexually apart from their desires to have a home, children and work done by a suitable spouse. Since there was no room at all in the primitive society for repressed sexual feeling, this never became a prime motive and prostitution is very rare as compared with its incidence in large civilized cities. Naturally a savage prefers a handsome woman for a wife, but he sees to it, before committing himself, that she has other substantial recommendations as well.

Vanity love begins directly there are classes within the community and the possession of several wives or of one rich one is a mark of social distinction. Polygamy, as we have seen, usually implies such social classes and is often the method used by a *nouveau riche* to acquire merit and to promote envy; but sometimes it is nothing more than a capital investment, for though a wife costs a good deal in the first instance, her labour brings in an excellent return for money invested. Women, too, are vain of the strength of their husbands and their skill in the hunt; but as with all their other property each sex regards its mate from the standpoint of use rather than of show.

Gallant love, which is naturally the outcome of a very much more advanced state of sophistication, is curiously foreshadowed in the customs of the Shan tribes of Upper Burma, and a happy digression in this direction may be permitted as recompense for much that is depressing and even revolting elsewhere in the book.

The little Palaung girls put on their first skirt at the age of ten and are forced to receive parties of boys for an evening visit, during which they are pinched by the visitors without mercy, and unprotected by their parents. This is a sort of "coming out" ceremony, and is immediately followed by other visits, at which one boy, who has drawn the particular girl by lot, recites poems to her and she replies with more poetry. "We are friendly like paper flags," she says, "like flags with cut-out patterns. Thou art the sky, I am the earth; thou art the silk, I am the cotton; thou art the beeswax, I am the black lacquer; if thou sleepest near me thou wilt become ugly; to sleep a little while is not sweet; if thou sittest near me thou art in the mud; if thou walkest near me, thou walkest over a chestnut's prickly cover." The boy answers and the duologue continues with such verses as these, spoken by the boy: "I looked into the water as I dressed, I looked into the water as into a mirror. My heart ached in my body: I longed to be with thee. I ate my rice half cooked, the curry and vegetables were not ready, I ate only rice. I was in such haste my food did not reach my mouth. I was angry with my mother, I was angry with my friends and with my old mother. I did not think of my faults. I did not remember that there is a hell."

At first a young man is present to prompt the boy and a young woman to help the girl; but later the girl receives the boys alone, and these visits continue apparently until marriage. Moreover, people address one another in symbolic phrases as a general habit. Thus a young man says to a girl: "I have eaten the flowers of the cotton," meaning: "I long to have you." And the reply is: "I have eaten of the flowers of the paddy and the flowers of the cotton," meaning: "I also want you, but I am afraid." Readers of Marcel Proust will notice the anticipation of Swann's and Odette's "doing a cattleya."

Everything is carefully organized and the utmost trouble is taken to teach the children the art of flirtation. Apparently hundreds of poems are recited at these mock courtships. As the boys and girls grow older they continue to meet one another regularly, and each girl entertains a succession of young men every evening. If the girl's father or mother has scolded her during the day, she seeks for sympathy from the men who come to see her. When they ask her what she has eaten, she replies: "I ate a scolding today; today I ate nothing that was good."

They ask: "Who scolded thee?" But she does not tell them that it was her father or mother. She says: "I speak nonsense, no one was angry with me; at least if I was scolded I have forgotten who scolded me. I was deceiving you all. Who would dare to be angry with me? I am fierce as a tiger. No one dares to scold me for fear I would eat him up."

One of the young men says: "Thou art not a tiger, but perhaps today thou wert like a Chinese dog, yapping at the heels of the mules." She replies: "I am not a dog, I am a queen." Some one laughs and says: "How true! A queen of the tea leaves! A queen who goes to the spring for water." "If I am not a queen at present I shall certainly become one in my next life." Then one of the young men says: "Thou art rising very slowly to that height. Instead of being a queen I fear that in thy next life thou wilt certainly be that little dog, following a caravan from China." The girl who is best at repartee gets the most admirers, but she must be genial to all alike, and any girl who is asked must reply: "'Yes, I love thee," saying it in the same tone of voice as if she said to her mother: "The rice is cooked."

As in Stendhal's definition of gallant love, " 'tis a picture in which everything, to the very shadows, should be rose-colour"; it is a rare thing in early society and perhaps not of vast importance in the history of primitive women; but it will serve to show her infinite variety.

Chapter III

THE ANCIENT CIVILIZATIONS: ASIA, EGYPT, GREECE, ROME

§ 1. *The Eastern Mother-Gods* FROM the innumerable suggestive details of primitive societies so-called, we must pass to the fragments which are all that can be gleaned about the ancient civilization. Our own history springs largely from Rome, influenced by the still more ancient Greece, and the Jewish background of Christianity. But behind all these there loom the shadows of an earlier Eastern world, of Egypt, and of Babylon, and of Asia Minor.

These first civilizations were in some sense the flower of the social systems we have so far been discussing; their institutions and their ideas are the same as these, only thrust further to a logical conclusion. The history of their women is the history of primitive women modified by growing cultures and huger imperialisms. Here are the same problems, the same contradictory solutions, the same attitude to women leading to the same degradation or exaltation, as the case may be.

We can distinguish among them two main types, differentiated along this very division: in the one the degradation of women has reached a further stage, in the other the exaltation of women has conquered new fields of thought and activity. At the beginning of this chapter we must begin with the second and leave the first to the chapter which follows.

A thousand years or so before the Birth of Christ we see the threshold of human history occupied by a group of noble empires based upon a life of agriculture. Babylonia and Syria, Egypt and Phrygia, built up a wider and higher culture than had ever been seen before. Each of them developed a religion which taught the worship of an omnipotent feminine power personified under different names as a supreme goddess of fertility.

In Phrygia and throughout Asia Minor along the rich river valleys each year were celebrated the death and rebirth of all nature. Cybele, the Great Mother of the Gods, was worshipped by orgiastic dances, fertility rites and human sacrifices; and so powerful was the effect of her cult upon the imagination that it spread to Greece and later also to Rome. There two hundred years before the birth of Christ her yearly mysteries were performed in a hysterical frenzy of excitement: her lover Attis, a god who died, was mourned with wild self-mutilations, and his resurrection hailed with every manifestation of unbridled joy; carnival broke loose; every man was free to do or say what he pleased; the resurrection of Attis was hailed not only as the rebirth of vegetation, but as a promise of man's own resurrection from death. These Roman rites grew wilder with the

decline and decadence of later days, and we shall return to
them again later.

In Babylonia a great mother-god Ishtar yearly mourned
her dead lover Tammuz: she followed him "to the land
from which there is no returning, to the house of darkness,
where dust lies on door and bolt"; and during her absence
the world was chilled, the fields were barren and love
ceased in man and nature. The women wept over the corpse
of Tammuz and tore their hair. In Phœnicia Ishtar became
Astarte or Ashtoreth; in Greece Tammuz became Adonis,
and his lover, Aphrodite. Everywhere his death was followed by a resurrection, giving promise of new life for
nature in the spring and for man after death.

Among all these mother-gods, alike save only in name,
none other gained so wide an influence as Egyptian Isis.
Originating as the sister and wife of Osiris, himself a god
of fertility in one of his many aspects, she became eventually even greater than her spouse—the Queen of Heaven,
the Earth Mother. She passed from country to country absorbing all the local deities until Greece and Rome identified
her with Selene, with Demeter or Ceres, with Aphrodite,
Juno, Nemesis, Fortuna and Panthea.

"I am Isis," reads an old Greek inscription—"the mistress of every land; I laid down laws for mankind, and
ordained things that no one may change; I am she who governs Sirius the Dog Star; I am she who is called divine
among women; I divided the earth from the heaven; I made
manifest the paths of the stars; I prescribed the course of

the sun and the moon; I found out the labours of the sea;
I made justice mighty; I brought together man and
woman; I burdened woman with the newborn babe in the
tenth month; I ordained that parents should be beloved by
their children; I put an end to cannibalism; I overthrew the
sovereignty of tyrants; I compelled women to be beloved
by men; I made justice more mighty than gold or silver; I
made virtue and vice to be distinguished by instinct."

In short, Isis, the fertile mother, the feminine principle,
had taken to her the attributes of most minor deities and
triumphed over the civilized world. It is well to remember
that this signifies the full worship of women as the givers
of fertility and their exaltation over all mankind; it is, like
the customs of the Khasis and the Pelew Islanders, the logical outcome of woman's chief claim to power, of her one
gift which no man can share with her.

In the most famous of old romances, the Golden Ass of
Apuleius, Lucius, on whom has fallen, Bottom-like, an ass's
head, prays to Isis to remove it, confessing that he is completely at a loss to know which of her innumerable names is
the right one, and she replies: "Lo, Lucius, I am come, I,
nature's mother, mistress of all the elements, the first-
begotten offspring of all the ages, of deities mightiest, queen
of the dead, first of heaven's denizens, in whose aspect are
blent the aspects of all gods and goddesses. With my rod I
rule the shining heights of heaven, the health-giving
breezes of the sea, the mournful silence of the under-world.
The whole earth worships my godhead, one and individual,

under many a changing shape, with varied rites and by many diverse names. There the Phrygians, first born of men, call me the Mother of the Gods that dwell at Pessinus; there the Athenians, sprung from the soil they till, know me as Cecropian Minerva; there the wave-beaten Cyprians style me Venus of Paphos; the archer Cretans, Diana of the hunter's net; the Sicilians with their three-fold speech, Stygian Proserpina: the Eleusinians, the ancient goddess Ceres. Others call me Juno, others Bellona, others Hecate, others the Rhamnusian; but those on whom shine the first rays of the Sun God as each day he springs to new birth, the Avii and the Ethiopians and the Egyptians, mighty in ancient lore, honour me with my peculiar rites and call me by my true name, Isis the Queen."

Such was Isis: "When her cult finally broke down through the development and mighty spreading of Christianity in Egypt, Isis was to her votaries the type and symbol of all that is greatest and best in woman in her character of the unselfish, true, tender, loving and eternal World Mother,"—World Mother and Earth Mother, the exaltation of the soil because of its fertility, and of women in general because they by their mysterious *mana* made this earth fertility possible. With us today, in spite of two thousand years of another religion, these ideas are the natural begetters of poetry which is religious in its deepest essence.

> Who is that goddess to whom men should pray,
> But her from whom their hearts have turned away,
> Out of whose virgin being they were born,

Whose mother nature they have named with scorn
Calling its holy substance common clay?

Yet from this so despised earth was made
The milky whiteness of those queens who swayed
　　Their generations with a light caress,
　　And from some image of their loveliness
The heart built up high heaven when it prayed.

Lover, your heart, the heart on which it lies,
Your eyes that gaze and those alluring eyes,
　　Your lips, the lips they kiss, alike had birth
　　Within that dark divinity of earth,
Within the mother being you despise.

Ah, when I think this earth on which I tread
Hath borne these blossoms of the lovely dead,
　　And makes the living heart I love to beat,
　　I look with sudden awe beneath my feet,
At you with erring reverence overhead.

These words from the pen of the twentieth-century Irish
poet, who signs himself Æ, and who has bicycled all over
the country roads of Ireland in an effort to induce her peas-
ants to learn to make her soil more fruitful, are a proof of
the immortality of a religious faith which was based upon
homage to the fruitfulness of women and to their genius as
priestesses to nature.

§ 2. *Early*　　WE see then that the first great civilizations
Codes: Exal-　which influenced our own history through
tation of
Women.　　Greece and Rome, developed imposing re-
　　　　　ligions based upon the worship of women as
the fertile force in nature. We wish to know now if such a

fact corresponds to any exalting of the status of women as compared with other societies which had no such worship. Clearly, this is a history of women, and therefore goddesses are of secondary importance to us compared with their woman worshippers. The evidence pieced together from fragmentary ancient monuments is not so rich in suggestive detail as that which we have hitherto studied, nevertheless there are certain bodies of evidence of the very greatest importance for our quest.

Most noteworthy of all is the evidence for women's superior status given us by the code or laws of Hammurabi, a king of Babylon about B. C. 2350. This very ancient code differs from most other ancient bodies of law in that it gives women a good and independent legal position.

Marriage, while being as usual a form of purchase, was also a contract to be man and wife together: it was monogamous, but a childless wife might give her unmarried servant to her husband to raise up seed. She remained mistress of her maid and might degrade her for insolence, though she could not sell her if she bore children to her husband. If she refused to give her servant to her husband, he might take a concubine, but otherwise not; this concubine had her own rights and was not under the jurisdiction of the wife; she was free and her children legitimate; she could be divorced only on the same terms as a wife.

If a wife became ill her husband was bound to support her unless she preferred to go back to her father's house, in which case she took her dowry. The husband of a chronic invalid could remarry and have legitimate heirs.

The marriage was usually arranged by the parents; the bridegroom's father paid the bride price, which was presented ceremoniously to the bride's father by the bridegroom; on the completion of the marriage it was usually given by her father to the bride herself, and so came back with her dowry to her husband. This dowry, which might include real estate, remained the property of the bride and descended from her to her children; or if she was sterile it returned to her family on her death. The actual marriage ceremony included the recitation of a formula by the bridegroom, such as the following: "I am the son of nobles, silver and gold shall fill thy lap, thou shalt be my wife, I will be thy husband. Like the fruit of a garden I will give thee offspring." In the marriage contract all sorts of stipulations could be inserted affecting the conduct of either man or woman.

The man was responsible for his wife's debts, including those contracted before marriage. A man might make his wife a settlement by deed of gift, which gave her a life interest in his property; he might reserve to her the right to bequeath it to a favourite child, but she could never bequeath it to her own family.

Divorce was optional with the man, but he must return the dowry, and the woman kept custody of the children and was given sufficient means from real estate to pay for their upbringing. If she had been a bad wife, the husband might send her away without dowry or degrade her to the position of slave, but she could bring an action in such a case against him and seek judicial separation on the ground of cruelty. If she failed to prove her case, she was drowned. If her husband failed to support her during absence, she could cohabit with another man, but must return to her husband if he came back, the children of the second union remaining with their father.

A widow took the dead husband's place, his house and his property, all of which must be used for the children: if she married again, the whole estate was transferred to her and her second husband in trust for the children. If she did not marry she received her dowry, anything willed to her by her husband, and a child's share with the children when they grew up. Adultery was punished by the death of both parties by drowning, unless the husband cared to pardon his wife, when the king might pardon her lover also.

Moreover, women could be judges, elders, witnesses and scribes; so that in every way their position was high and in many ways higher than in nineteenth-century England or America; and yet the code of Hammurabi is more than four thousand years old. This fact should weigh heavily with those who take it as an axiom of their faith that the Christian religion must necessarily have exalted women above their status under ancient pagan goddesses whose worship was stained with orgiastic fertility rites.

We can add to this account of an ancient code formed

under the eye of Ishtar some small account of women under the eye of Isis in Egypt.

For centuries women owned property in Egypt to such an extent that in some households the husband was practically nothing but a boarder. In the writings which go by the name of Ani we read: "Be not rude to a woman in her house if thou know her thoroughly. Do not say 'Where is that? bring it to me' when she hath put it in its right place and thine eye hath not seen it; when thou art silent thou knowest her qualities, and it is a joy for thine hand to be with her." It is clear from this that the woman owned her house, and as late as Ptolemaic times marriage contracts made over all possible property of the man entirely to the woman.

In other cases it would seem that the husband is owner of the household, but even here he is commanded to treat his wife very well. "If thou art successful and hast furnished thy house and lovest the wife of thy bosom, then fill her stomach and clothe her back. The medicine of her body is oil. Make glad her heart during the time that thou hast. She is a field profitable to its owner." This last sentence will not sound well in the ears of a modern feminist, but it shows the outlook which in primitive days was most satisfactory for a woman.

Moreover in Egypt the man was forced to shoulder the responsibility of any irregular conduct in which he might see fit to indulge. Often enough in communities even of a highly civilized kind the woman who has been the partner in an immoral act is left to bear the consequences without help or sympathy from the man, but in Ptah-hotep we read: "If thou makest a woman ashamed, wanton of heart, whom her fellow townspeople know to be under two laws (i. e. in an ambiguous position), be kind to her for a season, send her not away, let her have food to eat. The wantonness of her heart appreciateth a straight path."

Other moral precepts commanded affection and care of mothers: "I gave thee to thy mother, who carried thee as she carried thee and without any help from me she carried thee—a heavy burden. When after thy months in the womb thou wast born, she put herself under the yoke; for three years her breasts were in thy mouth. When thou wast sent to school to be taught, day by day unfailingly she came to thy teacher, bringing bread and beer for thee from her house. Now that thou hast become a young man, and art married and hast a house, watch well thy child and bring him up as thy mother brought thee up. Make it not necessary for thy mother to suffer, lest, if she lift up her hands to God, he will hearken to her complaints and punish thee."

It is not surprising that Herodotus, who, as a Greek, was used to the women being kept very much in their place, wrote: "No country possesses so many wonders and has such a number of works which defy description. The people also, in most of their manners and customs, exactly reverse the common practice of mankind." Indeed, even the king had to acknowledge his wife at least as his equal and often as his superior: to her belonged to a great measure the land of Egypt itself, and the king was the man who married the royal princess. This custom of female ownership gave rise to the most surprising of all Egyptian customs: in palace and in cottage, as often as not, brother married sister, in order to keep the property in the family.

§ 3. *Athens:* OUT of civilizations such as these came the *Debasement of* elements which combined to make ancient *Women.* Greece; and what we know from Homer of the earliest ages seems to correspond in its general lines with other east-Mediterranean societies. In Homer the position of women is dignified and free; by the time we reach the golden age of Pericles, women are cloistered slaves.

It is difficult to maintain continuity of thought, when we pass from the history of women in primitive societies to their history in communities like those of ancient Greece; so many new elements have entered in and the scene of action has been so changed. Ancient Greece was at once more civilized and more intellectual than any modern community; and as barbarous or rather as "primitive" as any of the communities we have so far been studying; both these elements are, however, alike in their effect upon women— both tend to her degradation.

If we consider Athens and Sparta in their greatest periods, we find that the individual was sacrificed to the State, was identified with the needs of the herd, as completely as in any savage tribe: what individualism there was must be exercised in the service of the State; more-

over, individuality was allowed only to a small minority of
one sex; the rest were slaves without minds, and women
without minds.

This then is the first point to be realized in studying the
history of women at this period: their lives were passed as
slaves in a slave state. When we think of the incredible
galaxy of great names, Socrates, Plato, Sophocles, Æschy-
lus, Euripides, Aristophanes, Pericles, Alcibiades, Themis-
tocles, Demosthenes, Herodotus, Aristotle, Thucydides,
Praxiteles, Xenophon, who lived and flourished within a
very few years of one another, who are known, every one,
by name at least to every educated person; it is important
to remember that those sons of women achieved their
eminence at the cost not only of a horde of male slaves,
but of the enslavement of the whole female sex.

Plato classes together "children, women and servants,"
precisely as the tenth commandment of the Hebrew and
Christian religions classes together one's neighbour's wife,
his servants, his ox, his ass and the rest of his property.
Pericles, in the most famous funeral speech in human history, is made by Thucydides to say: "If I am to speak of
womanly virtues to those of you who will henceforth be
widows, let me sum them up in one short admonition: To
a woman not to show more weakness than is natural to her
sex is a great glory, and not to be talked about for good or
for evil among men."

What then was the duty of women in a slave-owning
State? To produce children who should be healthy and

valuable as soldiers. What was their discipline? To be shut up in the house to breed. "A free woman should be bounded by the street door," says a character in one of Menander's plays. "War, politics and public speaking are the sphere of man; that of woman is to keep house, to stay at home and to receive and tend her husband." Xenophon describes the perfect wife in his *Œconomicus:* she has been brought up "that she might see, hear and ask as little as possible," and her outlook to her husband is summed up in a phrase: "Everything rests with you; my duty, my mother said, is simply to be modest."

Not only was this attitude no advance on the primitive attitude; it was positively retrograde, for the practical sphere of women's activities was curtailed by the presence of slaves. To the ancient Athenian all forms of manual labour, commerce and business were degrading and no free citizen could think of soiling his hands with them; his activities, apart from war, were purely intellectual, and he did not feel any lack of interests because he had this new field to explore, the field of reason, which for him compensated for the relegation of hunting, fishing, manual work and commerce to a subject class. In the same way, his wife lost nearly all her occupations—no longer could she even go out into the fields and sow the crops; but she had no compensations—the intellect and its exercise were absolutely denied her; she became not even an overworked companion, but an isolated reproductive organ. "They dip their wool in hot water according to the ancient plan, all of

them without exception, and never make the slightest inno-
vation. They sit and cook as of old. They carry upon their
heads, as of old. They wear out their husbands, as of old.
They buy sweets, as of old," says a character in Aristophanes; female inertia had reached its limit.

Perhaps there is no better way of realizing the position
of the citizen's wife under the Athenian social régime than
to consider the attitude of public opinion to Euripides and
his plays. The great dramatist, "the human, with his drop-
ping of warm tears, and his touching of things common till
they rose to greet the spheres," was throughout his long
life the butt of the wits and the target of public abuse; he
was the first, they said, to show his public on the stage the
disgusting spectacle of a woman in love; he was certainly
among the first to paint a woman as a personality having
her own feelings and using her own mind, instead of regarding the female sex as a whole as a standardized factory
product supplied for one purpose only to her husband, to
the State, to mankind.

"To the average stupid Athenian," says Professor Gilbert
Murray, "it was probably rather wicked for a woman to
have any character, wicked for her to wish to take part in
public life, wicked for her to acquire learning or to doubt
any part of the conventional religion, just as it was wicked
for her to deceive her husband. Such a woman should not
be spoken about; above all, should not be treated with understanding and sympathy."

Euripides, a sort of Greek Ibsen in this particular, proceeded to do precisely what should not be done; he talked about women of an independent type of mind and sympathized with them; he even showed how loathsome were some of the pillars of society, the heroes of Greek legend, in their conduct towards women. Thus in the play of *Alcestis* he treats a legend which was absolutely familiar to every Athenian, but he treats it at an angle different from the conventional. Admetus, king of Thessaly, is fated to die, but is promised a respite by the gods if he can find someone else to die for him. Alcestis, his wife, willingly offers to sacrifice herself; Admetus accepts her offer, and in doing so clearly feels that Alcestis could hardly do otherwise, seeing that she was a dutiful wife. Generations of Athenians had agreed with Admetus to the extent of hardly finding Alcestis's sacrifice worthy of praise, her action was so necessary in a decent wife and woman. Euripides introduced a new note; he makes Admetus talk in such a way as to make him revolting in his selfishness: and in so doing shocked his Athenian audience, male and female, by calling in question the very ideal of a womanly woman, as they understood it.

In *The Cretan Women,* Euripides did even worse: Aërope, a Cretan princess, has a lover; her guilt is discovered; her father behaves as any good Athenian would, and gives her to a sailor to be drowned in the sea. Euripides did not sympathize very much with the orthodox outlook and in his version gives Aërope such beautiful love songs that he was never forgiven by the righteous populace. In *Ion* he deals with the amour of a god for a mortal woman, and does everything to make the woman beautiful and the god contemptible. In *Medea,* "he states the cause of a barbarian woman against a Greek man who has wronged her. . . . When Jason had to defend an obviously shabby case, no gentleman cared to hear him; but Euripides insisted on his speaking . . . when Medea was revealed as obviously a wicked woman the plain man thought that such women should simply be thrashed, not listened to. But Euripides loved to trace all her complicated sense of injustice to its origins, and was determined to understand and to explain rather than to condemn."

Such an attitude was altogether foreign to the public opinion of the day; nothing which departed from convention was desirable and the generations of men who perhaps of all the children of men most revered wisdom and intelligence, substituted for them a savage reign of taboo in all that concerned their wives. We have seen in Phrygia and Egypt women as natural priestesses of vegetation goddesses; in ancient Greece we see them as vegetables.

§ 4. *The Birth* CAN we explain why women should have been
of Reason.   so stricken by the first society where philosophy and logic mingled with the mysticism and superstition hitherto all-powerful? For the importance of ancient Greece in the history of humanity is largely that it introduced into social thought and activity the use of reason: the savage whom we have been studying was neither rational nor logical, neither he nor his wife; we now pass to a significant

stage; men are interested in reason, believe they can or should be reasonable, even though in fact they are unsuccessful practitioners, but no one suggests for a single moment that women can or should make any such claim.

Hitherto women have been reverenced for fertility, a genius which is their peculiar attribute; now there has come a new fertility, a giving birth to children of the mind, to ideas, and from this new fertility women are excluded, and men take their place. In Plato's Symposium we find the clearest expression of this new element in the history of women; the philosopher is telling us of how Diotima of Mantineia taught him the elements of love:

"Those who are pregnant," she tells Socrates, "in the body only, betake themselves to women and beget children, —this is the character of their love: their offspring, as they hope, will preserve their memory and give them the blessedness and immortality which they desire in the future. But souls which are pregnant,—for there certainly are men who are more creative in their souls than in their bodies,—conceive that which is proper for the soul to conceive or contain. . . . And such creators are poets and all artists who are deserving of the name 'inventor.' And he who in youth has the seed of those implanted in him and is himself inspired, when he comes to maturity desires to beget and generate. . . . When he finds a fair and noble and well-nurtured soul, he embraces the two in one person . . . and they are married by a far nearer tie and have a closer friendship than those who beget mortal children, for the children who are their common offspring are fairer and more immortal. Who, when he thinks of Homer and Hesiod and other great poets, would not rather have their children than ordinary ones? Who would not emulate them in the creation of children such as theirs which have preserved their memory and given them everlasting glory? . . . Many temples have been raised in their honour for the sake of children such as theirs; which were never raised in honour of anyone for the sake of his mortal children."

Is it not clear that women met here in Greece almost for the first time one of their greatest enemies,—the human intellect? Men had discovered how to become pregnant themselves with children of the mind. If we ask why the new fertility was confined to men, why women also did not share in the joys of the intellect, we may find an answer in the mode in which the habit of philosophy came into the world. The greatest of the Roman poets, Lucretius, describes it thus: "When human life lay foully prostrate on earth, crushed beneath the weight of religion, which showed itself hideously lowering from the quarters of heaven upon mankind, a man of Greece ventured for the first time to lift up his mortal eyes to its face and to withstand it face to face. Him neither story of gods, nor thunderbolts, nor heaven with threatening roar could quell, but they only stirred up the more the eager courage of his soul, filling him with desire to be first to burst open the locked doors of nature. . . . Hence religion in its turn is put down and trampled under foot: and by his victory we are brought level to heaven."

In short, philosophy and the use of reason came as rebels and revolutionaries to turn over custom and belief and convention; since therefore women were the chief repositories of these, and since also their inertia beneath them was the sole sanction of existing order, the new wine of the mind did not appeal to them, nor did their husband wish it to. The centuries of taboo and fear and contempt had frozen them to stone, and they were the anchors which men used at moments of repose. Nothing could be gained by altering this condition, either by men or by women.

Moreover, the new knowledge was eminently practical in its nature: it found a meaning in politics and statecraft which it could never find in the loom, the kitchen and the bedroom: clearly it belonged to the men's sphere and was without interest or application in the women's; it was animal, not vegetable.

It was clear that with such a wife the Greek husband could find no basis for an intellectual friendship, even had he wished to do so; but he had no such desire; the wife of a citizen was there, as we have seen, for one purpose only, to provide authentic, legitimate children to the State, to keep up the stock, and to keep it pure. Just as a mongrel dog is allowed more freedom to go abroad than is accorded to a thoroughbred, so there were women in ancient Athens who were not the victims of such an incarceration as befell the citizen matron; these were for the most part foreign women, who were often intelligent and educated. Their life was very different; they were free and at the same time respected; at least it was respéctable to associate with them. They were the famous Hetairæ, among whom Phryne and Aspasia are well known to this day. Probably their intellect has been exaggerated by sentimentalists, but Aspasia at least seems to have been remarkable in this way. She was the mistress of Pericles, and Plato says that she even composed the famous Funeral Oration. However that may be, it is of great significance to the history of women to note this example of a division of labour and of morality, of a dual standard between women in one society. Besides the enlightened courtesans there were also common prostitutes to whom men resorted less overtly.

What does all this imply? It implies that in ancient Athens men tried to solve the inevitable contradictions in their own attitude to women by creating three types, three rigid divisions of the sex, from each of which they could obtain a special sort of gratification. Philoprogenitive Love requires above all absolute certainty that the mother shall be faithful, and to produce this, Greek women's minds were stunted, their inclinations decreased to the smallest possible number, their physical liberty curtailed to the limit of the front door. Such a being could not inspire any form of Passion Love, which, as we have seen, requires above all individuality and imagination, or the power to stimulate it: hence the need, limited as we shall soon see, for Aspasias.

Moreover we can be quite certain that the practical mind of the Greek, as well as his residuum of primitive taboo, made his wife a poor vehicle for the satisfaction of Physical Love, for which purpose existed then as now the common prostitute. Vanity Love and Gallant Love were totally unrepresented in Greek society; the first because a general contempt for property or possession would not lead men to marry in order to show off a remarkable wife to their friends; and indeed the wife was never seen in any circumstances; the second because effeminacy, without which Gallant Love cannot exist, never entered into the Greek composition.

But there is one more factor which directly affected the position of women; and that is the degree to which the Greeks indulged their passionate friendship for other men. The most inspiring, the most ennobling, the most permanent of all affections felt by them were these. "Their ideal," says Lowes Dickinson, "was the development and education of the younger by the older man, and in this view they were recognized and approved by custom and law as an important factor in the State." Two such passionate friends were Achilles and Patroclus, and when the latter was killed, "Achilles wept, remembering his dear comrade nor did sleep that conquereth all take hold of him,—but he kept turning himself to this side and to that, yearning for Patroclus' manhood and excellent valour, and all the toils he achieved with him and the woes he bore, cleaving the battles of men and grievous waves. As he thought thereon, he shed big tears, now lying on his side, now on his back, now on his face; and then anon he would arise upon his feet and roam wildly beside the beach of the salt sea."

It was for attributing such feelings to women that Euripides was ridiculed by his audiences, even though they admired his art and at his death mourned his loss. It is curious also that the first-century Tatian, more Christian than the Pope or St. Paul, so much so indeed that he died a heretic from overzeal, prayed fervently that the immoral works of Euripides should be blotted from the face of the earth.

§ 5. *Sparta:* In Athens then we have an example of a state
Eugenists' where women were treated absolutely ration-
Paradise. ally; but it was possible only by refusing to treat them as rational beings. Public opinion laid down that a woman was nothing but a means of procuring a supply of citizens, and therefore men set about to ensure this result in the most logical manner, remembering that the most important object was to avoid the slightest chance of spurious blood entering the sacred company of the elect. "The women could not be trusted in this matter to their own sense of propriety. Even men were powerless before irresistible love, and much less self-control could be expected from weak women. Means must therefore be devised to prevent the possibility of anything going wrong, and accordingly, the citizen-women had special apartments assigned to them, generally in the upper story, that they might have to come downstairs, and men might see them if they ventured out.

Then they were forbidden to be present at any banquet. The men preferred to dine by themselves rather than expose their wives to their neighbours' gaze. And in order to defy all possibility of temptation, the women must wrap up every part of their bodies. In addition to these external arrangements, laws were passed such as might deter the most venturesome."

Such an outcome to logical sex relations is a warning to those who believe that reason freed from superstition would solve every human desire; it is also evidence that however successful and exalted the life of a community may be in some respects—and who does not look back to Athens as to a golden age of enlightenment and fine living?—there are always shadows in the picture. But we have only to turn to another of the Greek city-states to find a second example of these depressing realities, and an example which must be pondered deeply by certain advocates of what they are pleased to call scientific citizenship.

If Athens is a state where everything, including women and slaves, is sacrificed to intellectual accomplishment, Sparta is the paradise of the Eugenists. In Sparta it was not purity of blood which was the ruling passion, but strength of muscle, and the women were not sacrificed to chastity but to war. "The Spartans wanted strong men: the mothers therefore must be strong. The Spartans wanted brave men: the mothers therefore must be brave. The Spartans wanted resolute men, men with decision of character: the mothers must be resolute."

Just as in Athens, the woman's life was ruled in Sparta by the ruling idea; but whereas in Athens that idea led to seclusion and degrading emptiness, in Sparta it led to a rigorous and public discipline, a hardening process such as the world has not yet seen fit to repeat.

The whole education of a Spartan woman was aimed to fit her for bringing forth not only a Spartan citizen but, what was in fact the same, a Spartan soldier; there was no other purpose in her life, her greatest reward was to hear of the death of her son in battle. Sexual passion so gravely feared by the Athenian husband was crushed out in Sparta by cold baths and athletics. The softer sentiments associated with motherhood in our eyes were also destroyed by a rigorous discipline, which required each new-born child to be brought before a committee of hygiene in order to be judged strong enough to live, or weak and therefore fit only for death by exposure. The man or woman who did not marry could have only one excuse, that he or she was weak and unfit for the parenthood of strong children; all others were forced by the most degrading consequences of non-compliance to propagate the species. "If a man did not marry on reaching a certain age, he was forbidden to be present at the exercises of the young girls. The whole set of them were taken one wintry day in each year, and, stripped of their clothing, went round the *agora* singing a song that told how disgraceful their conduct was in disobeying the laws of their country—a spectacle to gods and men. The women also, at a certain festival, dragged these misguided individuals round about an altar, inflicting blows on them all the time."

Modesty in the sense we know it, that is largely a fear and horror of the naked body, nakedness being defined in accordance with the sartorial fashions of the moment, was, fortunately, utterly unknown. Just as the Athenians covered their women up to the eyes and hid them at home lest they should excite the concupiscence of their friends, so the Spartans stripped theirs of all covering and sent them into the market place, so that their health and physical suitability might be marked by all potential fathers. All girls went through a course of gymnastics, and wrestled and threw the javelin: their superb health must have been exhilarating, and their morals were by all accounts singularly pure. Since the supreme good of the state was the production of healthy children, there was nothing immoral in free intercourse between people outside the bonds of matrimony, always provided that the men and women who indulged in it conformed to the necessary high standard of physical excellence. Such free love was therefore not discouraged and brought no disgrace, whereas celibacy was, as we have said, a sin and a crime. Adultery was, however, unknown; all testimony agrees upon this point.

The great freedom of the Spartan women excited the contempt of the Athenians; and it was a constant source of sarcastic comment that the Spartans were ruled by their wives. It is certain that their women had a voice in politics and that their influence on conduct in general was omnipotent; but it was hardly more than the influence of the young chorus girl who presented men during the late war with white feathers unless they wore uniform, save that the Spartan woman had the supreme virtue of being willing and even anxious to take part in warfare and dangers herself.

If we consider the case of Spartan women, therefore, we are bound to admit that, just as the Athenian state, though the first to curb conduct with intellect, and superstition with reason, was unable to give posterity any enlightened example of a noble solution of the difficulties of womanhood; so the Spartan state, though it placed men and women on a plane of equality scarcely equalled elsewhere or at any other time, could do so only by a rigid devotion to the ideal of a healthy animal for both sexes alike. There was no woman question in Athens, because all the women were vegetables, and there was no woman question in Sparta, because both men and women were little better than animals. Moreover, Sparta, the eugenic paradise and the first and only practitioner of the equality of the sexes, has left literally nothing to posterity but a record of implacable attachment to life, like that of a dog which has its teeth fixed immovably in the neck of an enemy ten times its size.

It is remarkable, also, that Sparta never called forth from man or woman a single comment, or criticism, or revolt about the standard and ideals to which her social creed bound every individual. In Athens, on the other hand, the country where though women were bound the intellect was free, there were signs of unrest and of a questioning of existing conventions. We have already mentioned the attitude of Euripides; we cannot do better than close our short view of Greek women with the famous speech of Medea, wherein we can find a lively protest against the subjection of women, and an early example of a voice which re-echoes often in later centuries. "Of all things that have life and sense," says Medea, "we women are most wretched. For we are compelled to buy with gold a husband who is also— worst of all!—the master of our person. And on his character, good or bad, our whole fate depends. For divorce is regarded as a disgrace to a woman and she cannot repudiate her husband. Then coming as she does into the midst of manners and customs strange to her, she would need the gift of divination—unless she has been taught at home— to know how best to treat her bedfellow. And if we manage so well that our husband remains faithful to us, and does not break away, we may think ourselves fortunate; if not, there is nothing for it but death. A man when he is vexed at home can go out and find relief among his friends or acquaintances; but we women have none to look to but him. They tell us we live a sheltered life at home while they go to the wars; but that is nonsense. For I would rather go into battle twice than bear a child once."

But Greek civilization never succeeded in giving redress to this eternal complaint: Athens for all its intellectual grandeur died out; Sparta for all its eugenics became hopelessly degenerate: all that was good and valuable as human experience passed by way of Greek literature to later times and younger civilizations.

§ 6. *Roman*   IN primitive societies the history of women
Legal Evolu-   largely consists of customs and conventions
tion.   from which we can draw a picture of their life
and status; but with the advent of the first great civilizations
we have to supplement custom and convention, that is the
unwritten laws, with the written law itself.

We have already seen how one of the earliest of written
legal codes, the code of Hammurabi, gives women a very
exalted position indeed, almost on the same level with men;
this was important evidence for our general history and
helped us to correlate the worship of fertility with reverence
for women.

We must now take a rapid glance at the most important
body of law the world has ever seen, the law which evolved
under the practical genius of the Romans. Just as the Greeks
gave us our philosophy and our art, and the Jews our religious outlook, so Rome gave us government, roads, baths,
architecture and law; thus completing the main outlines of
what some people like to call our Protestant, Anglo-Saxon,
Nordic civilization.

How did Roman law regard women? If we look at the
earliest times, the rigid days of the granite virtues, we find
women in a very primitive and dependent condition. They
were under the perpetual tutelage of their fathers, or near-
est male kind before marriage, and then passed bag and
baggage to the power of their husbands. Early Roman law
indeed did not hear of a woman as a wife; she was in its
eyes the *daughter* of her husband. As such she could not, of

course, exercise any public or civil office; she could not act as witness, she could not sign a will, she could not make a contract, she could not inherit property from anyone dying intestate except from her husband or brother. Owing to her *imbecility*—the exact Latin word—she was given certain minor privileges; for example, she could plead ignorance of the law in some circumstances and she was on occasion exempted from torture.

Another type of law shows, however, that from quite an early time, women were often wealthy, for they were forbidden by the Lex Oppia in B. C. 215 to own more than half an ounce of gold, to wear parti-coloured dresses, or to ride in carriages within a mile of Rome except on certain public festivals. Similar laws had been passed in ancient Greece by Solon and others, who prohibited the wearing of expensive clothes by any woman *except prostitutes;* many laws of the same nature were passed later in Europe, as we shall see.

Gradually, however, these disabilities disappeared, or rather were evaded by clever fictions and deliberate avoidance of the spirit of the laws: thus in 159 B. C. a law had forbidden women to be made heirs to fortunes above a certain sum: the law said that if a man was registered as having more than this he could not leave it to any woman; instead of abolishing the law, rich men evaded it by not registering, or by leaving the fortune on trust. By subterfuges such as this the whole legal position was changed to mark time with women's growing social importance; until their actual position became far better than it has ever been since, until very recent times. For instance, the perpetual guardianship of women died out entirely, although, according to Maine, "the laws of the Scandinavian nations respecting women preserved it until quite recently. The invaders of the Western Empire had it universally among their indigenous usages and indeed their ideas . . . were among the most retrogressive of those which they introduced into the Western World. But from the mature Roman jurisprudence it had entirely disappeared. We should know almost nothing about it, if we had only the compilations of Justinian to consult."

To describe how the change came about in the legal position of women we cannot do better than to quote Sir Henry Maine at length:—"Ancient Law subordinates the woman to her blood-relations, while a prime phenomenon of modern jurisprudence has been her subordination to her husband. The history of the change is remarkable. It begins far back in the annals of Rome. Anciently, there were three modes in which marriage might be contracted according to the Roman usage, one involving a religious solemnity, the other two the observance of certain secular formalities. By these . . . the Husband acquired a number of rights over the person and property of his wife, which were on the whole in excess of such as are conferred on him in any system of modern jurisprudence. But in what capacity did he acquire them? Not as *Husband,* but as *Father* . . . that is, in law she became the *Daughter* of her husband. She was included in his *Patria*

Potestas, she incurred all the liabilities springing out of it while it subsisted, and surviving it when it expired. All her property became absolutely his, and she was retained in tutelage after his death to the guardian whom he had appointed by will.

"These three ancient forms of marriage fell, however, gradually into disuse, so that, at the most splendid period of Roman greatness, they had almost entirely given place to a fashion of wedlock—old apparently but not hitherto considered reputable—which was founded on a modification of the lower form of civil marriage . . . I may describe it as amounting in law to little more than a temporary deposit of the woman by her family. The rights of the family remained unimpaired, and the lady continued in the tutelage of guardians whom her parents had appointed and whose privileges of control overrode, in many material respects, the inferior authority of her husband.

"The consequence was that the situation of the Roman female, whether married or unmarried, became one of great personal and proprietary independence, for the tendency of the later law was to reduce the power of the guardian to a nullity, while the form of marriage in fashion conferred on the husband no compensating superiority."

In short, it is clear that Roman history gives us a picture of women attaining gradually more and more liberty, a higher legal status and in general greater power; but even though in early days the law treated her with ignominy, the Roman matron was always a formidable figure. The story which we read in Livy of the opposition to the Lex Oppia, mentioned before, and the success with which it met, reads like a passage from the annals of modern feminism. The matrons canvassed all voters and finally surrounded the houses of their leading opponents and threatened them with vengeance if they persisted in their attitude. The women won the day after speeches for and against them of such a perennial nature that they too might be discovered within the pages of quite recent volumes of Hansard. "If men," said Cato the Consul, "had retained their rights and dignity within the family, the women would never have broken out publicly in this matter. If women had only a proper sense of shame, they would know that it was not becoming in them to take any interest in the passing or annulling of laws. But now we allow them to take part in politics. If they succeed, who knows where they will end? As soon as they begin to be equal with us, they will have the advantage over us. And for what object are they now agitating? Merely to satisfy their inordinate craving for luxury and show, which will become only the more intense the more it is gratified."

"Cato is wrong," replied Lucius Valerius the Tribune, "in asserting that women make a public appearance on this occasion for the first time. The wives of the first Romans stepped publicly between fathers-in-law and sons-in-law. Roman matrons went on deputations to Coriolanus, they interfered at the Gallic invasion, they performed public services in religious matters. Then the prosperity following the

Punic Wars has brought advantages to all classes of the community; why should the matrons alone be excepted from this good fortune? And why should men grudge them their ornaments and dress? Women cannot hold public offices or priesthoods, or gain triumphs; they have no public occupations. What, then, can they do but devote their time to adornment and dress? Surely then men ought to let them have their own way in these matters."

With these arguments did the cause of feminism in ancient Rome succeed in asserting the right of all women to adorn themselves in many-coloured dresses, to wear jewels and to ride in chariots; a victory which, as we shall see, was lost again to the new asceticism of Christianity.

§ 7. *Character in the Roman Matron.* IT is clear, therefore, both that Roman law constantly ameliorated the position of women and that even when the law was most definite in its oppressive tendencies there were many women with personalities capable of rising above the low level which formalism dictated to them.

As early as the Lex Oppia women could make their opinions respected and by the later days of the full-fledged law they had obtained a position, not only actual, but legal, above that which they were to experience for the next thousand years and several centuries more. James Donaldson, from whose excellent study we have already quoted, has accumulated the examples of exceptional power, talent and character on the part of women which Roman history af-

fords us, and they comprise a list which is remarkable when
compared with the barrenness of Greek history.

First among great Roman matrons, and typical of them
in her virtues, was Cornelia, the mother of the Gracchi.
Plutarch gives us a story about her husband which compares
very favourably with that of Admetus and Alcestis: Tiberius Gracchus found two snakes under his bed and the
diviners to whom he applied for an explanation told him
that if he killed the male snake he would himself die, while
if he killed the female his wife Cornelia would die; but that
on no account must he let both snakes go alive. Without
hesitation he condemned himself and the male snake. However that may be, Cornelia was left in B. C. 151 a widow
with twelve children, who did not prevent her from receiving
many offers of marriage, all of which she, in the interests of
their education, refused. Of her children two became famous, and one for a period well nigh omnipotent, as the
defenders and representatives of the people against the
aristocracy. They were carefully educated by their mother,
and the older, after a distinguished military career, became
Tribune at the age of thirty and passed agrarian laws which
gave land to poor citizens, and generally reduced the power
of the large capitalists; in consequence of the opposition this
aroused in the richer classes, Tiberius Gracchus was murdered.

The younger son, Gaius, attained to even greater power
and used it to pass vindictive legislation against his brother's murderers; but this legislation was never carried into

effect owing to the influence of Cornelia. Gaius carried on the work of his brother and by B. C. 112 ruled Rome as the hero of the proletariat and the poor farmer; but a year later he too was murdered. Cornelia, who had been the inspiration behind all these political activities, now retired to the country and, though she must have been more than sixty, became the centre of a literary salon and devoted herself to the study of Greek and Latin literature. She was known as a stylist and her letters were read for their beauty as literature; we may even have fragments of them in the history of Cornelius Nepos, but the genuineness of these is highly doubtful. Thus Cornelia, the mother of the Gracchi, gave birth to twelve children, was so fascinating as to be a much-desired widow in spite of this, was a leading influence in the stormiest of political epochs and was an author on her own account, a scholar and a friend of scholars. She rivalled Aspasia in wit and intellect, and at the same time displayed all the matronly virtues which in Greece left no memorial.

A remarkable group of women surrounded Julius Cæsar and contributed to his career. First there was his mother, Aurelia, to whom Tacitus attributes much of her son's ability as a statesman, coupling her name in equal honour with that of Cornelia, the mother of the Gracchi. Then there was his own wife, Cornelia, for whom he had such esteem that he risked his whole career for her, since when Sulla commanded him to divorce her he refused and was deprived of property and honours and would have been deprived of life also but for the intercession of the Vestal Virgins. Finally, there was his daughter, Julia, who became the wife of her father's great rival, Pompey: her character was equal to the task of keeping the rivals on good terms until her influence was withdrawn by her death; whereupon the smouldering jealousy broke out into open enmity.

Pompey married a second remarkable woman, another Cornelia, of whom Plutarch says: "The young woman possessed many charms besides her youthful beauty, for she was well instructed in letters, in playing on the lyre, and in geometry, and she had been accustomed to listen to philosophical discourses with profit. In addition to this, she had a disposition free from all affectation and pedantic display, which such acquirements generally breed in women."

Another player in the tragedy of Julius Cæsar, Marcus Antonius, was possessed of a remarkable wife in Octavia, sister of the Emperor Augustus. All authorities speak of her virtues with great respect, and her importance and reputation can be gauged by the fact that she herself took troops and money out to her husband, while he was at the court of Cleopatra. Marcus Antonius refused to see her and formally divorced her; whereupon she returned to Italy to look after her husband's children by herself, by Fulvia and by Cleopatra. Octavia is yet another example of the way in which domestic virtue and charitable sensibilities were combined in Roman matrons with political acumen and public service.

We pass to the wife of the younger Pliny, Calpurnia by name, and we can quote a passage from her husband's letters which describes a charming marriage relationship wherein intellectual tastes are shown to be common ground and the whole companionship as complete as any is likely to be: "She has my books," writes Pliny. "She reads them again and again; she even commits them to memory. What anxiety she feels when I am going to make a speech before the judges, what joy when I have finished it! She places people here and there in the audience to bring her word what applauses have been accorded to my speech, what has been the issue of the trial. If I give readings of my works anywhere, she sits close by, separated by a screen, and drinks in my praises with most greedy ears. My verses also she sings, and sets them to the music of the lyre, no artist guiding her, but only love, who is the best master." The picture is a little too androcentric to satisfy the modern feminist, and it is to be doubted if even the modern lecturer would desire such obsequious love; but it is better than love in Athens or in the Middle Ages, and it compares favourably also with the outlook of an Addison.

Finally, we may glance at the two Agrippinas, mother and daughter, the first of whom was the granddaughter of Augustus and wife of Germanicus, the second the sister of Caligula and mother of Nero. These two are excellent examples of the good Roman woman of affairs and the bad Roman woman of affairs.

The first Agrippina is noteworthy for her constant assistance to her husband on his military campaigns, whither she followed him, though the mother of nine children; and especially for her active retaliation on his enemies when Germanicus died, as she believed, of poison, inflicted by another woman of affairs, Plaucina, wife of Piso. This event took place in Syrian Antioch and Agrippina returned to Rome post-haste with her husband's ashes and an implacable desire for revenge. She publicly accused Piso of the poisoning, and he made the proof and his own defence alike impossible by committing suicide. She became so powerful that Tiberius had her banished to a little island off the Campanian coast where she maintained her reputation to the last by starving herself to death.

Her daughter and namesake, the mother of Nero, was of like metal, save that, whereas the energetic genius of the mother showed itself in stern virtue and impeccable morality, the daughter went in for wholesale intrigue, in the prosecution of which she sacrificed truth and several other virtues. She may even have poisoned her second husband, and it is perhaps a pity that she did not poison the first before he had begotten her notorious son, the future Emperor Nero. Her third husband, relict of another famous lady, Messalina, was the Emperor Claudius, whom she did undoubtedly poison, after he had adopted Nero as his heir. Agrippina was not even yet, however, within sight of her goal, for the uninterrupted rule over Nero and the Roman Empire which she had promised herself was threatened by the influence of a concubine named Acte. She resolved to throw Nero over for an old rival in the popular esteem, Britannicus, doubtless hoping to find him more pliable; but she reckoned without the enterprise which she had imparted with her own blood to the Emperor, who thwarted her decisively. He invited her to Baiæ and put her on board a ship which had been constructed in a way which made it certain to sink. The plan fell through, however; Agrippina swam ashore and had to be murdered on land. Mother, poisoner, politician, Agrippina was also a writer of memoirs, but these have not come down to us: she stands at the opposite end of the scale of human virtues to Cornelia, mother of the Gracchi; but, like her, bears witness to the versatility of the feminine Roman genius.

§ 8. *Roman Licentiousness.* THIS glance at the younger Agrippina brings us to a problem of the greatest importance in the history of women, which we must now state as clearly as possible in the limited space which can be spared.

The popular conception of the Roman world at the coming of Christianity is that a moral and intellectual degradation had settled on all alike; that the position of women was submerged by a general licentiousness, unique in the world's history, and that there were no signs of a healthy growth away from this devastated condition. Agrippina and Messalina have been taken as typical women of their period, everything that Juvenal wrote in the bitterest satires ever written has been assumed to be true; and too often historians and others have been uncritical in sorting the evidence, because they have wished to show the new religion against the darkest background for better contrast. The question, important as it is, cannot be settled here, but it is essential to remember that certain definite facts have convinced many excellent authorities that with all its manifest faults, amounting often to infamous immoralities, the pre-Christian period of the Roman Empire offered many advantages to women over those of early Christianity.

In the first place, we must never forget that the Stoic philosophers taught a moral code and an outlook towards women quite as high as that of later times; for example, Musonius Rufus, a Stoic of the degraded period of Nero's reign, wrote in the following strain: "I say that, as in the human race men have a stronger and women a weaker nature, each of those natures should have the tasks assigned to it which are most suited to it, and the heavier should be allotted to the stronger, and the lighter to the weaker. Spinning as well as housekeeping would therefore be more suitable for women than for men; while gymnastics as well as out-of-door work would be fitter for men than for women; though sometimes men might properly undertake some of the lighter tasks and such as seem to belong to women; and women again might engage in the harder tasks, and those which appear more appropriate for men, in cases where either bodily qualities or necessity or particular occasions might lead to such action. For perhaps all human tasks are open to all, and common both to men and women, and nothing is necessarily appointed exclusively for either; not that something may not be more suitable for one, and others for the other nature, so that some are called men's and others women's occupations. But whatever things have reference to virtue, these one may rightly affirm to be equally appropriate to both natures, since we say that virtues do not belong more to the one than to the other."

We see at once that the Stoic had risen entirely above the taboo attitude which occupied us so largely in the preceding chapter; there is no artificial division into a man's sphere and a woman's sphere, for though such a division exists it is not water-tight and it is based upon reasonable considerations. Moreover, he distinguishes certain qualities as above sex differences; virtue, he tells us, is equally appropriate to both natures; an attitude which compares favourably with the ideas of a special feminine virtue, which Mary Wollstonecraft had to combat seventeen centuries later. Donaldson sums up what is known of Musonius's practical applications, as follows; "Musonius applies his principle of equality to sexual relations and to marriage. He held that what was wrong in a woman was equally wrong in a man, or rather was more disgraceful to a man, inasmuch as he claimed to be a stronger being, and therefore more capable of controlling his passions. He therefore denounced all illicit amours as unjust and lawless. He also propounded a view which was afterwards adopted by the Christian writers, that all indulgence of the flesh not requisite for the propagation of the race was unworthy of a philosopher. But he differed from the great mass of the Christian writers, and regarded marriage as the happiest condition of life. He describes it as a community of life, and a mutual care for each other in health and sickness, and in every occurrence of life, and he brands a marriage when there is no community of feeling as worse than a desert. He argued that the man who does not marry must be inferior in his experience and usefulness to the man who does, and that therefore the solitary life is not advantageous even for the philosopher. And he urges that the whole of civilization rests upon the institution of marriage. "For," says he, "the man who takes away marriage from the human race takes away the household, takes away the State, takes away the human race."

Musonius and the Stoics undoubtedly had a great influence upon their countrymen, for though it would be absurd to look for any wide acceptance of such high ideals, then or now, the despotic rule of a series of benevolent emperors applied what they had learned from the philosophers to altering and refashioning the law of the land in accordance with the best ethical principles. The laws of Augustus attempted to support the cause of morality and also the equally pressing cause of an increase in population, and there are various signs of a healthy and a satisfactory outlook on women throughout the period.

In the second place, in judging the effect of Christianity upon Roman women, we must not forget the legal advantages which they enjoyed. Christianity undoubtedly diminished these, as we shall see in the next chapter; and it is the opinion of Sir Henry Maine, one of our best authorities, that "no society which preserves any tincture of Christian institution is likely to restore to married women the personal liberty conferred on them by the middle Roman law."

In the third place, we must remember that our authorities for the vices and decadence of the early Roman Empire are "a bitter satirist, a pessimist historian and a scandal-mongering biographer." Everybody likes to believe that the period in which he lives is excessively vicious, and if we compare the picture even of Juvenal, we find it no worse than what the historian Ammianus Marcellinus has to tell of the Roman nobles of A. D. 353–378, more than fifty years after the first Christian Emperor, Constantine, had accepted Christianity as a State religion. This historian paints the prevailing decadence in lively colours, and among other strange side-lights upon women's lives describes how "it has happened that in the same house, though in different apartments, a husband and a wife, with the laudable design of overreaching each other, have summoned their respective lawyers, to declare, at the same time, their mutual but contradictory intentions";—much else that is relevant is not so suitable for transcription from the history of Ammianus Rufus.

Again, Salvian, a Christian historian of the fifth century, who wrote to confute those who suggested that the miseries of his day were due to the forsaking of the Pagan gods or to the fact that the Christian God was nodding and no longer steering the ship of creation, paints the blackest of pictures of Christian manners and morals. Gaul, Spain and, worst of all, Carthage, were, according to him, inconceivably licentious. We shall see also that the Christians were accused by their opponents of scandals no less abominable than those of Nero or Elagabalus, and that the orthodox always barbed their dogmatic arguments against heretics with accusations of the worst immoralities. From these considerations we may assume that when Christianity and Roman Imperialism joined hands the world was not at its worst, and that it did not proceed to get better immediately: the good and the bad intermingled and fought each other then as now, and probably the first noteworthy influence of the new religion was in the direction of nullifying the legislation which aimed at encouraging marriage, and glorifying in its place a strict and sterile chastity. In this way, though undoubtedly Christian ethics did a great service as an enemy of licence, they also did harm as an enemy of fertility.

§ 9. *Some*   IF we compare what we have learned about
Conclusions.   primitive communities with the Greek and
Roman civilization, we notice the rise of several vast problems for women's history. Above all we notice the following:

I. The distinction between woman and woman and the rise of separate classes of women within the community, obeying different laws and receiving different treatment.

II. The primitive division of labour between the sexes with its consequent production of a man's sphere and a woman's sphere begins to press hardly upon women's happiness, because every new economic change tends to diminish the women's sphere and to increase the man's sphere.

III. The birth of reason as a social force is regarded by many communities as part of the man's sphere, thus denying women the right to be educated or the need of being able to think.

IV. The growth of individualism and the acknowledgment that the individual has rights and interests apart from those of the State tends to begin among men, who gradually achieve personality, while women are considered together as "the sex."

 V. The complication of life brings another element into the conscious happiness of women: hitherto happiness consisted largely of natural good luck and conformity to convention; now it also includes a comparison with other women and an emulation between one woman and another.

Let us examine some of these and their consequences. In the first place, the distinction between woman and woman and the rise of separate classes of women, is due to a division of labour between them based upon the incompatibility of men's desires. Men, as a whole, want a good wife for themselves and a bad one for their next-door neighbour: the means which a man takes to secure his wife's faithfulness are disastrous for her capacities as an intriguing and exciting lover, or as a vivacious and intelligent companion. Men therefore meet together one with another and make a social contract; their own wives and daughters shall be respected by their friends, in return for the reciprocal arrangement: for other purposes groups of women shall be set apart. The final and necessary outcome of this is that in every civilized community there are groups of good women and of bad women. We call the phenomenon prostitution.

Prostitution scarcely exists in any primitive community; until the coming of the white man the institution was seldom allowed and even less often tolerated in savage society. In Greece it was the necessary corollary to the ideal of a Greek matron; though, it is true, stern virtues and a general lack of interest in women from the sexual or any other point of view kept it in check. In Rome it prospered, especially when Rome became the centre of an overwealthy empire. Ever since it has been an overwhelming problem which is unsolved even today, and we must therefore remember that its beginning was due not to innate depravity on the part of men or of women, but to a social institution which deprived the good woman of any quality except that of reproduction. The existence of the bad woman is and has always been due to the existence of the good woman, and one will not be modified without the other;—it is not a historian but a statesman who must solve the problem implicit in these words.

The second characteristic of our two periods is that as civilization advances the men's sphere expands, but the woman's contracts. Part of the degradation of Athenian women was due to the existence of slaves, who deprived them of all occupation. This, like prostitution, is a problem which exists today unsolved. A well-known writer on women's emancipation wrote that the ideal wife at a certain epoch was hardly to be distinguished from a domestic servant; but a domestic servant is also a woman, and women's emancipation must free not only the rich wife from being almost a domestic servant, but the domestic servant from being one in actuality. In other words, since work is better for anyone than idleness, it is better for a wife to be a house drudge than a parasitical ornament; nothing could degrade women more than the Victorian ideas, which dug holes in the ground and sealed up some women in the basement, and built drawing-rooms aloft and sealed up the other women in an atmosphere of idleness and pampas grass. Which of the two groups were most miserable nobody knows, but at least it is degrading to all women to believe that it is better to have servants than to be one.

We can put it in another way: in primitive society one woman's good was another's; in civilized society, where individualism triumphs, some women are happy at the expense of others. The woman's sphere is more and more given over to the women slaves, whether true slaves, serfs or wage slaves, and the rich woman left alone face to face with luxury.

With the effect of reason we have already dealt; we may notice here once more the birth of a vicious circle of argument about women:—their sphere does not call for the use of reason, therefore they need not be educated; since they are not educated to use their reason they are clearly devoid of it; since they are devoid of it, they must remain within their own women's sphere and take no part in public affairs. We must also remember that since happiness springs from slavery to convention, the average Greek woman was content to remain as she had always been, and her man-imposed inertia militated more and more against her emancipation because it met with her approval. The subjection of women would not have lasted so long, had not even subjection had its compensations.

A last consideration: women are set against one another directly civilization introduces a division of their labours along emotional and sexual lines. The existence of one Aspasia is a challenge and a temptation to all matrons in every society. Aspasia has manifest advantages over Medea; she is free in body and she is free to possess a mind, she is a person as well as a woman. She will be hated and despised by every matron who envies her, but her presence is the beginning of the end, though the end will be long in coming; so long indeed that more than two thousand years later, Hannah More could write: "If the ambition of an excellent British lady should be fired by the idea that the accomplished females of those polished states were the admired companions of the philosophers, the poets, the wits and the artists of Athens; and their beauty and talents so much the favourite subject of the muse, the lyre, the pencil and the chisel, that their pictures and statues furnished the most consummate models of Grecian art; if, I say, the accomplished females of our day are panting for similar renown, let their modesty chastise their ambition by recollecting that these celebrated women are not to be found among the chaste wives and the virtuous daughters of the Aristideses, the Agises and the Phocions; but that they are to be looked for among the Phrynes, the Laises, the Aspasias, and the Glyceras. I am persuaded the truly Christian female, whatever be her taste or her talents, will renounce the desire of any celebrity when attached to impurity of character, with noble indignation . . . in all polished countries an entire devotedness to the fine arts has been one grand source of the corruption of the women; and so justly were these pernicious consequences appreciated by the Greeks that they seldom allowed them to be cultivated to a very exquisite degree by women of great purity of character." Hannah More has been saved the pain of reading what a talented modern woman, who unlike her is feminine enough to have a husband and children into the bargain, has to say about Aspasia as she undoubtedly exists today. But we are anticipating. Aspasia may not have been the first educated woman, but she is a symbol of what must happen when education gives women the delights of the mind; namely, that *if the choice has to be made,* women would rather go to hell with Aspasia than remain in Heaven as the wife of a famous man whose ideals of womanly virtue are modelled on Attic lines. Hannah More thought differently, but then she was no prophetess.

Chapter IV

WOMEN AND THE EARLY CHRISTIAN CHURCH

§ 1. *"Pan Is Dead."* AMONG all the vast assembly of gods and goddesses who people the mountain of Olympus or the woods and fields of Greece, some were more human than others. Zeus and Athene, Hera and Apollo, for all their interferences and all-too-human commerce with the sons and daughters of men, were aloof and afar, the seigneurs of the castle, who did not stoop to the nights and days of ordinary people's lives.

Not so the nymphs and satyrs, the Naiads and Silenuses, and especially not so the Great God Pan. Rather than superhuman, these were exaggeratedly human, and hid nothing of their mortal form, though clothed in the mantle of immortality. They were nature gods, and by peopling the wild and desolate countryside, the mysterious cave, the untrodden mountain, the treacherous marsh, the hidden stream, robbed these of their loneliness and terror, bringing friendliness and companionship to the isolated herdsman and hunter. They tamed by their presence the weird and magnificent forces of earth and sky, and transmuted them into something whimsical, humorous, childlike; if they did not make nature harmless or altogether kind, at least they made her less terri-

fying, less overpoweringly tragic; they had their little mal-
ices, but they were not crushing and fatal.

And among them all, the chief was Pan: "everywhere in
groves and marshes, on the peat moor or the rocky heights,
floating in the current of the streams or traversing untrodden snows, in the day at the chase, and as evening closes
in solitude fingering his flute, seen and heard by shepherds,
alone or with his dancing train, is to be met the horned and
goat-footed, the sunny-smiling Pan."

> The Sileni and Sylvans and Fauns,
>   And the Nymphs of the woods and the waves,
> To the edge of the moist river-lawns,
>   And the brink of the dewy caves,
> And all that did them attend and follow,
> Were silent with love, as you now, Apollo,
>   With envy of my sweet pipings.
>
> I sang of the dancing stave,
>   I sang of the dædal earth,
> And of heaven and the giant wars,
>   And Love and Death and Birth.
>   And then I changed my pipings,—
> Singing how down the vale of Mænalus
>   I pursued a maiden and clasped a reed.
> Gods and men, we are all deluded thus!
>   It breaks in our bosom and then we bleed.

This human god, of like passions with ourselves, not
built upon the heroic scale, was the patron of the village
festival, the familiar of the village girls, in spite of his
horns, his goat's beard and his hooves, and his very hairy
body. Like the villagers he hunted and fished; like them he

made love; he sported and danced with nymphs and often chased mortal girls who ventured into the forest. He made the flocks fertile and was a friend to all shepherds; and even today, high up in his Pyrenees, can be heard the shrill voice of his pipes, played by an isolated man among his sheep, who probably does not know whence his instrument of music came to him.

In short, Pan is a Puck-like figure and a genial personification of the powers of fertility and physical love; for him no sonorous rites were performed, it is true, but he was all the more loved for his homeliness and lack of dignity. A god willing to wink and to play indecent pranks is a relief after the bloodstained, grand and terrifying higher powers. His worship was universal and he received homage wherever a man and a woman made love, and he wanted little else.

At the time of the birth of Christ a schoolmaster named Epitherses was sailing in a ship bound from Greece to Italy; at nightfall the wind died down as the ship was floating near the little island of Paxos, and in the silence they came very close to the shore. The passengers had hardly finished dinner and were lingering over the wine. Suddenly a loud voice was heard from the shore crying out: "Thamus, Thamus, Thamus," thrice. Unknown to the passengers there was on board at the time an Egyptian pilot of that name; and when he heard himself called a third time, he answered the voice and bade it speak.

Louder than ever the voice replied: "When you are come to Palodes, tell the people that the Great Pan is dead."

Astonishment and fear fell on all, and after debating the matter this way and that, Thamus resolved to pass Palodes in silence if the wind continued, but if it became calm again to obey the voice.

Palodes was reached; the last breath of wind fainted away; Thamus accepted the omen. "The Great Pan is dead!" he cried, and in answer to his voice there came the sound of multitudes weeping and wailing for the dead god; a sound which died away in muttered and ominous echoes around the shores of the wine-dark Mediterranean sea.

When the Emperor Tiberius heard of what had happened, he questioned Thamus and caused enquiries to be made about the god: the story spread rapidly and soon the whole of Rome and the neighbouring world knew that Pan, the whimsical, sportive, lewd god of domestic and youthful pleasures was no more; the god of fertility, to whom every woman was a priestess, was dead.

What did this portend to the women who came home from the village wells that evening, smiling at some secret thoughts and perhaps blessing the Pan who added salt to their daily lives? Certainly they never gave a thought to the provincial life of far-away Judæa, where at that very time a new mystery was coming alive.

§ 2. *The Old Testament View.* THE death of Pan, explain the idle tale as we will, came at the moment when the forces of hate and contempt were preparing their worst blow against women; when the one great virtue and strength which compensated for every bodily weakness, was to be taken from them; when fertility was to be dishonoured and the fifteen-century reign of sterility to be inaugurated over the broken images of the old gods and goddesses.

It is not to impugn the beauty of the solitary Nazarene, nor to question a word of His wisdom, to assert that beyond all possible doubt the first centuries of Christianity degraded women, filled them with despair, made their life purposeless, to an extent which has rarely been equalled in the whole history of mankind. Nor was this the result of a period of decadence and degeneracy; what is more significant is that the very hope of mankind, the most advanced thought and striving after truth, proved to be the messenger of despair to one-half of humanity.

It is only to be expected that such a statement will be received with incredulity and resentment by many readers, and in order to prepare our minds for the evidence which is to follow it will be well to consider what Christianity means to the historical student.

To most of us Christianity means the group of beliefs which we were taught in childhood and in which we find our justification for human existence. It is a personal thing and, to use William James's expression, our "total reaction to life." We measure our own shortcomings and perhaps those of our neighbours against the fullness of the stature of Christ. Beyond this we include in our conception of Christianity a certain number of habits and ceremonies which represent nothing particular to us but which have their charm of tradition, coming as they do from a time when they meant something concrete to our ancestors. Few Catholics, for example, know why they eat fish on a Friday but not meat; it is as we shall see originally because fish are not the result of an act of sexual copulation and therefore were considered less impure by people several thousand years ago. Thus the forgotten original reason would today be rejected scornfully, but its effect, become a tradition, is still with us.

Now to the historian Christianity must mean nothing personal, it must be the mold into which the metal of human thought and feeling has been poured at different epochs. To him the early church was not bent so much on justifying the ways of God to man as on justifying the ways of man to God. The church could not produce anything except what was in the nature of the raw material she had to use.

And so when we see the appalling doctrines about sex, women and marriage expressed in the writings of the early church, we must remember that these were the primitive traditional reactions to life of savages, who wanted to find justification for their feelings in the new teaching. We can find an analogy in our own time. It was not the fault of Christianity that bishops and others found a justification in their ideas of Christianity for turning churches into recruiting offices during the war, and in the same way it was not the fault of Christianity that it became the meeting-point and distributing centre for all the primitive taboo feelings towards women existing in the world at the time of its birth and early success.

But as a historical fact it remains true that women have little to thank the early church fathers for; and this remains true even though every doctrine about deity, immortality, sin and divine revelation and purpose may be equally true.

It is only natural that we should expect Christianity to have broken by its very advent the continuity of savage superstition: we expect a sort of analogy of the psychology of individual conversion, but history shows us nothing of the kind. Christianity, to be intelligent about women, had to wait for human nature to become intelligent about them— and this did not happen in the twinkling of an eye.

To show this most clearly it will be best to trust as often as possible to the words of the original authorities, to the men who were the spokesmen of the early church; these words cannot be regarded merely as matters of opinion, they are matters of fact.

Christianity, the fierce, passionate, revolutionary force that it was in the early days, assailed with bitterness and cruelty all that in savage belief, in paganism, high or low, ministered to joy in women and respect for them; and accentuated and exalted all that brought them suffering and contempt. To read the early Church Fathers is to feel sometimes that they had never heard of the Nazarene, except as a peg on which to hang their own tortured diabolism—as a blank scroll upon which to indite their furious misogyny.

"I have not left any calamity more hurtful to man than woman. O assembly of women, give alms, although it be of your gold and silver ornaments; for verily ye are mostly of Hell on the Day of Resurrection."

"The sentence of God on this sex of yours lives in this age. You are the devil's gateway. You destroy God's image, Man."

What does it matter that the first of these sentences comes out of the mouth of a man named Mohammed, and the second out of the mouth of one named Tertullian—the one founder of a religion which to this day is regarded as the most degrading for women; the other the greatest Christian, and the most influential, of his age? Clearly it is the same lying spirit, the same tortured emotionalism, the same sick soul, which speaks through each. If Christianity treats women better today than Islam, then it is because Christianity has changed and Islam remained the same, for in their early years they were indistinguishable.

Tertullian, the great African, felt towards women as his Moorish descendants do today; not only do these believe women defective in understanding and religion, but they think that God has excluded them from His mercy, that they are the friends of the devil; nay, that an old woman is often worse than the devil, and that many women are devils in disguise.

"The woman's lot," writes Doughty in *Arabia Deserta*, "is here unequal concubinage and in this necessitous life a weary servitude. The possession in her of parents has been yielded at some price to an husband, by whom she may be dismissed in what day he shall have no more pleasure in her. The Arabs are contrary to womankind, upon whom they would have God's curse; some say the Beduw are poisoners of husbands, and there are many adulteresses. The *woman* they would have under subjection; admitted, they say, to an equality, the ineptitude of her evil nature will break forth. They check her all day at home, and let her never be enfranchised from servitude. The woman's sex is despised by the old nomad and divine law in Moses."

Here we see the contrary spirit to that which we studied at the beginning of the last chapter: there we saw the agricultural philosophy of the great river valleys of Asia Minor and Africa producing as its fruit a medley of goddesses, and a synthesis of them all in the Great Mother of the Gods; we saw too that women prospered under the eye of these fertile deities; they were protected by remarkable codes of law, their daily life was sweetened by the admonishments of which we read in the Egyptian papyri.

Now there appears the spirit of the wilderness, the nomadic philosophy of pastoral peoples whose women were a nuisance to the group, rather than the fountain of their prosperity; the arid nightmare of desert sorrows. "In this desert there are a great many evil spirits and also hot winds; those who encounter them perish to a man. There are neither birds above nor beasts below. Gazing on all sides as far as eye can reach in order to mark the track, no guidance is to be obtained save from the rotting bones of dead men, which point the way." So wrote Fa-Hsien of the Gobi about 400 A. D.; and when the evil spirits and hot winds of desert life settle upon the life of women, they leave it arid and rotten. Christianity was born out of the desert.

Not only were the first great Christians of the early Church the inheritors of the nomadic philosophy, but they acquired their outlook on women from a written source, which was itself a relic of a nomadic time embedded in elements of a later date and a more advanced culture. It was through the Mosaic law that there flowed in all the most hateful superstition of primitive man, to meet and colour the simple clear waters of the new dispensation. The naked back of woman felt the sting in the Christian Church, even more so than before, of five lashes, and their names were Genesis, Exodus, Leviticus, Numbers and Deuteronomy. We have only to quote from the book of the law to understand the truth of this: and here are the passages which show it:—

"And the Lord spake unto Moses, saying, Speak unto the children of Israel, saying, If a woman have conceived seed, and born a man child: then she shall be unclean seven days; according to the days of the separation for her infirmity shall she be unclean. And in the eighth day the flesh of his foreskin shall be circumcised. And she shall then continue in the blood of her purifying three and thirty days; she shall touch no hallowed thing, nor come into the sanctuary, until the days of her purifying be fulfilled.

"But if she bear a maid child, then she shall be unclean two weeks, as in her separation: and she shall continue in the blood of her purifying threescore and six days.

"And when the days of her purifying are fulfilled, she shall bring . . . a young pigeon . . . for a sin offering, unto the door of the tabernacle of the congregation, unto the priest: who shall offer it before the Lord, and make an atonement for her; and she shall be cleansed from the issue of her blood." (Levit. 12).

Here we have precisely the same elements of belief as we have already seen common among all savages: childbirth makes a woman unclean; she must be cleansed with an offering for her sin; if moreover it is a girl child the penalties are double—she has not even the excuse of adding one of the desired sex to the population; finally, it is the blood which is the dangerous element. Childbirth involves the expenditure of the symbol of life, and as long as there is any risk of a man coming in contact with this, so long must she be strictly secluded. The fifteenth chapter of Leviticus goes into further details about the uncleanness which results from any kind of "running issue out of his flesh." The man with such an issue is unclean, so are his bed and his clothes, the chair he sits on, his saddle, the cup from which he drinks; all must be segregated. Since also a woman is periodically so afflicted, the restrictions and taboos are most strongly felt by her.

"She shall be put apart seven days: and whosoever toucheth her shall be unclean until the even. And every thing that she lieth upon in her separation shall be unclean: every thing also that she sitteth upon shall be unclean. And whosoever toucheth her bed shall wash his clothes, and bathe himself in water, and be unclean until the even . . . And on the eighth day she shall take unto her . . . two young pigeons . . . and the priest shall offer the one for a sin offering . . . and the priest shall make an atonement for her before the Lord for the issue of her uncleanness."

Again, we see precisely the same outlook at work which produced the seclusions and restrictions of menstruous women among savages; and it is worth while observing that the restrictions are clearly for the same reason as was then given:

"I have commanded thee, and thou shalt eat in thy gates whatsoever thy soul lusteth after. . . . Only be sure that thou eat not the blood: for the blood is the life; and thou mayest not eat the life with the flesh. Thou shalt not eat it; thou shalt pour it upon the earth as water. Thou shalt not eat it; that it may go well with thee, and with thy children after thee, when thou shalt do that which is right in the sight of the Lord." (Deut. 12.)

These passages explain in part the strange degradation of women which we are about to study: but still earlier in the books of Moses comes the passage which more than any other is to influence their position among the early Fathers.

"Now the serpent was more subtil than any beast of the field which the Lord God had made. And he said unto ... woman, Yea, hath God said, Ye shall not eat of every tree of the garden? And the woman said unto the serpent, We may eat of the fruit of the trees of the garden: but of the fruit of the tree which is in the midst of the garden, God hath said, Ye shall not eat of it, neither shall ye touch it, lest ye die.

"And the serpent said unto the woman, Ye shall not surely die: for God doth know that in the day ye eat thereof, then your eyes shall be opened, and ye shall be as gods, knowing good and evil.

"And when the woman saw that the tree was good for food, and that it was pleasant to the eyes, and a tree to be desired to make one wise, she took of the fruit thereof, and did eat, and gave also unto her husband with her; and he did eat. And the eyes of both of them were opened, and they knew that they were naked; and they sewed fig leaves together, and made themselves aprons. And they heard the voice of the Lord God walking in the garden in the cool of the day: and Adam and his wife hid themselves from the presence of the Lord God amongst the trees of the garden.

"And the Lord God called unto Adam, and said unto him, Where art thou? And he said, I heard thy voice in the garden, and I was afraid, because I was naked; and I hid myself. And he said, Who told thee that thou wast naked? Hast thou eaten of the tree, whereof I commanded thee that thou shouldest not eat? And the man said, The woman whom thou gavest to be with me, she gave me of the tree, and I did eat.

"And the Lord God said unto the woman, What is this that thou hast done? And the woman said, The serpent beguiled me, and I did eat. And the Lord God said unto the serpent, Because thou hast done this, thou art cursed above all cattle, and above every beast of the field; upon thy belly shalt thou go, and dust shalt thou eat all the days of thy life: and I will put enmity between thee and the woman, and between thy seed and her seed; it shall bruise thy head and thou shalt bruise his heel.

"Unto the woman he said, I will greatly multiply thy sorrow and thy conception; in sorrow thou shalt bring forth children; and thy desire shall be to thy husband, and he shall rule over thee.

"And unto Adam he said, Because thou hast hearkened unto the voice of thy wife, and hast eaten of the tree, of which I commanded thee, saying, Thou shalt not eat of it: cursed is the ground for thy sake; in sorrow shalt thou eat of it all the days of thy life; thorns also and thistles shall it bring forth to thee; and thou shalt eat the herb of the field; in the sweat of thy face shalt thou eat bread, till thou return unto the ground; for out of it wast thou taken; for dust thou art, and unto dust shalt thou return. . . .

"And Adam knew Eve his wife; and she conceived. . . ."

It is hard to believe that any words written by man have ever done so much harm to women as these, which generations have claimed were written by the Holy Spirit. Without any doubt they have set the seal for Christian peoples upon the degradation of women. They were interpreted by a line of teachers, beginning with St. Paul, in such a sense as to make women expiate eternally the bringing of death into the world and all our woes. In them has been found adequate sanction for treating women as inferior beings, for subjecting them to wrongs, both spiritual and temporal, for carrying on the reign of the most savage of all superstitions.

Finally one more quotation, well known as it is, will be given to complete the raw material of early Christian belief about women:

"And the Lord God said, It is not good that man should be alone; I will make him an help meet for him. . . . And the Lord God caused a deep sleep to fall upon Adam, and he slept: and he took one of his ribs, and closed up the flesh instead thereof; and the rib, which the Lord God had taken from man, made he a woman, and brought her unto the man.

"And Adam said, This is now bone of my bones, and flesh of my flesh: she shall be called Woman because she was taken out of Man." (Genesis 2.18 and 2.21–23.)

The burning faith and fanaticism of a small group of men, haunted by memories of the evil spirits and dead bones of the desert whence they came, was to spread the literal belief in these words throughout the world, until all the enemies of women dwelling in men's complexes and mental conflicts could roost in its branches.

§ 3. *St. Paul's* SINCE it was through St. Paul's teachings that
View.   Christianity finally took its shape, before
studying the outlook of women among other early thinkers,
we will watch the leaven of the Law of Moses working in
his Epistles. Through St. Paul, Genesis and Deuteronomy
became the basis of Christian doctrine with regard to
women: here then are the critical passages of his message.

"I will therefore," says St. Paul in the First Epistle to
Timothy, "that women adorn themselves in modest apparel,
with shamefacedness and sobriety; not with braided hair,
or gold, or pearls, or costly array; but (which becometh
women professing godliness) with good works. Let the
woman learn in silence with all subjection. But I suffer not
a woman to teach, nor to usurp authority over the man, but
to be in silence. For Adam was first formed, then Eve. And
Adam was not deceived, but the woman being deceived was
in the transgression. Notwithstanding she shall be saved in
childbearing, if they continue in faith and charity and holiness with sobriety."

In the Epistle to the Ephesians it is written: "Wives, submit yourselves to your own husbands, as unto the Lord.
For the husband is the head of the wife, even as Christ is
the head of the church: and he is the saviour of the body.
Therefore as the church is subject unto Christ, so let the
wives be to their own husbands in every thing." In the First
Epistle to the Corinthians it is written: "I would have you
know, that the head of every man is Christ; and the head of
the woman is the man . . . Every woman that prayeth or

prophesieth with her head uncovered dishonoureth her head: . . . for a man indeed ought not to cover his head, forasmuch as he is the image and glory of God: but the woman is the glory of the man. For the man is not of the woman; but the woman of the man. Neither was the man created for the woman; but the woman for the man. . . . Judge in yourselves: is it comely that a woman pray unto God uncovered?"

St. Paul also treats in this epistle of the general subject of marriage. "It is good," he says, "for a man not to touch a woman. Nevertheless, to avoid fornication, let every man have his own wife, and let every woman have her own husband. . . . I say therefore to the unmarried and widows, It is good for them if they abide even as I. But if they cannot contain, let them marry: for it is better to marry than to burn. . . . He that is unmarried careth for the things that belong to the Lord, how he may please the Lord: but he that is married careth for the things that are of the world, how he may please his wife. There is a difference also between a wife and a virgin. The unmarried woman careth for the things of the Lord, that she may be holy both in body and in spirit: but she that is married careth for the things of the world, how she may please her husband."

It is clear from these that whatever else in his own life and experience and in his own intimate psychology moulded St. Paul's attitude to women, he was deeply influenced by a literal belief in the story of man's fall and also by a literal belief in the story of woman's creation from man's side: but even without such a belief he would doubtless have shown the same temperament and the same spirit as that which chose in an earlier age, but among a similar people, such allegories to explain and define woman's nature and relationship to man: and although we are tempted to criticize St. Paul, since it was through him that the offensive attitude towards women was finally expressed in the Catholic Church, we must remember that it was necessary that offence should come. The attitude was not simply that of one man, but of a stage in mankind's development. The rival sects which struggle with Pauline Christianity had little or nothing better to offer women. If, as might well have happened, the religion of Mithras had conquered the religion of Jesus, it would have had to incorporate precisely the same symptoms of the world's sickness of soul, and just the same disreputable opinions about women would have been expressed by the early Mithraic church fathers.

§ 4. *Ascetic Contempt for Sexual Life.* THE triumph of the Christianity of St. Paul, with its consequent effects upon the history of women, was brought about by the defeat of two main internal enemies, and the struggle which preceded it produced a wealth of material illustrating the outlook of the times on women.

But first we should remember that before the coming of the new faith there were three chief forces in the world, or rather in that part of it in which our interest lies: first, Greek philosophy, second the Roman practical genius, and third the amorphous fertility-religions of Asia Minor. Of these, the first offered women nothing, not even an embryonic reasoning power; the second was breaking down under the corrosion of luxury, militarism and imperialism, and could no longer guarantee a dignified status to women amid the animal passions of a society in decay; the third gave women much, but was bound to become an anachronism in a world where logic had come to temper mysticism.

The new religion finally conquered by absorbing all three, but in a changed form. The Great Mother of the Gods, stripped of her licentious attributes and in the process stripped of all feminine qualities as well, became the Virgin Mary; the militarism of Rome, at the word of Constantine, became the secular arm of a Church militant, which soon learned to persecute, where once it had been persecuted; Greek philosophy in the guise of neo-Platonism, sapped of all which gave it value to mankind, had a very small influence, but was buried for the most part beneath the onrush of emotionalism and contempt of reason.

In order to perform this task of absorption, the Church had to pass through a period of "syncretism," that is, a period during which as much as possible of all current beliefs must be accepted, in contrast to the later period, which began at the Council of Nicæa, A. D. 325, and was marked by the possession of a dogma, an accepted body of belief, outside which everything was damnable heresy. In this earlier period some very remarkable teachings were abroad within the ample bounds of Christianity, of which two were, as we have said, the chief enemies of Pauline Christianity. What had these to say about women?

First there were the Christians who desired to incorporate the whole letter of the Mosaic law; who felt that to be a good Christian, one must first be a good Jew. These Ebionites, as they were called, carried with them much of the noble, ascetic faith of the Essenes, a Jewish monastic body who existed before Christ. The Essenes would not marry, but adopted children, because they would have nothing at all to do with women owing to their low estimation of the female character.

All the Ebionite Christians did not carry things so far: they desired that young people should be encouraged to marry, and aimed merely at absolute purity of morals; they regarded adultery as worse than homicide: and marriage as a necessary social institution. In the pseudo-Clementine literature we have a picture which approximates to the point of view of a rather liberal Ebionite:

"He that desires a chaste wife," says the author, "lives chastely, pays her conjugal duties, eats with her, lives with her, comes with her to be sanctified by the preacher, does not grieve her or find fault with her unreasonably, seeks to please her, and procure her all the pleasures in his power, and makes up for what he cannot give her with caresses. Not that the chaste wife requires these caresses to do her duty. She looks on her husband as her master. If he be poor, she bears with his poverty; she hungers with him if he be hungry. If he go to a foreign land she goes with him. She consoles him when he is sad. . . . The prudent woman is temperate in her eating and drinking. She never remains alone with young men, she even avoids old men, and she shuns unseemly mirth. She takes pleasure in grave discourse and flies from all that is not decorous."

Nobody can find fault with such a charming, temperate picture as this; it is the mildest admonishment to be found in the period, a simple praise of chastity. "The chaste woman," he says, "is the fairest thing in this world, the most perfect token of God's just creation; . . . she aids the pure to be pure, she delights God himself. God loves her, desires her, keeps her for himself; she is his child, the bride of the Son of God, robed as she is in holy light." But behind these writings lay the intolerable weight of the Mosaic law with its inevitable tendencies towards the degradation of women. The Ebionites and Judaising Christians denied St. Paul as an apostate, but their importance to Church history is far greater than their importance to the history of women; so that we may leave them with the suggestion that at best they approached the simplicity of Quakers, while at worst they kept alive the same spirit as St. Paul in an exaggerated form.

But at the earliest date there was a more extreme set of sexual doctrines which even St. Paul fought to eradicate; and though they never existed as a sect apart, the Encratites, as they were called, sought to impose upon the church the dogma of the utter wickedness of marriage. They demanded that no Christian convert should marry and that those already married should dissolve the tie; they encouraged the practice of "spiritual wives," that is, marriages which were not to be consummated; they even advocated self-mutilation. We see here traces of the Manichæan doctrine, which believed that "in every act of begetting, human or otherwise, a soul is condemned afresh to a cycle of misery by imprisonment in the flesh." They therefore incidentally abstained from eating all animals whose birth was due to copulation, and hence ate fish only, thereby originating the Catholic rule of fasting.

These origins are of importance for our understanding of the later growth of reverence for virginity: they indicate one source for it. Another was found in the belief in the coming end of the world, which led to more than one curious practical application. Thus Montanus arrived on the scene from mystical and hysterical Phrygia with two women, Priscilla and Maximilla, prophesying as they went. To them the end of the world was so near that at first the sexual act lost all significance, or rather, its prohibition was not even worth while, with the result that many scandals arose. Moreover, Priscilla forestalled Catherine of Siena in some particulars and was even visited by Jesus in the form of a woman and inoculated by him in a mystic embrace with a superior wisdom. Montanus went to the opposite extreme from the Encratites, and in his hands "poor motherless Eve" was transformed into a saint, women became eligible for bishoprics and all Church offices, and in the earlier period of Montanism much licence abounded. "Seven virgins clad in white and bearing torches, entered the church, uttering groans of penitence, shedding torrents of tears, and deploring with expressive gestures the misery of human life." People prophesied, had fits of ecstasy, preached and went mad with enthusiasm; crowds came from the four corners of the Christian world; chaos reigned. Gradually however there came a change; a rigid asceticism sprang up where earlier there had been laxity; and at last Tertullian himself left the Church he had served so well and joined the Montanists. But their burning zeal, their mysticism, their probable early debauchery and their undoubted later asceticism burned out and the ashes were scattered to the wind.

In all these attacks on marriage there is, of course, a recrudescence of the primitive fear of women's *mana;* it is the taboo system that reigns. We shall shortly pass to the second internal enemy of Pauline Christianity and the Christian struggle with the old fertility rites and religions, where we shall see a different outlook illustrated; but on the way it will be cooling to look at a very curious critic of marriage, Epiphanes, the son of Carpocrates, who died at the age of seventeen after displaying a wealth of erudition and scholarship worthy of a chess prodigy. His church resembled in some ways a sort of modern Ethical church: it contained statues of Jesus, Pythagoras, Plato and Aristotle, to which worship was given; one feels that at a later date William Morris, Tolstoi and Bernard Shaw would have been added. "God," said Epiphanes, "is just and

good; for nature is impartial. The light is equal to all; the
sky is the same for all; the sun makes no distinction between
rich or poor, male or female, free men or slaves. None can
take another's share of the sun to double his own. Nature
offers to all men equal cause for happiness. It is human
laws which, violating the Divine laws, have brought into the
world evil, the distinction of mine and thine, inequality and
enmity." Applying these principles to marriage, Epiphanes
denies its justice and necessity. "The desires we have by
nature are our rights, on which no human institution may
set limits." The result, according to his critics, was unbridled licence, and it may have been so: Epiphanes is
nevertheless a curious figure for his time, and not unlike
Shelley at Oxford.

Ebionites, Encratites, Montanists, Epiphanes, all of them
help us to understand the intense importance at the birth of
Christianity of the problem of the relations between the
sexes: as often as not God is forgotten in the wrangling and
casuistry about women. Even when Tatian, for example,
argued and expounded about the nature of Christ, coming to
the conclusion that he had no earthly genealogy, but as "The
Word of God" was born without fleshly parents or fleshly
body, he was not really thinking of God or Jesus, but of his
loathing for women and the sexual act. "The advent of the
Kingdom of God appeared to him as the suppression of
sex and shame." He was expelled from the Church, since
his views led to absolute nihilism, but he left behind him
plenty of less extreme upholders of the same view.

§ 5. *Survival of Fertility Religions.* WE pass now to the other great enemy of Pauline Christianity near to which we have already come in noticing Epiphanes.

If one group of thinkers, or rather "feelers," wished to eradicate sex from the Church, either because it was evil or because it was useless, another group brought the peril of licence with their doctrines. These were the Gnostics, spiritual descendants of the worshippers of the Great Mother of the Gods, who taught that Jesus had lived in retirement for a period after his Resurrection, during which he had taught a secret, esoteric doctrine, which was their property. Their principles varied widely, but in most cases their practice tended to debauchery.

First there were the Valentinians: their priests seduced women openly and claimed immunity from sin owing to their superior wisdom and spiritual status. Next there were the followers of Marcos, "who was wont to seduce women by a strange manner of celebrating the Eucharist, and by the audacity with which he made them believe that they had the gift of prophecy. His fashion of administering the sacraments entailed the most perilous intimacies. Feigning to be the dispenser of grace, he persuaded women that he was in the confidence of their guardian angels, and that they were destined to high rank in his church; and commanded them to prepare for mystic union with him. 'Of me and by me,' he said to them, 'shalt thou receive grace. Be as a bride that welcometh her bridegroom, that thou mayest be what I am, and that I may be what thou art. Prepare thy bed to receive the seed of light. Behold grace descending on thee; open thy mouth and prophesy!' 'But I have never prophesied—I know not how to prophesy,' the poor woman would reply. He redoubled his invocations, terrified and stunned his victim: 'Open thy mouth, I say unto thee, and speak; all that thou shalt say shall be prophecy.' The neophyte's heart beat fast; expectancy, embarrassment, the idea that perhaps she really was going to prophesy, made her lose her head, and she raved at random. Then what she had said was represented to her as being full of sublime significance. From that moment, the unhappy woman was lost. She thanked Marcos for the gift with which he had endowed her, asked what she could do in return, and recognizing that to resign her possessions to him was but a slight recompense, offered him herself, if he would deign to accept her." The poor women thus duped threw themselves upon the mercy of the orthodox Church and lived out the rest of their lives in penitence and perpetual confession.

This sort of thing, always frowned upon by the orthodox Church, was full of the greatest dangers for all true Christians: it represented, of course, the decadent worship of the Mother Cult of Phrygia debased by charlatans; and its excesses were laid at the doors of all Christians whatsoever by their enemies. These represented the young Church as a den of debaucheries, a confederation of licensed profligates; it was in vain that less virulent detractors pointed to the ascetics and the worship of chastity, to the sincere puritanism and sustained austerities; the Pauline Christians, whom we criticize from quite a different angle, had to bear the scandal of these Gnostic poltroons and abracadabra seducers. Cæcilius, the apologist, gives us in the mouth of a typical calumniator the stories which were circulated about his fellow religionists.

"They recognize one another by marks and secret signs; they love one another almost before they are mutually acquainted. Next, debauchery becomes their religion, the bond that unites them. . . . On holy days people of all ages, men and women, assemble for a banquet with their children, sisters and mothers. After much feasting . . . a dog is fastened to the candlestick and is then coaxed and made to jump out of the space in which it is confined by a little cake being thrown to it. The candlestick is overturned. Then, disembarrassed of every gleam of importune light, in the midst of a darkness that favours all shamelessness, they mingle, as chance will have it, in embraces of infamous concupiscence. . . ."

Amid all this orgy of extremism, this sensual asceticism, this sensual debauchery, these false accusations and all the obscurity of changing faiths and new feverish revelations, what was the truth? Where did the Church stand in its early days with regard to women? The persuasive words of another apologist, Athenagoras, a Greek of Plato's city and with something of the philosopher about him beneath his Christian garments, may tell us:

"According to differences in age, we treat some as sons and daughters, others as brothers and sisters, others as fathers and mothers: but these terms of relationship entail no stain of impurity. The Word says indeed: 'If anyone repeat the kiss to obtain enjoyment . . .' and it adds 'we must be highly scrupulous concerning the kiss, more especially in the case of adoration, since, were it defiled by the least impure thought, it would deprive us of eternal life! . . . Each of us uses his wife according to certain rules which we have laid down, and in such measure as serves for the procreation of children; even as the husbandman, having left his seed in the ground, awaits the harvest without sowing anything more. You will find among us many persons of both sexes who wax old in celibacy, hoping thus to live nearer God. . . . Our rule is that each must remain as he is born, or be content with a single marriage. Second marriages are nothing more than decorously disguised adultery."

There is little in this which transcends normal asceticism; nothing to shock the sensibilities of man or woman; and yet we know that it is not the whole picture: it represents however one thread in the tangled skein. If we are to try and sum up the heterogeneous and jangled elements out of which later Christian ages formed their practice, we will suggest that in all these reactions there is an underlying current of loathing for sex and that this is transmuted into a contempt for women. Yet even the chastity is tricked out in terms of lubricity, and is the chastity of men not really chaste in mind. We are soon to see that though lust in action may lead to the expense of spirit, lust dammed up as these men tried to dam it, leads to catastrophe. Meanwhile there are the very words of the Fathers themselves as proof that Athenagoras was milder than the spirit which was abroad and which was shortly to triumph.

§ 6. *The Church Fathers on Women.*   WE have quoted familiar passages from the Old Testament and from the writings of St. Paul; they have all been read several times by every worthy Christian and also by every man or woman who has been decently educated. It is probably correct to say that most of us have refused to accept these passages at face value; for though we may not mind the idea that men are descended from anthropoid animals, we certainly object to thinking that women are themselves devils, or unclean inferior beasts. We have shut our minds to their significance and gone on our way untroubled. But the effect of early Christianity upon women was so serious and so different from what we might presume that we need to ponder it most carefully; and we must add to these well-known passages a selection from the mouths of the men who controlled the destinies of the new religion during the first two or three centuries of its existence. In doing so it will be best to let the words speak for themselves and to offer but little comment of our own, but to rely upon a passage from the works of James Donaldson, who is without doubt a most competent historian of the period.

The opinion of Clement of Alexandria as to how women should be dressed for going to church:

"Let her be entirely covered, unless she happens to be at home. For that style of dress is grave, and protects from being gazed at. And she will never fall who puts before her face modesty and her shawl; nor will she invite another to fall into sin by uncovering her face. For this is the wish of the Word, since it is becoming for her to pray veiled." (Pædagogia iii, 11, 79.)

The opinion of Commodian as to the clothing of a Christian woman:

"It is not right in God that a faithful Christian woman should be adorned." (Book ii, 19.)

The opinion of Tertullian on the same:

"Natural grace must be obliterated by concealment and negligence, as being dangerous to the glance of the beholder's eyes."

Clement of Alexandria on hair-dressing:

"Head dresses and varieties of head dresses, and elaborate braidings, and infinite modes of dressing the• hair, and costly mirrors in which they arrange their costume, are characteristic of women who have lost all shame."

Cyprian upon cosmetics:

"Are sincerity and truth preserved when what is sincere is polluted by adulterous colours, and what is true is changed into a lie by the deceitful dyes of medicaments? Your Lord says Thou canst not make one hair black or white, and you, in order to overcome the word of your Lord, will be more mighty than He, and stain your hair with a daring endeavour and with profane contempt; with evil presage of the future, make a beginning to yourself already of flame-coloured hair. . . . You cannot see God, since your eyes are not those which God made, but those which the devil has spoiled. You have followed him, you have imitated the red and painted eyes of the serpent. As you are adorned in the fashion of your enemy, with him also you shall burn by and by. . . . Let your countenance remain in you incorrupt, your head unadorned, your figure simple; let not wounds be made in your ears, nor let the precious chain of bracelets and necklaces circle your arms or your neck; let your feet be free from golden bands, your hair stained with no dye, your eyes worthy of beholding God."

Tertullian's opinion upon the expediency of motherhood:

"Further reasons for marriage which men allege for themselves arise from anxiety for posterity, and the bitter, bitter pleasure of children. To us this is idle. For why should we be eager to bear children, whom, when we have them, we desire to send before us to glory (in respect, I mean, of the distresses that are now imminent); desirous as we are ourselves to be taken out of this most wicked world and received into the Lord's presence.

"Let the well-known burdensomeness of children, especially in our case, suffice to counsel widowhood—children whom men are compelled by laws to have, because no wise man would ever willingly have desired sons.

"What has the care of infants to do with the Last Judgment? Heaving breasts, the qualms of childbirth, and whimpering brats will make a fine scene combined with the advent of the Judge and the sound of the trumpet. Ah, what good midwives the executioners of the Antichrist will be!"

Clement of Alexandria interprets an infant's wail:

"Why, O mother, didst thou bring me forth to this life, in which prolongation of life is progress to death? Why hast thou brought me into this troubled world, in which, on being born, swaddling bands are my first experience? Why hast thou delivered me to such a life as this, in which a pitiable youth wastes away before old age, and old age is shunned as under the doom of death? Dreadful, O mother, is the course of life, which has death as the goal of the winner. Bitter is the road of life we travel, with the grave as the wayfarer's inn."

Tertullian on how much better he feels himself away from his wife:

"Let us ponder over our consciousness itself to see how different a man feels himself when he chances to be deprived of his wife. He savours spiritually."

Tertullian in a letter to his wife on the joy of the Resurrection morning:

"There will at that day be no resumption of voluptuous disgrace between us."

The Testament of the Twelve Patriarchs on all women whatsoever:

"By means of their adornment they deceive by the glance of their eye, and then they take them captive by their doings . . . men should guard their senses against every woman.

"The angel of God showed me: that for ever do women bear rule over king and beggar alike; and from the king they take away his glory, and from the valiant man his strength, and from the beggar even that little which is the stay of his poverty."

Tertullian on the same:

"Nothing disgraceful is proper for man, who is endowed with reason; much less for woman, to whom it brings shame even to reflect of what nature she is."

The Apostolic Constitution on the duties of widows:

"Let the widow mind nothing but to pray for those that give and for the whole Church, and when she is asked anything by anyone let her not easily answer, excepting questions concerning the faith and righteousness and hope in God. . . . She is to sit at home, sing, pray, read, watch and fast, speak to God continually in songs and hymns."

Tertullian on women's part in Christian religious work:

"For how credible would it seem that he (Paul) who has not permitted a woman even to learn with over-boldness, should give a female the power of teaching and baptizing. 'Let them be silent,' he says, 'and at home consult their own husbands'!"

The Apostolic Constitutions on the same:

"But·if we have not permitted them to teach, how will anyone allow them, contrary to nature, to perform the office of a priest? For this is one of the ignorant practices of the atheism of the Greeks to appoint priestesses to the female deities."

Tertullian on the wickedness of certain heretics:

"The very women of those heretics how wanton they are! For they are bold enough to teach, to dispute, to enact exorcisms, to undertake cures, it may be even to baptize!"

Epiphanius sums up:

"The race of women is prone to slip and is unstable and low in their thoughts."

So much for the words of the Christian Fathers. We will now quote the opinion of their effect which James Donaldson gives after having considered a mass of similar evidence in the early Church writings. "Such ideas," he says, "had necessarily a very powerful effect on the place and position of woman and on the conception of her nature. What was that effect? I will attempt to describe it in a few words. I may define man to be a male human being, and a woman to be a female human being. They are both human beings, both gifted with reason and conscience, both responsible for their actions, both entitled to the freedom essential to this responsibility, and both capable of the noblest thoughts and deeds. As human beings they are on an equality as to

their powers, the differences in individuals resulting from
the surroundings and circumstances of spiritual growth.
But man is a male and woman is a female, and this distinction exists in nature for the continuance of the race.
*Now what the early Christians did was to strike the male
out of the definition of man, and human being out of the
definition of woman.* Man was a human being made for
the highest and noblest purposes; woman was a female
made to serve only one. She was on the earth to inflame the
heart of man with every evil passion. She was a fire-ship
continually striving to get alongside the male man-of-war
to blow him up into pieces. . . . How then were men to
treat this frivolous, dress-loving, lust-inspiring creature?
Surely the best plan was to shut her up. Her clear duty was
to stay at home, and not let herself be seen anywhere. And
this duty the Christian writers impress upon her again and
again."

§ 7. *Evolution* It is necessary to attempt some estimate of
of Roman   the actual effect upon women of these doc-
Law.
            trines; and first of all we must remember that
during these early years of Christianity, the whole body of
believers was an illegal and persecuted assembly. Its members became so because they were impelled to do so by their
own souls and in order to save themselves from spiritual despair. They were not a normal sample of the population,
upon which as a whole they produced absolutely no effect. It
is clear that the women who became Christians could not

have been in any way typical of their period, except in so far as we find both in Greece and in Rome an enthusiasm for religion continually appearing among women, doubtless as a solace and a reaction from their unsatisfactory everyday lives.

At first sight women would seem to have had little to hope from these stern ascetics, who were as contemptuous of them as they were terrified of their possible fascinations: nothing but an ardent faith and hope of immortality to be gained only through the crucified Christ could have drawn them from their ordinary life: that and the example of chaste, kindly, charitable communities of believers, radiant in a faith which was still youthful and green, amid the chaotic and feverish turmoil of Roman social life. Christianity appealed first to the slaves and the oppressed, and later to the matrons of even noble families, who had a distaste for their ordinary occupations.

To these women the Church offered in this world the work of deaconesses, which was little more than that of a pew-opener and minor lady almoner; but in the next world it offered them life and salvation. It was those last gifts that were craved. The road to them often lay through martyrdom, and the type of woman who became a Christian was ready and willing to undergo that with all its accompaniments of torture and degradation. The martyrdom of the slave girl, Blandina, was the great example of these women, who, though they defied the beasts, the red hot chair, the wheel, boiling oil, were blessed with a poorness in spirit which could stand without flinching the loathsome detractions of a Tertullian.

But when under the Christian Emperors Christianity became respectable and *de rigueur,* all this changed. Women were not attracted by hopes of a martyr's crown, and it was no longer only the poor in spirit who found themselves seated in the congregations of the State religion. The severe code of morality and the ascetic outlook on life ceased to have the same relevance; there grew up a dualism of conduct and ideal, and while one group of Christians aimed at a higher exercise of faith, the majority were well content to dilute the strong wine of early practical doctrine. The dictum that whereas all things are possible, all are not expedient, conveniently opened the way to the assertion of a major and a minor rule of expediency.

Nevertheless we must always remember that the ideals towards which all alike were exhorted to strive in a greater or less degree were dictated and interpreted by a hierarchy of powers which believed in celibacy as a virtue and practised it as a natural state. To these women were nothing more than a temptation, as we have abundantly seen; in their hearts were still alive every savage fear and savage taboo; as we have traced our history there has been no lack of continuity in this. The ethical instructors did not expect every Christian woman to remain a virgin, but if they permitted a limited exercise of the functions of sex, it was as a sop to the devil, a necessary concession to feminine frailty; and never as a natural right or as a gift of God.

We may see in part what practical effect these ideas produced by a consideration of the changes of Roman law with regard to women. James William, All Souls Reader in Roman Law at Oxford, has summarized these as follows:

1. The influence of the Church was exercised in favour of the abolition of the disabilities imposed by the older law upon celibacy and childlessness.
2. There were increased facilities for entering a professed religious life.
3. Wives were secured due provision.
4. Differences in the law of inheritance from intestate persons as between males and females were abolished by Justinian.
5. The Church supported the power of Roman empresses and others who were her best friends (e. g. Pulcheria and Irene).
6. Justinian sanctioned the appointment of mothers and grandmothers as tutors.
7. The principle that the mother of three (or if a freed woman of four) children succeeded to the property of her intestate children was extended to all cases.
8. Widows had increased rights of succession.
9. Restrictions on the marriage of senators and other men of high rank with women of low rank were extended by Constantine and entirely removed by Justinian.

10. Second marriages were discouraged, and in the ninth century third marriages were punishable.

11. In the ninth century the benediction of a priest became necessary for a legal marriage.

12. Adultery was punished with death by Constantine, but the penalty was reduced by Justinian to relegation to a convent.

13. An adulteress could not re-marry, and a marriage between a Jew and a Christian was technical adultery.

14. Severe punishments for procurement and incest and other offences against chastity.

15. Capital punishment for abducting or assaulting a nun.

It should be clearly understood that these are the supposed effects of Christianity upon Roman law and that they have nothing at all to do with the Canon Law, which of course constitutes the main body of Christian legal doctrine. We are not therefore at liberty to regard them as necessarily innovations due to the new religion: and in many cases they are clearly the next natural step in the evolution of Roman thought and needs.

The first mentioned is, however, an obvious change of attitude; beginning with Augustus and the Lex Papia Poppæa of A. D. 9, the Roman law had made strenuous efforts to encourage marriage and to chastise celibacy. We have seen in ancient Sparta that marriage and parenthood were protected and multiplied by disgracing those who avoided them, and even in our own days there is a constantly recurring chatter about the propriety of taxing all bachelors. Augustus found himself faced with a diminished population and a growing aversion to marriage: he imposed fines on all bachelors between twenty and sixty, and extra taxation and civil disabilities on bachelors and spinsters alike. The very existence of these laws suggests two points of significance to women's history; first that the time was long past when women were silently given to men in marriage, if they were to be considered as blameworthy for remaining single; and second, that the marriage laws and customs must have been hard on men if they were so averse to contracting such an obligation.

Under Christian influences this situation would naturally change radically; and no legal power which contained within it the slightest tinge of the religion of the Church Fathers could be expected to encourage what they thought at best a necessary fall from complete virtue.

A glance at the list printed herein reveals that numbers 1, 3, 4, 6, 7, 8 were all of them in the direct line of Roman legal evolution and probably quite unconnected with Christian influences: numbers 2, 5, 10, 11, 13, and 15 were obvious and logical effects of Church influence and for the most part are intended to satisfy the needs and secure the position of the religious community rather than to affect for good or ill the status of woman. But we must make one exception: the discouragement of second marriages, whatever its ethical basis in the minds of early bishops, undoubtedly struck at one of the great abuses of later Roman times. Easy divorce had made all marriage precarious and undignified. "The causes of the dissolution of matrimony," says Gibbon, "have varied among the Romans. . . . In the first ages, the father of a family might sell his children, and his wife was reckoned in the number of his children; the domestic judge might pronounce the death of the offender, or his mercy might expel her from his bed and house; but the slavery of the wretched female was hopeless and perpetual, unless he asserted for his own convenience the manly prerogative of divorce. The warmest applause has been lavished on the virtue of the Romans, who abstained from the exercise of this tempting privilege above five hundred years; but the same fact evinces the unequal terms of a connection in which the slave was unable to renounce her tyrant, and the tyrant was unwilling to relinquish his slave. When the Roman matrons became the equal and voluntary companions of their lords, a new jurisprudence was introduced, that marriage, like other partnerships, might be dissolved by the abdication of one of the associates. In three centuries of prosperity and corruption, this principle was enlarged to frequent practice and pernicious abuse. Passion, interest, or caprice suggested daily motives for the dissolution of marriage; a word, a sign, a message, a letter, the mandate of a freedman, declared the separation; the most tender of human connections was degraded to a transient society of profit or pleasure. According to the various conditions of life, both sexes alternately felt the disgrace and injury; an inconstant spouse transferred her wealth to a new family, abandoning a numerous, perhaps a spurious, progeny to the paternal authority and care of her late husband; a beautiful virgin might be dismissed to the world, old, indigent and friendless. A specious theory is confuted by this free and perfect experiment, which demonstrates that the liberty of divorce does not contribute to happiness and virtue. The facility of separation would destroy all mutual confidence, and inflame every trifling dispute; the minute difference between an husband and a stranger, which might so easily be removed, might still more easily be forgotten; and the matron who in five years can submit to the embraces of eight husbands, must cease to reverence the chastity of her own person."

In such words does Gibbon paint the customs of the Romans with regard to divorce and his own respectable opinions. The effect of Christianity was excellent in most particulars; for the precarious position which overtakes women when divorce is so free that they are likely at all times to be left stranded in middle age, is almost worse than that in which they find themselves when divorce remains a "male prerogative." Constantine and his successors to Justinian were influenced now by the Church, now by the pagan traditions; "In the most rigorous laws," said Gibbon, "the wife was condemned to support a gamester, a drunkard or a libertine, unless he were guilty of homicide, poison or sacrilege, in which case the marriage, as it should seem, might have been dissolved by the hand of the executioner. . . . The obstacles of incurable impotence, long absence and monastic profession were allowed to rescind the matrimonial obligation." The husband, however, could always divorce his wife for adultery. In these vigorous laws we see of course the hand of the Church; and Justinian's successor was forced to yield "to the prayers of his unhappy subjects, and restored the liberty of divorce by mutual consent: the civilians were unanimous, the theologians were divided; and the ambiguous word, which contains the precept of Christ, is flexible to any interpretation that the wisdom of a legislator can demand." In short, the effect of Christianity upon the Roman law of divorce mitigated the scandals of frivolous beginnings and endings of marriages, but would have substituted a heavy load of hidden sorrow upon a basis of matrimonial indissolubility; ever since civil practice has attempted to steer a middle course between these dangerous extremes, while the Roman Catholic Church at least has constantly preferred to conceal natural frailty and to forbid escape from its consequences.

It remains to consider for a brief space the nature and effect upon women of that distinctively Christian fabric, the Canon Law.

We saw in the last chapter that later Roman law left the wife in a position of great personal and proprietary independence; from the very beginning Christianity tended to modify this. Whenever in later Europe the Canon or Ecclesiastical Law prevailed, the status of the married woman was degraded; whenever the secular Roman law prevailed

it was raised. "But," says Sir Henry Maine, "the Chapter
of law relating to married women was for the most part read
by the light, not of Rome but of Canon Law, which in no
particular departs so widely from the spirit of the secular
jurisprudence as in the view it takes of the relations created
by marriage. This was in part inevitable, since no society
which preserves any tincture of Christian institution is
likely to restore to married women the personal liberty
conferred on them by the middle Roman law, but the proprietary disabilities of married females stand on quite a
different basis from their personal incapacities, and it is by
keeping alive and consolidating the former that the expos-
itors of the Canon Law have deeply injured civilization.
There are many vestiges of a struggle between the secular
and ecclesiastical principles, but the Canon Law nearly
everywhere prevailed. In some of the French provinces
married women, of a rank below nobility, obtained all the
power of dealing with property which Roman jurisprudence
had allowed, and this local law has been largely followed by
the Code Napoleon; but the state of the Scottish law shows
that scrupulous deference to the doctrines of the Roman
jurisconsuls did not always extend to mitigating the disabilities of wives. The systems, however, which are least in-
dulgent to married women are invariably those which have
followed the Canon Law exclusively, or those which from
the lateness of their contact with European civilization,
have never had their archaism weeded out. . . . Indeed
the part of the Common Law which prescribes the legal sit-

uation of married women may serve to give an Englishman clear notions of the great institution which has been the principal subject of this chapter. I do not know how the operation and nature of the ancient Patria Potestas can be brought so vividly before the mind as by reflection on the prerogatives attached to the husband by the pure English Common Law, and by recalling the vigorous consistency with which the view of a complete legal subjection on the part of the wife is carried by it, where it is untouched by equity or statutes, through every department of rights, duties and remedies."

In short, Canon Law, which has been followed in this particular more than Roman Law, translated into the practice and precept of legislation the spirit of St. Paul: "the head of every man is Christ, and the head of the woman is the man." The innumerable disabilities which orthodox and official Christianity put in the way of women's legal emancipation were not swept away until the twentieth century, and then it was not to religion that women owed their tardy freedom, but to their own education.

Whether then we judge by the utterances of the early Church writers or by the dogmas and injunctions of the early Church law, we are forced to the conclusion that among all the enemies of women, none has waged more implacable war against them than the religion which grew up and was called Christianity. It brought a blast from the desert which made all nature sterile, and we still suffer from its effects.

Terrible, however, as the indictment may seem, we must remember that all these old fathers, these founders of the Christian Church, were not only the sons of God, but sons of their own age: their attitude towards women was no integral part of their new faith, it was typical merely of the continuity and permanence of early reactions between men and women, reactions which had to wait upon the growth of reason and intelligence before they could be purified.

Chapter V

THE MIDDLE AGES: THE WITCH, THE VIRGIN AND THE CHATELAINE

§ 1. *Barbarian Womanhood.* THROUGHOUT the periods of world history at which we have been glancing hitherto, our own immediate ancestors have remained savages unaffected by the forces which have been accumulating like an avalanche. We must now try to form a picture of how that avalanche, which we call civilization, engulfed the savage women of the German forests and made with the remains of their primitive virtues and vices the modern history of women.

On the one hand we have a mighty mixture of complicated elements, sophisticated, unstable, in many ways decadent; on the other, we have the Teutonic barbarians with their raw human nature, their untainted blood, their uncritical and un-self-conscious energy. Let us stand back and look at both these phenomena before they begin their interplay.

In previous chapters we have tried to build up a diagram of what we may call the civilized attitude to women, as civilization existed at the time of the Council of Nicæa, in A. D. 325. That episode in human evolution is suitable as a surveying point because it represents the exact moment when Christian doctrine and Roman practice fused together and became a single force for the moulding of the future. Naturally the Council did not fashion a code or a programme for the future of women, nor did it represent a complete fusion of the chief elements of civilization; but when Constantine summoned the princes of the church and met them in conclave, he gave the Church the material power with which to enforce its spiritual message, and at the same time he forced Christianity far out of the orbit contemplated by its founder, or by St. Paul or by Tertullian: instead of a religion for slaves, hermits and humble folk, he made it a religion for conquerors, courtiers and soldiers. He decreed that not Christ, but Constantine, should Christianize Europe and the whole world. The effect on women's history was, of course, as great as the effect upon history as a whole, for it ensured that her lot in European society would be conditioned by a diluted form of St. Paul's and Tertullian's outlook and that, not merely a few, but all women would find themselves in a society where religion and idealism preached their inferiority and practised their subjection.

Both Roman thought and Christian thought about women were the production of a particular social evolution and both of them were tinged with the savage and primitive customs of thought and feeling from which those divergent social evolutions had begun. In A. D. 325 these two mixed and henceforth became one: if, then, we divide our mental avalanche into its component parts we find them to be the

primitive taboo outlook on women evolved into the outlook
of St. Paul and Tertullian on the one hand, and, on the
other, the primitive taboo outlook on women evolved into the
practices of later Roman society; and of the two we are
bound to suggest that the latter was at least from the sole
point of view of sexual equality and women's happiness,
more exalted and less dangerous.

We have quoted elsewhere Sir Henry Maine's statement
that Roman law gave greater personal freedom to married
women than can ever be given them in any society preserv-
ing the least tincture of Christian institutions: and if recent
legislation has in great part brought twentieth-century
women on to a level with third-century Roman women, it
is not, as also we have said, due to Christian institutions but
to their own educated efforts. It is this which justifies our
judgment as between Roman and Christian influences on
women; and the real importance of such a judgment lies in
the fact that as far as women are concerned the Christian
point of view has dominated the Roman: whatever views
Constantine's generals may have had on the subject, as
Romans and the husbands of Romans they influenced the
course of history far less than the views of Constantine's
priests as Christians never to be defiled by the touch of a
woman.

So much for the avalanche of civilization. What of the
savages, who were to be swamped by it and transformed
into part of it in its onward course down the mountain-sides
of time? Tacitus paints, and possibly exaggerates, their

virtues in his *Germania*. They respected their women, he tells us, and exacted from them an equal share of toil and hardship; chastity was an esteemed virtue and an actual fashion, divorce was unknown, and also polygamy; neither luxury nor indolence corroded the family, and a hardiness of body was the natural begetter of a hardiness of soul. "Although the progress of civilization," says Gibbon, "has undoubtedly contributed to assuage the fiercer passions of human nature, it seems to have been less favourable to the virtue of chastity, whose most dangerous enemy is the softness of the mind. . . . The elegance of dress, of motions, and of manners gives a lustre to beauty and inflames the senses through the imagination. Luxurious entertainments, midnight dances, and licentious spectacles present at once temptation and opportunity to female frailty. From such dangers, the unpolished wives of the barbarians were secured, by poverty, solitude, and the painful cares of a domestic life. . . . The Germans treated their women with esteem and confidence, consulted them on every occasion of importance, and fondly believed that *in their breasts resided a sanctity and wisdom, more than human.* Some of these interpreters of fate, such as Velleda in the Batavian war, governed in the name of their deity the fiercest nations of Germany."

In short, the barbarians maintained in their social conventions more than a shadow of the worship of women as givers of fertility; but to what extent this trait was common to all the warring tribes we cannot know. We are told, however, by Tacitus, that they did not for the most part even practise the art of agriculture and we can therefore be certain that fertility rites were not universal. Moreover, in many ways, we find that the position of women among the barbarians was not higher than in Christian law, let alone in Roman law, and even the evidence that Tacitus gives us, for instance, that there was no divorce, is not entirely satisfactory. To Tacitus, no doubt, absence of divorce seemed to indicate a higher position of women than the easy degradation of Roman marriage, but we must remember that when Romans refrained from divorcing wives for five hundred years it was because they killed or enslaved them instead.

However, we may pass from the study of the uncivilized Teutonic tribes without too nice enquiry into the details of their society and take up the story at the point when the fusion had begun to bear its peculiar fruit. Whatever we do not know, we do at least perceive that the complicated and contradictory Romano-Christian avalanche found an added impetus from the unspent force and energy of barbarian blood. The old institutions were remodelled, women were re-enslaved, enlightened, degraded, exalted in different ways from the old which we have so far studied.

§ 2. *Chivalry.* THE fusion between Romano-Christian civilization and the barbarians produced two great social institutions, feudalism and chivalry: and nothing in women's history has been of such supreme importance as the way in which these affected it.

Feudalism may be defined, for our purposes, as a relationship between overlord and tenant whereby the overlord secures the tenant in the enjoyment of his lands in exchange for the tenant's assistance in warfare. The value of the fief to the overlord was that it secured him the services of a given number of soldiers under the command of the tenant; the claim to the fief on the tenant's part was based upon his fulfilling this claim to his service as a soldier. Feudalism in this sense was a Roman institution adopted and developed by the new barbarian powers of northern Europe.

Chivalry on the other hand was an adaptation of barbarian usages by the Christian Church for its own purposes. Chivalry was the army of the Church, the band of knights who fought for the Church against its enemies, in contrast to the Roman army which fought for the Church against the enemies of Rome.

The Knight of Chivalry had to obey ten commandments, which were as follows:—

    I. Thou shalt believe in all that the Church teaches and thou shalt observe all its commandments.

    II. Thou shalt protect the Church.

    III. Thou shalt respect the weak, and appoint thyself their defender.

IV. Thou shalt love the country where thou art born.

V. Thou shalt never retreat before the enemy.

VI. Thou shalt wage on Infidels a war without truce and without mercy.

VII. Thou shalt acquit thyself of thy feudal dues with exactitude, if they are not against the laws of the Church.

VIII. Thou shalt never lie, and shalt be faithful to thy given word.

IX. Thou shalt be generous, and give largess to all.

X. Thou shalt be everywhere and always the champion of the Right and of the Good against injustice and evil.

Thus Chivalry was the culmination of the movement which gave fire and sword to the hand of those who would propagate the belief in the preacher of the Sermon on the Mount. Nothing could be a better example of the secular nature of the Church teaching after the conversion of Constantine. It was the idealizing of war as a Christian virtue and the spiritual twin of the Islamic belief that he who died fighting for Allah against the Christian was heir to paradise. Beyond all else, we must superpose a negative. Chivalry had nothing whatever to do with chivalry either as an ideal of decent behaviour towards women or, in its later sense, as a conventional code exemplified by a man taking his hat off when women are in an elevator.

Feudalism and chivalry reached their culminating point

about the twelfth century when they became a force equal
to if not greater than that of Christianity itself in the shaping of convention and morality. Indeed, it would be more
correct to say that they became the medium through which
alone Christianity enforced any of its practical precepts.
Let us see how women fared amid barons and knights and
the odour of sanctified war.

In the first place feudalism had a very powerful effect
upon the legal position of women: we have already stated
that the tenure of land involved the duty of fighting for the
overlord in all his battles; now clearly a woman could not
fulfil this duty and therefore her holding of land was regarded almost as a conspiracy to defraud the overlord of his
lawful rights. If therefore a young girl inherited land from
her father, or if a widow inherited land from her husband,
their position was precarious and wretched. The overlord
demanded and could enforce marriage or remarriage with
all the force of justice and custom on his side. A fief being
land held in return for military service, what right had a
woman to hold a fief? Clearly it was her duty to change the
anomalous position in which she found herself and that
with the least possible delay.

In the Chanson de Geste called *Charroi de Nîmes* we
read the following scene: " 'One of these days,' said the
King to the Knight William, 'one of my peers will die; I
will give you his land and his wife, if you wish to take
them.' He then suggests various vacant inheritances and
finally says: 'Take the land of the Marquis Berenger who

has just died, and take his wife with his fief.' William is angry and replies: 'You have sure a very short memory. Do you not remember one day how, in the midst of a battle with the Saracens, you were unhorsed and in great danger of death. One of your counts saw you in danger: he ran up and made a space round you with his sword as a wild boar with the hounds: then he got off his horse, held the stirrup for you, and put you in the saddle. It was Marquis Berenger whose wife you now offer me. But he has left a son who is still very young. I will kill the first who touches the child.' "

This is, doubtless, an excellent example of the manners of the period. William is, of course, a hero, and another would have accepted Berenger's widow without a murmur, but even then it is not for the widow's sake, but for Berenger's, and especially for his son's. Had the widow been childless doubtless the affair would have turned out differently. Then again we must remember that though the position of women, as the gift of the overlord and a sort of vitalized deed of conveyance for landed property, may seem low to us, it did not necessarily seem low to them. We can pour out too many tears for the widow's feelings. In the Chanson de Geste called *Girars de Viane*, we read: "My husband has just died: but what are the use of widow's weeds? It has always been since Moses' time that some have died and others lived. Find me a husband who is strong, for I need one such to defend my land."

In another Chanson de Geste, called *Garin de Loherains*, we read how Helissent of Ponthieu has lost her husband,

and within a month her brother, Beaudocim of Flanders, offers her another. He chooses out two possible suitors and advises her to choose one of them, since "he is the richer of the two." For a moment the widow pretends to make some resistance, but almost at once she agrees; immediately the brother takes her by the hand and gives her to the knight; the marriage takes place at once; the celebrations are joyous; the fief passes to a new husband, and, incidentally, the woman too.

In the same way Charlemagne on his return from his wars in Spain remarries en masse all the widows of the knights who have fallen there: land tenure, title deeds, are more important than sentiment, and, truth to say, sentiment scarcely exists. These various examples tell us a great deal about the position of women under chivalry: as women they did not exist, as property holders they were the pawns of the kings and knights: what were they to the bishops? We shall see that later; for the moment we must enquire what lay behind this unlovely situation. What sort of person was the lady of the castle?

As far as marriage was concerned, she was Medea's sister: she could have echoed the famous speech word for word, but she was even less likely to see through the conventions than Medea's countrywomen in the days of Euripides. It was not only the widow who married again and as fast as possible, nor was it only the orphan who took what was given her in the way of a husband with hopeful thanks for her good fortune. No girl was consulted in the matter; for her father she was, we repeat, a pawn, to be moved up to the eighth square in order to become a queen: that is, to be given in marriage to whomsoever promised a desirable military alliance.

In the Chanson de Geste called *Département des enfans Aimère*, the father says to his son, Garin: "You will be very foolish to hope for my inheritance, for you will not get Narbonne: go, Garin, to Bavaria, and tell the Duke of Naunes to give you his daughter, and the town of Auseune, its ports and its shores. True this land is now in the hands of the Saracens, but you will only need to regain it." Garin sets off and reaches Naunes, greets the Duke and tells him why he has come. "You are of high descent," replies the Duke, "and I am going to give you my fair-faced daughter." He calls the young girl. "Pretty child," says he, "I have given you a husband." "Thanks be to God," she answers. They send for Archbishop Samson; the marriage is performed. Of course the girl had consented freely, but what can we think of the promptitude? It suggests a vacant enough mind and a too facile discrimination; such things must have led to the massacre of many an innocent.

It would be wrong, however, to assume that the Lady of Chivalry was a perennial ingenue: she knew what she wanted and had various means of attaining it. Her easy way of transferring her affections to one man or another according as one husband died, or a father required an alliance, is curiously reminiscent of Homeric days. The women of Homer were captured by warriors, or became the

property of one side or the other according to the fortunes
of war, but they bore it with an ease and a grace which must
have made their happiness less insecure however much it
may have lowered the dignity of their position in our eyes
as we look back: and so it was with the feudal lady. She was
better off than the Athenian and better off than Tertullian
would have made her had he had his way.

§ 3. *The Lady* WHAT sort of life did the lady of chivalry
of Chivalry. lead in her castle? In the first place, she had
in many cases some rudiments of an education. She had
probably spent many hours as a child with a tutor or in an
amateurish sort of school where she had been taught to read.
She could recite stories and romances, which she bought
from itinerant minstrels; and when this is said, we must
remember that her brothers were incapable of any such
thing as reading. Such as it was, the woman's learning ex-
ceeded the man's. The Lady could, of course, sing a little,
and accompany herself or others on the harp or the viol.
She was an astronomer, so far at least as to know the con-
stellations and the brighter stars and to be able to point out
the Milky Way to her parents. She could play chess, though
it is impossible to judge her standard; if she was capable
of thinking one move ahead she was more advanced in this
subject than ninety-nine out of a hundred of her grand-
daughters today. She knew a little falconry and enough
medicine to set a broken arm, to pound herbs in a pestle
and mortar and to dress a wounded knight; and, of course,

she could sew, weave and embroider, and repeat a few words of Latin, with a greater or less consciousness of their meaning.

This list of accomplishments is meagre, but, as has been said, it far surpassed the proudest boast of the average knight; and it contained enough to set an occasional mind afire with vague desires. Probably a lady was as much better educated than a knight as an American woman is compared with an American man; and the effect in both cases was about the same: to raise timid doubts whether war in one case and business in the other is really the end of things created.

So much for the lady's mind. Her body is sophisticated, with traces of a Christian anti-sexual ideal. She has indeed a boyish figure, slender, narrow-waisted, with small breasts and low hips; and, above all, she is deathly white in colour, "so white that February snow is less white than she; whiter than snow on ice, than snow in sunshine." This ideal has appeared at recurring intervals in women's history but on this occasion it did not go with the character of an ingenue; from this unformed body, supplied with what most would call an unformed mind, came a plentiful supply of worldly wisdom expressed in forcible and even coarse vocabulary. She was not expected to know as little about sex and physiology as might have been expected from her unemphatic body; she could take care of herself whenever she felt disposed to do so.

The age of chivalry is notable for the great lack of interest shown by the average young man in the opposite sex, but we would perhaps be less disposed to show surprise at this if we divested ourselves of our associations with the word "chivalry" and remembered that it has less to do with ladies and more to do with horses than people allow themselves to think. In the age of chivalry women were hardly as important as horses: save, as we have said, as living titles to landed property. Here is a conversation from a Chanson de Geste called *Girbers de Metz:* the daughter of Auseis sat one day at her window; there pass beneath two young men, Garin and Girbert: "Look, cousin Girbert, look. By Saint Mary, what a pretty girl!" "Ah, what a beautiful beast is my horse," Girbert answers without turning his head. "I have never seen so charming a girl, what beautiful colouring and dark eyes." "I know no charger fit to be compared with my horse," and so the two pass on. A little incident, but significant; for lack of interest breeds contempt. "They are ill-advised, those princes, who go and ask counsel in the women's quarters," is the logical outcome of a man's thought, if his feelings begin by rating a young girl on a level with his horse.

Indeed, the age of chivalry affords us some excellent examples of such contempt: take, for example, the incident in the Chanson de Geste called *Mort de Garin.* Blancheflor goes to her husband, the Emperor Pepin, and asks him to help the Lorrainers. "The king hears her, he grows enraged, he strikes her nose with his fist, four drops of blood fall from her and the Lady says: 'Thanks be to thee; when thou wilt, give me another blow.'" This is not isolated. Often enough the very words are repeated as if they were a formula. In the age of chivalry a woman who dared to counsel her husband was greeted with a closed fist on her face; but the chivalrous among us will be glad to hear that there were rules which ought to be obeyed in the matter. A husband may strike his wife with his fist on the face or on the back for adultery, or for contradicting him: by the thirteenth century manners had so far been softened that Beaumanour lays down that the beating of a wife should not be severer than is reasonable.

If, then, a woman was married on the spur of the moment, often to a man she had never seen, simply to facilitate warlike alliances, military strength or real estate transactions; if, moreover, when married to a war-mad knight, of no intelligence and even illiterate in most cases, she could be beaten for contradicting him; could the Lady of the Castle find redress or succour for a miserable life or from an unworthy husband? On this point it will be of double interest to quote Léon Gautier, the great French authority on Chivalry, and the quotation will be of service also because it illustrates the difficulty in which the student of women's history constantly finds himself; the authorities have their own private axes to grind, and Monsieur Gautier deliberately leaves out, refuses to believe or discounts every fact which contradicts his main theses, the perfection of French women in all centuries and the goodness of the Church in its dealings with them. "In spite of so much poetry," writes Gautier, "passions were not extinguished in men's hearts, and there were some which were wearied by the banality of marriage: but then they found before them the terrible Church barring the way. We must indeed admit that she was not always very powerful, and that there were even in the ranks of the clerical army, regrettable and shameful fallings away. Until the eleventh, indeed into the twelfth century, we find cases of divorce; but it is wrong to confuse later 'separation' with divorce. The separation, allowed by the Church, is merely physical separation, which does not allow the wife or husband to contract a new marriage."

The rules laid down by the Church were:

I. Separation is a true physical separation which allowed the man or woman to live separately but not to contract another marriage.
II. Separation is pronounced only for grave and specific causes.
III. Voluntary separation for which all that is needed is the consent of the pair is permitted if one or other desires to become a religious recluse.
IV. In all other cases the consent of the pair does not suffice, and an enquiry into the stated grievances is necessary.
V. It is the ecclesiastical jurisdiction, alone competent in questions to do with marriage, which must carry out this enquiry.
VI. In case of separation children under seven go to

the mother and the father contributes a half-share
to the costs of their upbringing.

We find in one of our oldest chansons (we are condensing
the words of Gautier) a notable example of this cruel and
rare separation. Poor Count Ainis becomes a leper. His
wife, Lubias, is horrified by the diseased man and comes
to the Bishop to ask for separation, which requires an ecclesiastical inquiry before it can be granted. Lubias points
out the disease and begs to be separated. The Bishop replies: "Madam, the last person who ought to unveil thus
your husband's disease is yourself." Eventually the Bishop
grants the separation, influenced by the mob whose sympathies are with the lady, seeing that she is married to a man
so horrible with disease that no one can bear to look at him.
"The Bishop," continues Gautier, "who ought to have re-
sisted to death, the Bishop thinks he must yield, and calls
three other prelates uselessly to the judgment. The poor
leper, in face of his universal desertion, ends by himself
asking for judicial separation . . . he is taken to a hut outside the town, where there comes to visit him one consoler,
one friend. This consoler, this friend, is his son, his little
seven year old Girard, God bless him. God curse Lubias.

"In spite of the perfidy of certain Lubias, in spite of the
criminal compliance of certain bishops, in spite of all, the
great principle of the indissolubility of marriage has triumphed in Christian society."

It is hard to realize as we read the last few lines of

Gautier's remarks that all the wretched Lubias is asking
for herself is the legal right not to have physical relations
with a leper: she does not ask for the right to marry anyone
else, but simply for the right to keep her body from the
danger of contracting a foul disease. Gautier shows himself a worthy descendant of Tertullian, with the same outlook in the nineteenth century as that which we have studied
in the third; yet his point of view is perfectly orthodox over
much of the earth's surface today.

§ 4. *Church* Besides the dogma of the indissolubility of
Regulations marriage, the Church concerned itself chiefly
of Marriage. with three points about the wife: her age, her
free consent, and her non-relationship with her husband;
and it is clear that with regard to the first two its influence
would be of supreme value. We have seen that feudalism
treated a woman with scant consideration; she was the complete slave of a system of militarism and land tenure which
regarded her personal feeling as of quite secondary importance. How far could Christianity, which, of course, could
not oppose the feudalism which gave it strength, mitigate the
abuses of such a system?

In the first place the Church attempted to lay down a
minimum age at which a girl could be married; this age was
fixed at twelve. The age of marriage is at all times and in
all places a useful indication of women's social position;
in primitive society the age of puberty was, as we have seen,
the age of marriage; and in that period of human history

the result was beneficial to women's happiness, for marriage was a function and not a sacrament nor a companionship. But when we reach a later stage where intellectual factors begin to play a large part in human relationships, it is perfectly clear that early marriages are deleterious to a woman's happiness. What discrimination can be expected of a girl of twelve, save between an ugly and a handsome man? Yet in fixing the age at twelve, the Church was fighting against still earlier marriages. In the age of chivalry a girl of five years was frequently a bride, in spite of the power of the Church, simply because marriage was a matter of military tactics and territorial alliance. " 'The man cannot take a wife before the age of fifteen, the woman cannot take a husband before the age of twelve.' This prudent rule," said Gautier, "this formal decision of the Church was not made to please noble families, who scouted it. Feudalism had terrible needs indeed. That the same baron could one day have two fiefs instead of one; that sometime he could be twice Duke, or twice Count; to round off their manor and their property they did not stop at any sacrifice, and they went so far as to marry scandalously children of five. The Church protested, but the laws of the Church were good enough for the bourgeois and the villains. They let her protest and married at all ages."

If then the Church was not very successful in imposing a minimum age for marriage, what effect had it upon the woman's freedom of choice? In theory this free consent was throughout the middle ages the *summa vis* of the sacrament of marriage: it was more important than the joining of hands by the priest; without it the marriage could not take place. In practice, we may very well ask what value such a precaution might have to a girl of twelve, brought up to assume that whatever her father decided for her was sure to be the best. The principle of consent, indeed, though laudable at all times, had to wait for other civilizing influences before it became significant in practice. If the attempts of the mediæval Church to impose upon feudal barons both an age limit and the principle of consent as concomitants of a just marriage were merely ineffectual, the third of her conditions was simply barbarous. Nothing could better illustrate how primitive superstition has been kept alive by Christianity than the mediæval laws regarding affinity and consanguinity and nothing could better illustrate the shallow justifications of superstitions so frequent among prejudiced historians than the words of Monsieur Gautier on the subject.

The first were a monstrous absurdity and their apologist made himself equally absurd; but lest these words may seem offensively strong to some readers, they may be coupled with a regret that the noble doctrines of the Nazarene should be so often encumbered by the rubbish of His prejudiced and foolish followers. According to the canon law of our period a man and a woman could not marry if they were related together within certain degrees; according to Gregory I these degrees included the seventh by civil computation, that is, if a man and a woman had the same ancestor, one four generations back and the other three generations back, they could not marry, or, more simply, first cousins are of the fourth degree of civil reckoning and people three degrees less closely related than cousins, could not marry. Charlemagne made this the law of the Empire and since most people then, as today, were unlikely to know all their relatives so distant as this, confusion was extreme. But this was only the beginning: since marriage made husband and wife "one flesh" all their relations reciprocally became of an equal degree of affinity—not only could I not marry my third cousin, but I could not marry my deceased wife's third cousin: a survival of this is seen till recently in the opposition to marriage between a man and his deceased wife's sister. Moreover, beyond these prohibitions of marriages on the grounds of consanguinity and affinity, it was held that a "spiritual affinity" was contracted between the baptizer and the baptized, the confirmer and the confirmed, between godparents, their godchildren and their godchildren's relatives: all these "spiritual affinities" constituted absolute bars to a marriage which would be, indeed, an incestuous relationship.

Now all this ridiculous superstition had, of course, two causes: first, it can be derived from the custom and habits of all primitive peoples among whom incest does assume a similar wide interpretation, and, second, it was due to the underlying desire of the Church to discourage marriage and to put every possible impediment in its way. We have already seen in our study of primitive men that the fear of incest was a powerful motive in social life, and we know from our study of the Church fathers that the coming of Christianity in no way broke the continuity of ancient superstitions; we must suppose therefore that the doctrines of the Church found ready acceptance in the mediæval mind. The old human fear of incest doubtless continued and the priests found no difficulty in enforcing the validity of their doctrines. Human beings were still sick in their souls as far as sexual relations were concerned. But though we cannot blame the Church for being human, all too human, we cannot give it any praise for being in the vanguard of intellectual emancipation. The results were lamentable, the search for an "unforeseen" affinity became popular as a substitute for divorce proceedings, and an unfortunate girl, so carefully protected from her desires to avoid the corruption of leprosy, might be cast out in middle age on the excuse that, quite unknown to everybody, her uncle had baptized her husband.

Now listen to Léon Gautier. "In spite of so many vexatious appearances, the law was good; one need not look here for anything but a neat plan on the part of the Church, which was to inspire in generations of Christians a profound respect for the family and the most profound horror for all that could, even at a great distance, approach incest. Above all, we owe to this fortunate severity beautiful races with the purest blood, which have not grown ugly, which have not diminished through these consanguineous unions condemned today alike by science and the Faith. If our barons were six feet high, with such rich colouring, with such large fists . . . they owed it without knowing it to the Church." No comment is required for a passage which is undoubtedly significant of the blindness afflicting historians. Though the fault of the Mediæval Church was simply that it was not ahead of the times, the fault of M. Gautier is that he was behind the times.

Thus we see that the Church, even when it would, could not help the Lady of the Castle to any great extent: she was always a civilian in a camp of armed men, always the useless holder of a barren fief. But there was an escape from the tedium of such an existence, indeed there were two escapes; and they were taken by a great proportion of those few women whose brains were enlightened and whose emotions were unsettled by a little learning. We will now proceed to glance at each of these in turn.

§ 5. *The Ro-* "A TRAIT peculiar to this epoch," writes
mantic Escape. Gautier in his *Social State of France During the Crusades,* "is the close resemblance between the manners of men and women. The rule that such and such feelings or acts are permitted to one sex and forbidden to the other was not firmly fixed. Men had a right to dissolve into tears, and women had a right to talk without prudery. . . . If we look at their intellectual level, the women appear distinctly superior. They are more serious, more subtle. With them we do not seem dealing with the rude state of civilization that their husbands belong to. . . . As a rule the

women seem to have the habit of weighing their acts; of not yielding to momentary impressions. While the sense of Christianity is more developed in them than in their husbands on the other hand they show more perfidy and art in crime."

This estimate of women is what we should expect from the facts at which we have already glanced: arm a girl with a little ability to read and put her in a camp of warriors with no culture and a contempt for everything but swords and horses, and she will either be queen or she will increase her pent-up energy until she bursts the dams of convention and carves out a new stream-bed for herself. The current doctrine of the end of the earth is not that we shall cool down to a pale and ghostly dead moon-like world, but that the radio-active substance imprisoned in the solid depths will gradually increase in heat until about forty million years hence they will melt the foundations of continents and ocean and swamp land and sea alike in molten rock. It was very much the same with the women of the early middle ages; their intellectual energy was imprisoned in the thick leaden folds of feudal society until it increased in force and overflowed into new channels.

Occasionally, of course, an accident allowed of a Queen Eleanor ruling the thick-skulled knights of chivalry; but the very nature of feudalism made a woman's activity within it dependent less upon her personal qualities and more upon her landed possessions, and even Eleanor was no exception to this rule.

It was outside the law that superior women found one of their two escapes. Shocking as it may sound illicit love became an attraction for all those who were intellectually above the very restricted sphere of a feudal daughter, wife and mother. If we return to Stendhal's classification of love and consider Passion Love, we have a thing compounded of mind and body; body alone entered into the married love of a girl wedded at twelve to her father's choice; when she grew to have a mind, she sometimes found herself attracted to a new choice of her own. It should not have been so, but it was so: we cannot hope to understand the history of women if we refuse on a priori grounds to believe it.

Of course there has always been a sort of nomadic affection born of boredom and the instability of human purpose; there has always been a roving tendency in the hearts of all men and women, undisciplined by religious, conventional or ethical considerations; but it is not of the gross results of this that we speak here. The phenomenon of which some notice is now to be taken was a refined, imaginative escape from the petty ties which were all that men chose for binding their women to themselves. It was the natural revolt of ardent women from the sort of young man who would not turn his eyes away from his horse to look at a woman, when that young man had grown to be their husband, the lord of their bodies, and, more important, of their lands.

We have seen how the Lady of the Castle, when still a young girl, bought romances from itinerant poets; she also listened to their recitations and learned from them quite another sort of love from the Philoprogenitive Love of her feudal barons. She found that there were men, noble, courteous, amusing, brave, who did not regard war as the object of existence, but rather love. Naturally she was capable of seeing that such a man was likely to exalt and serve her more whole-heartedly than the man who saw in her merely a title to lands, and, in daily life, a sort of sedentary camp follower. The troubadours, the first of whom was born about 1071, and the last of whom died about 1294, were not by any means cunning low fellows, hangers-on of courts and snappers-up of unconsidered trifles: twenty-three of them, including Richard I of England, were ruling princes. Guilhem IX, the first of them, was a Count in Poitiers and a Duke of Aquitaine, and "he knew well how to sing and make verses, and for a long time he roamed all through the land to deceive the ladies." Under their influence there grew up for the first time in the world's history that fusion of mind and body which has ever since been called after their language, Romantic Love, and which includes Stendhal's Passion Love and Gallant Love as well.

A remarkable result of this movement was the Court of Love, which, according to some old writers, became a common feature, especially in Provence. The Lady of the Castle, cramped by her feudal quarters, found in this institution a means to increase the poetry of existence and to exercise her faculties of imagination and creative poetry. Under a ruling judge, ladies gathered together and pronounced decrees upon the general theory of love, or gave judgments about

specific points brought to their notice by individual lovers.
Here is one such decree.

"Whether there can be love between married people.

"We pronounce and decree by the tenour of these presents, that love
cannot extend its powers over two married persons; for lovers
must grant everything, mutually and gratuitously, the one to the
other without being constrained thereunto by any motive of necessity; while husband and wife are bound by duty to agree the one
with the other and deny each other nothing. Let this judgment,
which we have passed with extreme caution and with the advice
of a great number of other ladies, be held by you as the truth, un-
questionable and unalterable.

"In the year 1174, the third day from the Calends of May."

The court which gave this remarkable decision was pre-
sided over by the Countess of Champagne; and her court,
like all the others, was guided by a written Code of Love
in thirty-one articles, which are so important that we will
transcribe them in full.

CODE OF LOVE OF THE TWELFTH CENTURY

1. Marriage is no good excuse against loving.
2. Whoever cannot conceal a thing, cannot love.
3. No one can bind himself to two loves at once.
4. Love must always grow greater or grow less.
5. There is no savour in what a lover takes by force.
6. The male does not love until he has attained to complete manhood.
7. A widowhood of two years is prescribed to one lover for the other's death.
8. No one, without abundant reason, ought to be deprived of his own love.
9. No one can love unless urged thereto by the hope of being loved.

10. Love is always exiled from its dwelling by avarice.
11. It is not decent to love one whom one would be ashamed to marry.
12. The true lover does not desire embraces from any but the co-lover.
13. Love that is known publicly rarely lasts.
14. An easy conquest renders love despised, a difficult makes it desired.
15. Every lover turns pale in the sight of the co-lover.
16. The lover's heart trembles, at the unexpected sight of the co-lover.
17. A new love makes one quit the old.
18. Probity alone makes a man worthy of love.
19. If love lessens, it dies speedily and rarely regains health.
20. The man prone to love is always prone to fear.
21. Real jealousy always increases the worth of love.
22. Suspicion and the jealousy it kindles increase love's worth.
23. Whom thought of love plagues, eats less and sleeps less.
24. Whatever a lover does ends with thinking of the co-lover.
25. The true lover thinks naught good but what he believes pleases the co-lover.
26. Love can deny love nothing.
27. The lover cannot be satiated by the delights of the co-lover.
28. The least presumption compels the lover to suspect evil of the co-lover.
29. He is not wont to love, whom too much abundance of pleasure annoys.
30. The true lover is haunted by the co-lover's image unceasingly.
31. Nothing prevents one woman from being loved by two men, or one man by two women.

These documents may at first sight seem to the reader so shocking, or so extraordinary, that their true significance may escape him. They reveal, however, the very important fact that when, in any historical epoch, women have been able to gather more intellectual pabulum than the men;

when this intellectual pabulum has expanded their imaginations and their ambitions; they burst the bonds of their conventional sphere and create something new and surprising on their own. It is true that the Courts of Love, the very existence of which has been denied by some authors, could have affected only a very few women, just as Shakespeare could have affected the life and pocket of only a very few contemporary tradesmen; but in both cases the ripples have gone out from the central splash to unexpected edges of the pool of life. Poetry, which by suggestion regulates men's everyday loves and emotions, was deeply tinged by Provençal wit and imagination; and it is hardly an exaggeration to say that the ladies who conspired with the troubadours, invented a new relationship between women and men. And to those who say that this relationship, disguised and tricked out as it may have been, was usually only illicit love, one can only reply that even illicit love is a higher ideal than war, however that too is disguised and tricked out in its turn.

Moreover, it is interesting to notice that women placed themselves on an absolute level with men in their Code of Love: this does not deal with lover and beloved, but with lover and co-lover; what was sauce for the goose was sauce for the gander. Again, consciously or unconsciously, women set themselves up as a power against the crudities of the orthodox Church, which knew a great deal about the Trinity but nothing whatever, naturally enough, about love, or the needs of women. If the Church showed itself so lacking in human values let it look out for itself. In *Aucassin and Nicolette* we read of the sort of people who go to heaven, and the sort of people who go to hell: "For into Paradise go none but such folk as I shall tell thee now: thither go these same old priests, and halt old men and maimed, who all day and night cower continually before the altars, and in the crypts; and such folk as wear old amices and old clouted frocks, and naked folk and shoeless, and covered with sores, perishing of hunger and thirst, and of cold, and of little ease. These be they that go into Paradise, with them have I naught to make. But into Hell would I fain go: for into Hell are the goodly clerks, and goodly knights that fall in tourneys and great wars, and stout men at arms, and all men noble. With these would I liefly go. And thither pass the sweet ladies and courteous that have two lovers, or three and their lords also thereto. . . . With these would I gladly go, let me but have with me Nicolette, my sweet lady."

This, doubtless, is a scandalous and immoral sentiment; but it must be placed against the background of its time: Aucassin has been driven to revolt against law and order, and with them against Christian morality itself, by the alternative offered him, and in this revolt Nicolette is his willing and equal partner. The whole spirit of these men and ladies in revolt was born of the speech of Aucassin's father: "Son, this may not be. Let Nicolette go, a slave girl she is, out of a strange land, and the captain of this town bought her of the Saracens, and carried her hither, and hath reared her and let christen the maid, and took her for his daughter

in God, and one day will find a young man for her, to win
her bread honourably; herein hast thou nought to make
or mend, but if a wife thou wilt have, I will give thee the
daughter of a King, or a Count. There is no man so rich in
France, but if thou desire his daughter, thou shalt have
her."

The whole of that spirit, moreover, is epitomized in
Aucassin's reply: "Faith! my father, tell me where is the
place so high in all the world, that Nicolette, my sweet lady
and love, would not grace it well? If she were Empress of
Constantinople or of Germany, or Queen of France or England, it were little enough for her; so gentle is she and
courteous, and debonair, and compact of all good qualities."
In short, a woman was more valuable and worthier of
friendship as a woman than as a landowner; when this was
fully appreciated feudalism and the feudal Church were
doomed. And it was the educated and intellectually vitalized women of the twelfth century who showed the way
towards this emancipation.

§ 6. *The Re-*   WE have seen that the first way of escape from
ligious Escape. their feudal dungeon led women to discover
Romantic Love, and that since this was a revolt against
convention it naturally took an illicit form. The second way
of escape was, however, eminently respectable. All day
long, in and out of season, the Lady of the Castle had
friends who thirsted and hungered not for her body but for
her soul. Not only did she read the romances of the passing

poets, she read and discussed the sacred literature which her
chaplains put in her hand. If she had a little intelligence, if
she was dissatisfied with the brainless brawn of her husband
or her brothers and their friends, she could always find in
the holy man an intellectual companion and a holy tempter,
whispering reports of a happy way out of boredom and
restraint.

Consider this Lady sitting alone and communing with
her inmost thoughts. "Generally," as Chaucer told us,
"women desiren to have soverainetee," and she certainly was
as womanly as the rest in this particular. What domination
could she have? How could she rule and alter the course of
events by her power? Perhaps there floats into her mind
some such story as that in the Chanson de Geste called
Garin de Loherains, where the King of Moraine, Thierri
by name, is mortally wounded by the Saracens, and sends
for Garin, to whom with his last breath he gives Blancheflor,
with all his land and country. Garin accepts conditionally
on the approval of Pepin, the Emperor, and he goes to the
imperial court to tell the news and to ask for Blancheflor. A
voice calls out in answer: "You forget, sire, that you have
promised me the first fief that falls vacant. It is to me that
Blancheflor belongs." The speaker is Garin's deadly enemy
and the enemy of all Lorrainers: a terrible war begins; they
fight around the ownership of Blancheflor; thousands are
killed, thousands are widowed and orphaned, and all for
Blancheflor. Another lady would envy Blancheflor, no
doubt, and think that this was power and honour and glory

indeed, to be the cause of such mighty wars; but the Lady we
are watching is subtler than this, her mind has been exercised with words and thoughts, she sees through all the pre-
tence, all the hollowness of this so-called power of the feudal
woman; what power, what honour, thinks she, would have
been Blancheflor's if she had had no lands, no marketable
qualities? Blancheflor is a landed prostitute.

Then this Lady thinks of another thing. Growing beside
this castle wall of feudalism is a green and sturdy creeper.
It is the Church, and there are possibilities of freedom, of a
sort, of power, of a sort, there. The Church will offer her
many negative joys, it will take her away from interminable
small talk about battles and tourneys, from the daily life
amid a quarrelsome band of proud ignoramuses; it will
perhaps give her more: as an abbess or a prioress she can
rule instead of being ruled; she can organize, innovate, give
counsel, instead of bending her back beneath a burden of
routine. The Church will offer her much that she desires and
lacks, even apart from its promises of rewards beyond death,
and in exchange it demands but one thing, that she, the
woman, the female human being, should strike female from
her definition, should cast off all her sex feelings, her love,
her maternity, like a soiled and worn-out garment and come
a naked unsexed being into her new kingdom. She can become a priestess of the last great goddess, and, like her ancestors who served Astarte, Demeter or Isis, serve the Virgin.

It is true, of course, that a great gulf has been fixed between the Virgin and the other goddesses; they were the guardians of fertility, she of sterility; their priestesses served her with liberal and licentious love, hers with renunciation and spiritual castration. But even a life of sterility was better for any intellectual woman than a life of small talk about wars and tourneys.

Maidens, widows and wives, all three could pass thus out of the Castle into the cloisters and become by rigorous training fit Brides of Christ. Even at home with her husband the wife was exhorted to practise chastity; she was taught that Joseph and Mary lived celebate lives and, though she and her husband might be granted the minor sin of getting a child or so, the sooner they achieved that ideal the better for both of them. Such married chastity was held to bring forth fruit thirty fold, widowed chastity sixty fold and virgin chastity one hundred fold; but best of all was the lot of a consecrated nun. Widows might well desire to escape into the cloisters to avoid the trouble and dangers of feudal life; wives also were able to dissolve a marriage, however little the husband desired it, by taking religious vows; and many parents got rid of surplus daughters in the same way. Thus the Virgin became one of the feminine types of the Middle Age, along with the Feudal Lady already described and the Witch to be described later.

True, the three together constitute a very small minority of the population; apart from them, as ever, lived and died the women without a history, they who toiled, bore children, prayed, wept, laughed and died, and left no memorial, nothing but an anonymous and fleshly immortality of which we ourselves are but a passing episode.

Yet the Nun, the Witch and the Lady were but this unknown woman exaggerated, raised to the nth power, and in studying them we study her also, or at least we study in what made or marred them, the same forces and ideas which made and marred her.

Let us now consider the consecrated virgin, she who has been chosen by her own choice to be the Bride of Christ; let us begin, not by theorizing about her significance, by placing her in her true niche in the history of women, but by observing the rule under which she lived, the practical ordering of her everyday existence. For this purpose there exists ready to hand a charming volume of doubtful authorship, called *The Ancren Riwle*. It is a treatise on seemly behaviour for those Brides of Christ who lived together in a small house and not a large nunnery, as recluses or anchoresses.

Vowed to a life of virginity, it was of course their first duty to keep that vow; she who bears a precious liquor in a frail vessel, would she not go out of the way of a crowd, unless she were a fool? This brittle vessel is woman's flesh. The liquor within it is her virginity. The brittle vessel is more brittle than glass and once it is broken it can never be mended. It breaks more easily than glass, for it is broken by one unchaste thought. Hence the Bride of Christ will leave the world and seek solitude.

"Thou, my dear spouse," says the Lord, her Bridegroom, "shalt thou follow goats a-field, which are the lusts of the flesh?" Solitude is the only bar against these lusts, and instead of unloosing it, the Bride should remain within and cry to her Husband: "Kiss me, my beloved, with the kiss of thy mouth, sweetest of mouths." This kiss is a sweetness and delight of heart, so immeasurably delicious and sweet that every savour in the world is bitter when compared with it: but the Lord kisses no soul that loves anything but Him. Let the Bride remain fast shut therefore and bolt her mouth, eyes and ears.

It is always the same symbolism, always the voluptuous delights of chastity, the sacrifice of earthly marriage for a heavenly one conceived in the most sensuous forms, described with all the imagery of a love poem.

"There was a lady," says the *Ancren Riwle*, "who was besieged by her foes within an earthen castle, and her land all destroyed, and herself quite poor. The love of a powerful king was, however, fixed upon her with such boundless affection that to solicit her love he sent his ambassadors, one after another, and often many together, and sent her jewels, both many and fair, and supplies of victuals, and the aid of his noble army to keep her castle. She received them all as a careless creature, that was so hard-hearted that he could never get any nearer to her love. What wouldst thou more? He came himself at last and shewed her his fair face, as one who was of all men the most beautiful to behold; and spoke most sweetly and such pleasant words, that they might

have raised the dead from death to life. And he wrought
many miracles, and did many wondrous works before her
eyes, and shewed her his power, told her of his kingdom,
and offered to make her queen of all that belonged to him.
All this availed nothing. Was not this disdain a marvellous
thing? For she was never worthy to be his scullion. But
through his goodness and gentleness, love at last so over-
mastered him that he said: 'Lady, thou art attacked, and
thy enemies are so strong that without help of me thou
canst not by any means escape their hands, so that they may
not put thee to a shameful death. I will, for the love of thee,
take upon me this fight, and deliver thee from those who
seek thy death, yet I know assuredly that among them all I
shall receive a mortal wound: and I will gladly receive it
to win thy heart. Now then, I beseech thee, for the love that
I show thee, that thou love me, at least after being thus
done to death, since thou wouldst not in my life time.' This
king did so in every point. He delivered her from all her
enemies, and was himself grievously maltreated and at last
slain. But, by a miracle, he arose from death to life. Would
not this lady be of a most perverse nature if she did not love
him, after this, above all things?"

The beauty of these words is all of this world: like a
vegetarian who has a chained carnivore within him and eats
his "nut chop" and his "vegetable beefsteak," so chastity
and life-long virginity must be rechristened with roses and
raptures and called a passionate marriage. And that fertile
love may seem a suitable name for sterility, abuse and loath-

ing must be poured upon all to which that name really belongs.

"Greek fire," we are told, "is made of the blood of a red man and it is said that nothing can quench it but urine, and sand, and vinegar. This Greek fire is the love of our Lord, and ye shall make it of the blood of a red man, which is Jesus Christ reddened with his own blood on the Cross. . . . Nothing remains, but to keep yourselves cautiously from every thing that quenches it, namely urine, and sand, and vinegar. Urine is stench of sin. . . . Urine . . . is stinking carnal love that quencheth spiritual love, which Greek fire betokeneth. What flesh on earth was so sweet and so holy as that of Jesus Christ? . . . Judge yourselves, is not he or she mad who loveth too much her own flesh, or any man carnally, so that she desire too fondly to see him, or to speak with him?"

It is curious to see how humanity, or, as the Middle Ages called it, the world, the flesh and the devil, will out: however often love is called carnal and stinking and urine, still the purer flame burns and dictates beautiful erotic descriptions of the love of Christ and his Brides. In these the buried humanity of man expresses its true feelings, though they are disguised at other times beneath a loathing of women.

This loathing of women, which marks almost every page of the early fathers and constantly appears in the teaching and precept of the whole Church, is also enshrined in mediæval sacred poetry. Sometimes the hatred is expressed in untranslatable metaphors of disgust and we can quote only some of the less obnoxious ones by way of illustration.

Thus Anselm of Canterbury in his poem, *De Contemptu Mundi,* "Concerning Contempt for the World," wrote:—

"Woman has a clear face and a lovely form, she pleases you not a little, this milk-white creature! But, ah! if her bowels were opened and all the other regions of her flesh, what foul tissues would this white skin be shown to contain."

How vile the imagination that stooped so low in an effort to discredit the beauty of the world of flesh: yet Odon of Cluny went further in a passage where he asks who could wish to embrace *ipsum stercoris saccum;* but we must refrain from translating the foul saint's words and leave their Latin context for those who wish to pursue it.

Marbode, Bishop of Rennes, embellished the eleventh century with many exceedingly interesting poems, but to him, though he was a true poet, women were so many Eves. "Of the numberless snares that the crafty enemy spreads for us over all the hills and fields of the world, the worst, and the one which scarcely anyone can avoid, is woman, sad stem, evil root, vicious fount, which in all the world propagates many scandals. Woman, sweet evil, honey and poison alike, anointing with balm the sword with which thou piercest even wise men's hearts. Who persuaded our first parent to taste the forbidden thing? A woman. Who forced the father to defile his daughters? A woman. Who tamed the strong by robbing him of his hair? A woman. Who cut off the sacred head of a just man with a sword? A woman. . . .

"Chimera to whom not unmerited is given a threefold

form, a lion in front, a dragon behind and in the middle naught but a very burning fire: an image which clearly shows forth the ways of the whore, who stretches out a lion's jaws to devour her prey, the while she feigns heaven knows what nobility, and having by these specious guiles caught her victims, she devours them with flames of lust."

Another and anonymous Christian poet thus describes woman. "Woman, man's confounder, mad beast, stinking rose, sad paradise, sweet venom, luscious sin, bitter sweet": in fact nothing could be found too vile for her. It is a pitiful spectacle to see these recluses, torn by what fevered spasms of disordered lust we can only guess, twisting the language of Catullus and Horace to the basest uses.

Yet we must admit that their poetry is a mirror of their faith, that the fierce savage misogyny had been exalted by it to the service of the Son of Man; and that their poetry came of the same spirit which in ordinary people degraded women in the practical walks of life, where there was little respite in intellectual pleasures for the toiling slaves of a sublunary world.

Surely we can imagine the racial memory of women looking back to the days before the voice had echoed round the Mediterranean, announcing: "The great Pan is dead": and in their unconscious wishes this death became a sleep, out of which the god one day awoke once more.

For this goat-like inspirer of physical love, this whimsical tempter of village girls, this fertile inventor of excuses for enjoying the life of the flesh, was far too valuable a stage property to be left buried and broken. The early Christian fathers did not content themselves with discrediting and crushing such gods as these, they knew a trick worth two of that: they gave them all their ancient powers and attributes but dyed as black as pitch; left them to whisper secrets into women's ears, but, instead of harmless witty little secrets, they were now execrably wicked ones, fit and able to "double them up and drag them down and damn their souls alive."

In short, the great Pan became the Devil; and as before he had specialized along certain lines of conduct and happiness, so now he remained a lewd, lascivious, degrading tempter, snatching at women's souls and winning them from God by their own weak bodies. A different figure this from the great Satan of the Bible and of the Jews: Satan who was great enough to challenge God Himself to war; Satan the slanderer, the accuser, the tempter, the evil one, the enemy, the prince of demons as he is in the Gospels; the prince of the power of the air, the deceiver of the whole world as St. Paul and St. John call him; sinner and murderer from the beginning, who enslaved man to sin, caused death, rules the present world and will be destroyed at last by Christ; Satan whom Milton could hardly help admiring and making the hero of *Paradise Lost,* a beaten hero, but a hero still who could say:

> "The mind is its own place, and in itself
> Can make a Heaven of Hell, a Hell of Heaven.

What matter where, if I be still the same,
And what I should be; all but less than he
Whom thunder hath made greater? Here at least
We shall be free; the Almighty hath not built
Here for his envy, will not drive us hence:
Here we may reign secure, and in my choice
To reign is worth ambition though in Hell:
Better to reign in Hell, than serve in Heaven."

The Pan-Devil on the other hand was a goat-man, with horns and hooves and a tail; he can be seen on the roof of Notre Dame, among the gargoyles of many old English churches, colleges and cathedrals; in slightly altered form he is to be found most suitably at every fancy-dress dance and carnival; he perches on the shoulders of torturers in sacred pictures of Christian martyrdoms, ready to carry off their souls to a far worse torment; his personal appearance grew up and was standardized between the eighth and the fourteenth centuries of our era; he and all his works were to be renounced by all Christians by command of the Synod of Leptina in 743; the bull of Innocent VIII in 1484 pronounced against demonology and witchcraft and described him in full realism.

At an earlier period his corporal presence was a matter of practical experience for St. Jerome and St. Anthony and the rest, who described all his attendants, the satyrs, the silenuses, the vampires, the incubi, the succubi and many other horrible forms. Day by day St. Jerome saw with his own eyes satyrs, little men with curved nostrils and the

horns and feet of a goat, and lovely female demons pros-
trated themselves before him in every languishing and
lascivious posture.

All these things were accepted as true and real by the
mediæval woman with even greater faith than Pan had
ever inspired in the days of his pleasant deity; and the key
to the next thousand years of the history of women is simply
this, that every woman feared to find a malicious face round
the door, feared to hear a tempting whisper from behind
her chair, feared to feel a wicked caress as she lay in bed,
feared always, everywhere, the presence and the influence of
the goat-man, the Pan-Devil, who was always at hand. In
these phobias which soon gave birth to hallucinations, the
priests encouraged her: instead of saying to her tormented
terrified mind, "Peace, be still," he told her that her phobias
were true, and he added the further information that she,
by her very womanly nature, had that within her which
might be trusted to succumb to the tempter; that she, daughter of Eve, was wayward and the devil's friend naturally;
that in her battle with the evil thing she was seeking all the
time to bring about the triumph of the enemy and her own
defeat. "Do you not know that you are each an Eve? You
are the Devil's gateway," Tertullian had thundered, and
every priestlet who was true to his calling echoed the words
and terrified the women still more.

It is hard for us who do not believe in ghosts, except very
late at night, to realize the concrete tangible belief in the
horned devil and his thousands of attendant spirits which

obsessed both Christian saint and peasant woman throughout these long centuries. The adherent of a faith which had
been tried by all the tortures of Roman tyranny, the beasts
of the amphitheatre, the wheel, the boiling oil, the red hot
chair, could imagine nothing less concrete than these in the
world to come. "You are fond of spectacles," hissed back
Tertullian to the infamous persecutors. "Expect the greatest
of all spectacles, the last and eternal judgment of the universe. How shall I admire, how laugh, how rejoice, how ex-
ult, when I behold so many proud monarchs and fancied
gods, groaning in the lowest abyss of darkness; so many
magistrates who persecuted the name of the Lord, liquefy-
ing in fiercer fires than they ever kindled against the Christians; so many sage philosophers blushing in red hot flames
with their deluded scholars; so many celebrated poets trem-
bling before the tribunal, not of Minos but of Christ; so
many tragedians more tuneful in the expression of their
own sufferings. . . ." And every woman in the Middle
Ages was obsessed with equally vivid, tangible, material
visions of what would be her lot in the world to come if she
once listened for a moment to the tempter. And, moreover, at
the same time she feared lest womanliness itself was not
doomed by its own corrupt nature to the sin and therefore to
the torment.

It is then not at all surprising that a number of women
tormented by these imaginings were glad to bury themselves
within the walls of holy places; and by renouncing the
ways of Pan in this world to secure hopes of much the same

sort of pleasures in the next. They became the Brides of Christ, in a mystical mood born of fear and hope.

§ 7. *The Life of a Bride of Christ.* WHAT did the ideal of being a Bride of Christ involve in everyday life? It involved the most minute precautions against the entering in of any temptation whatsoever. Christ the lover on the one hand, Pan the seducer on the other: between these two was the woman; would she turn to the left hand where Pan was forever whispering soft tempting suggestions into her ear, or would she turn to the right, where her promised Bridegroom stood waiting for her? We have seen enough to know that all this appeared to each woman as a concrete reality: she could hear the scuttling footsteps of the devil, she could feel the scented breath of Christ. Even Luther, a man of hard intellect, often saw the devil in the flesh. On one occasion, "as I found he was about to begin again," he tells us, "I gathered together my books and got into bed. Another time in the night I heard him above my cell walking on the cloister, but as I knew it was the devil, I paid no attention to him and went to sleep"; and if Luther believed thus concretely, what must have been the beliefs of the poor, bewildered, unhealthy Bride?

First, then, she must guard her eyes, fashioned peculiarly as a gateway for sin; she must not look out of her windows; they must be as small as possible, with a black cloth and a white cross drawn over them. "My dear master," she may say, "is it, now, so very evil a thing to look out?" "Yes, it is, dear sister, for the harm that comes of it is evil above evil to every anchorite. . . . For observe what evil has come of looking. Eve looked on the forbidden apple; thus did sight go before and prepare the way for guilty desire; and death followed, to which all mankind is subject. When thou lookest upon a man thou art in Eve's case; thou lookest upon the apple." "But," she asked, "thinkest thou that I shall leap upon him, though I look at him?" "God knows, dear sister, that a greater wonder has happened. Dinah was seen of men uncovered, and she lost her honour and became a harlot. God ordains that a pit be covered, and if any beast fall into an uncovered pit, woe betide him who uncovered the pit. A woman's fair face is such a pit, and so is her white neck, and her light eye, and her hand, if she stretch it forth in sight of a man. The beast is any man who may wish to fall into the pit, and his soul shall be required of the woman on Doomsday. She is to dread greatly this doom: and if a man is tempted so that he sin mortally even though it be not with her, if he seek to satiate on another her temptation she will certainly be condemned."

Moreover, to desire a man and to wish to be desired of a man are equal sins. Let her not look out of her window, therefore, lest she receive the devil's bolt between her eyes.

If, then, the eyes be so dangerous, so also is speech. Eve held a long conversation with the serpent, and hence our woes; the Virgin Mary was wiser with Gabriel and asked him briefly what she wanted to know. Let her believe secular men little and religious still less, nor let her desire their acquaintance. Eve spoke with the serpent without fear. Our Lady was afraid of speaking with Gabriel.

She is to hold no conversation with a man out of a church window; she is to preach to woman, nor ask any man advice; she is to shut not only her ears but her eye windows against idle conversation; that neither talk nor tidings of this world may come to her. The devil, it is said, is a liar, and the father of lies. She, then, who moves her tongue in lying maketh of her tongue a cradle to the devil's child, and rocketh it diligently as nurse.

If any man requests to see her, she is to ask what good may come of it, and if he insists immoderately he is to be believed the less. Two things are well beloved, a sweet voice and a fair countenance, and it is those who have these that Jesus Christ chooses for His Brides. If therefore she has them let no man see her countenance, nor hear her voice lightly; they are to be kept for Christ, the beloved Spouse, as He has demanded. These are his words: "Take good heed now, if thou knowest not whose spouse thou art, queen of heaven, if thou art true to me as a spouse should be. If thou hast forgotten this go out and depart, follow the lusts of the flesh. Feed thine eyes with looking about, and thy tongue with prating, thy ears with hearing, thy nose with smelling, thy flesh with soft feeling." These five senses he calls the kids, for as from a kid, whose flesh is sweet, there comes a stinking goat, so from a young sweet glance there grow a stinking lust and a foul sin.

But most dangerous of all the senses is the sense of touch.

Upon this the writer of the *Ancren Riwle* waxes even more
eloquent. "By those nails, I entreat you, anchoresses," he
cries, "not you but others, for there is no need, my dear
sisters—keep your hands within your windows. For hand-
ling or any touching between a man and an anchoress is
a thing so unnatural, and so lamentable a deed—so shameful and such a naked sin, and to all the world so hateful,
and so great a scandal, that there is no need to speak or
write against it; for, without writing, all the indecency is
apparent. God knows that I would a great deal rather see
you all three, my dear sisters, women most dear to me,
hang on a gibbet to avoid sin, than see one of you give a
single kiss to any man on earth in the way I mean. I say
nothing of the greater impropriety—not only mingling
hands but putting hands outward, except it be for necessity.
This is courting God's anger, and inviting His displeasure.
To look at her own white hands doth harm to many a recluse
that hath them too fair—as those who are idle. They should
scrape up the earth every day, out of the pit in which they
must rot."

Yet all these precautions and many more like them will
be insufficient to keep out temptation altogether. "Wherefore, my dear sister, as soon as ever thou perceivest that this
dog of hell cometh sneaking with his bloody fleas of corrupt thoughts, lie thou not still, nor yet sit, to see what he
will do, or how far he will go; and say not to him in a
sleepy manner: 'Friend dog, go out hence; what wouldest
thou have here?' This enticeth him toward thee. But take up

at once the staff of the cross and with thought in thy heart command him sternly to go out—the foul cur dog."

Beyond all else she must avoid the scorpion of lechery: sorry may she be who, with or without companion, hath so fed any of the progeny of licentiousness; for however it is done, willingly and awake, with the satisfaction of the flesh, except in wedlock only, it is a deadly sin. Solomon says: "He that hold hath of a woman is as though he held a scorpion." This scorpion is a "kind of worm that hath a face, as it is said, somewhat like that of a woman, and is a serpent behind, putteth on a pleasant countenance, and fawns upon you with her head, but stingeth with her tail. Such is lechery, which is the devil's beast, which he leads to market and cheateth many because they look only at the beautiful head."

There can be no defence, then, to the impeachment that the early Christian fathers incorporated into the new religion the old fear of woman's uncleanness, the old belief in her inferiority to men, the old desire to hold her in subjection; and the basis of the whole regimen, which the fathers sought to impose upon Christian women, was seclusion as strict as in any Arabian or Semitic household, but seclusion with a different end in view.

For the object of a Muslim husband is to secure for himself the undivided possession of one or more wives: in order to prevent any possibility of his male servants or of any other men seeing them unveiled he provides a special portion of the house for their exclusive use. No man at all save alone relatives can ever visit them there and no man who is a relative, and therefore privileged to see them unveiled, must ever describe their persons to anyone else. No man is allowed to see unveiled any woman but his own wives and female slaves and certain female relatives. It is the upper part of the head and the back which must be most closely veiled. Where in a small house there is no apartment on the ground floor for the reception of guests, these will call out as they go upstairs, "Permission" and "O Protecting God" in order to warn any woman who may be uncovered to veil herself in time.

E. W. Lane tells us that one friend of his did permit him occasionally to see his mother, a fat widow, about fifty years old. She would, however, never enter the room in which he himself was sitting. The man's wife he never saw, but spoke to once, in the presence of her husband, round the corner of a passage at the top of the stairs. Another man's mother, who wished to complain to him about her son's second and distasteful marriage, went so far as to put one hand within the door so as to help her words by adequate gesture, but the rest of her form remained completely hidden outside.

The early Church adopted a similar rigorous system of precautions, but instead of this being to provide a wife for a mortal husband, it was to provide Brides for Christ Himself. A nunnery was no more than a seraglio purged of all mundane love and filled instead with phantasies of a hardly more spiritual union.

§ 8. *The Witch.*   WE come now to the most amazing phenomenon in women's history, to the most peculiar
personality in all history, namely the Witch. We have tried
to show the vivid superstition and the implacable disgust
which women found kept alive by the Church for their own
special damnation. Let the reader remember that at this time
of which we speak, if the devil, with all his paraphernalia,
his Pan-body, his smell of brimstone, had walked into the
room, the average woman would have been terrified, but not
surprised. Let him also remember that if a devil had appeared on a fair lady's shoulder and torn her beauty to
shreds with teeth and nails, the average priest would have
been neither surprised nor sorry: moreover, he would perhaps even praise his God for such a miraculous intervention
against the wickedness of beauty.

Certainly the Church strove to attract women with threats
rather than with compliments, and only a horrible mental
picture of the world about them could possibly have attracted women within the gates of their sacred prisons. If
Pan drove some within the gates, others remaining outside
gave themselves up to him body and soul. These were the
worshippers of "the devil," who have become so familiar to
us as the victims of witchcraft persecutions, of burnings and
torturings almost beyond belief.

The witchcraft cult or delusion is not, as it might at first
be supposed, a pathological excrescence on the body of
women's history; it is an essential and integral part of the
whole, without which the whole cannot be understood. Let

us emphasize at the very outset that in studying witches we are studying women still and not wasting valuable pages through the seduction of the bizarre and spectacular.

Until quite recently it was assumed by all except the superstitious that witchcraft has never existed outside the minds of its deluded persecutors and their still more deluded victims: but the researches of anthropologists, trained in the knowledge of primitive beliefs and customs, have well-nigh proved that a widespread cult answering to all the descriptions of inquisitions and heresy hunts was in existence from pre-Christian days well into the seventeenth century and even later. Margaret Alice Murray's remarkable book, *The Witch Cult in Western Europe,* is to be recommended to all for its lucid and persuasive exposition of the evidence for the reality of witches and their worship of the devil.

We need not remind the reader of the primitive religions which centred in women and blossomed out into such manifestations of religious fervour as the cult of the Great Mother of the Gods; we have also noticed in passing that the Germanic tribes gave certain indications that before the penetration of Romano-Christian civilization they too practised fertility rites and the worship of gods and goddesses attended by women priestesses. Moreover, it needs nothing but common sense to feel sure that when the earliest missioners descended upon the British Islands carrying the cross and proclaiming Christ crucified, they did not preach to hearts utterly barren of any religious beliefs whatever. Miss Murray shows conclusively that the earlier religion which was superseded by Christianity was the same as that which was practised by witches hundreds of years later. The God which they worshipped was identified with the Pan-Devil, with Satan himself, and they, his children, were burned for refusing to deny him.

The evidence is absolutely clear for the continuity of this religious worship. In the first century the geographer Strabo wrote that "in an island close to Britain, Demeter and Persephone are venerated with rites similar to the orgies of Samothrace"; in the fourth century Dionysius in his *Periegesis* says that in islands near Jersey and Guernsey the rites of Bacchus were performed by women, crowned with leaves, who danced and shouted even louder than Thracian worshippers; in the seventh century Theodore, Archbishop of Canterbury, thus prescribes punishment for participation in the heathen cults celebrated in his own days, "not only celebrating feasts in the abominable places of the heathen and offering food there, but also consuming it. Serving this hidden idolatry, having relinquished Christ. If any one at the kalends of January goes about as a stag or a bull—that is, making himself into a wild animal and dressing in the skin of a herd animal, and putting on the heads of beasts— those who in such wise transform themselves into the appearance of a wild animal, penance for three years because this is devilish."

In 690, the laws of Wihtred, King of Kent; in the Penitential of Ecgberht, first Archbishop of York in the eighth century; in the Law of Northumbrian priests; in the laws of King Edgar, of 959; in those of King Cnut of the eleventh century,—devil-worship is expressly forbidden, so that we can be quite certain that it existed. Stranger, perhaps, in 1282 the priest of Inverkeithing was presented before his Bishop on the charge of having had a fertility rite dance at Easter round the phallic figure of a god; and in 1303 the Bishop of Coventry was accused before the Pope of having done homage to the Devil. Much more evidence of an equally conclusive sort is gathered by Miss Murray in her book, to which, however, we must refer the reader, so that we are at liberty to say that an old religion in which women played a noble and exalted rôle by reason, of course, of their time-honoured connection with fertility, remained in existence throughout Europe in spite of all the attempts of Christian missioners to win the folk from paganism.

It was this ancient cult which the Church fought as an implacable enemy and used as a useful ally; for it acknowledged the reality of the god which was thus worshipped and called him the devil of the New and Old Testament. The early fathers believed, as we have seen, most heartily in the corporeal reality of evil spirits, and the later schoolmen used all their ingenuity to evolve a subtle and dangerous "real presence" for witchcraft itself. Finally, in 1484, Pope Innocent VIII issued a famous Bull in which we read the following sentences: "It has come to our ears that numbers of both sexes do not avoid to have intercourse with demons, Incubi and Succubi; and that by their sorceries and by their incantations, charms, and conjurations, they suffocate, extinguish, and cause to perish the births of women, the increase of animals, the corn of the ground, the grapes of the vineyard, and the fruit of the trees, as well as men, women, flocks, herds, and other various kinds of animals, vines and apple trees, grass, corn, and other fruits of the earth; making and procuring that men and women, flocks and herds and other animals suffer and be tormented both from within and without, so that men beget not, nor women conceive; and they impede the conjugal action of men and women."

One last quotation will suffice to state the facts upon which we must comment; it is a translation from De Lancre's *Tableau de l'Inconstance des mauvais Anges* published in 1613 and it gives the statements of witches themselves about their attitude to the rites of their cult. "A witch of great reputation among the others told us that she had always believed that witchcraft was the best religion. Joan Dibasson, aged twenty-nine, told us that the witches' sabbath was the true Paradise, where there was much more pleasure than could be told. That those who go there find the time so short because of their pleasure and contentment, that they cannot depart without a marvellous regret so that it seems infinitely long, before they return there. Marie de la Raide, aged twenty-eight, a very beautiful girl, deposes that she had great pleasure from going to the Sabbath, so much so that when they came and summoned her to it she went off as if to a wedding: not so much from the liberty and licence which one gets from the intimacies together, which through modesty she says she has never shared or desired to share, but because the Devil had their hearts so bound and their wills also, that he scarce let any other desire enter there. Further she says that she did not think any evil of going to the Sabbath and that she had much more pleasure and content in it than in going to Mass, because the Devil made them believe that he was the true god and that the joy that witches had at the Sabbath was only the beginning of a much greater glory."

It seems clear from the evidence that in spite of the ridiculous credulity of the inquisitors and persecutors, who have cast a doubt on everything by the very absurdity of their believing everything, a tangible and important reality hides behind the stories and legends of the great persecution. We know that the greater intellects of the period believed in this reality, while the whole-hearted scoffers were very inferior men. Miss Murray points out that the believers included Bodin, Lord Bacon, Sir Walter Raleigh, Boyle, Cudworth, Selden, Henry More, Sir Thomas Browne, Matthew Hale, Sir George Mackenzie, whereas the sceptics were Weyer, a pupil of the occultist Cornelius Agrippa; Reginald Scot, a Kentish country squire; Filmer, whose name was a byword for political bigotry; Wagstaffe, who went mad from drink; and Webster, a fanatical preacher. None of these except Weyer had any first-hand evidence and most of the believers, on the other hand, had been present at the trials.

We must therefore believe that throughout the fifteenth,

sixteenth, seventeenth centuries, and even later, women in considerable numbers met together in remote country districts and worshipped the Devil. At their meetings they went through definite ceremonies and rituals; a man, often dressed as an animal, impersonated the god they worshipped, and the abundant details readily confessed by witches on trial show clearly that the whole cult was precisely similar to the fertility cults of earlier religions. The object of the worship was to induce the fertility of crops, animals, and people, though in the eyes of the Church, and perhaps actually in later degenerate forms, the object was exactly the opposite. In either case women were the central figures in the faith; they exercised their time-honoured genius to make all nature bring forth increase, or they used their mystical power over the forces of fertility to withdraw them from their proper functions, so that their enemies became sterile, they, their fields, and their cattle. The great legal authority, Lord Coke, defines a witch as "a person who hath conference with the Devil, to consult with him or do some act"; and five hundred and eleven witches were tried in England and Scotland in the seventeenth century; one continental judge put eight hundred to the torture in sixteen years; the Bishop of Württemberg burned nine hundred in one year; in Geneva five hundred were burned in three months; estimates vary as to the total number of witches burned but it is possible that several millions were tried, tortured or put to death, though other authorities put the number as low as a hundred thousand.

The last witch convicted in England was Jane Wenham in 1712; the last in Scotland was executed in 1722; in America there were the famous Salem witch trials in Massachusetts in 1691–2; a witch was burned in 1781 at Seville by the Inquisition and another beheaded by the civil authorities in 1782; the last German execution was in 1793 and perhaps the last witch-burning in the civilized Christian world took place in Peru in 1888.

It will be seen, therefore, that the phenomenon of witchcraft in Europe and the Christian world is extensive and moreover it did not reach its height until long after the period we have been studying in this chapter. Nevertheless its roots are deep in the Middle Ages and it is no great latitude to take the Witch along with the Nun and the Lady of the Castle as the third of the great types which are at once the flower of earlier days, and the seed of our more modern times.

§ 9. *Survival of the Three Types.* WHAT is the significance of witchcraft for the general history of women? It lies in the potentiality of every woman, given the right background, to become a witch. The Middle Ages set up an ideal of womanly life that had no sort of connection with primeval facts; a despotic and misogynist religious institution and a militarist and uncouth civil institution conspired together to make women's life miserable. Woman responded either by flouting the ideals and conventions imposed by her masters, both spiritual and temporal, by setting up her

Courts of Love, by turning from the soldier to the poet in man, by ignoring the virtues of ecclesiastical or feudal love and making a new virtue of romantic and often illicit love; or by accepting the Church's offer and surrendering all that constitutes womanhood in contradistinction to manhood; or, finally, by throwing off the garments provided for her by a pathologically modest Church and a boorishly ungraceful feudalism and standing up naked as womanhood itself, primitive, uncivilized, worshipper and dispenser of fertility. It is true that the woman made intelligent by book-learning did not become a witch; she qualified for Aucassin's hell by keeping a paramour, and constructed a poet's paradise, which many would call a fool's paradise, in Provençal ease and gracefulness; but she was doing exactly the same as her unlettered sister, who, terrified by priestly ghost-stories, and wearied by priestly injustice and human injustice as well, proclaimed that Astarte or Demeter under new names were preferable from the woman's point of view to the god whose priests blasphemed beauty and the body and even maternity and marriage.

It is not necessary to sentimentalize over witches; they were disgusting. From any sane standard their rites and beliefs require a catholic sympathy, if they are to be thought of with an open mind; but were the writers whom we quoted earlier on the foulness of women any less disgusting? For all that they belonged to a more respectable religion, could any woman listen to them without loss of as much dignity and self-respect as was lost in the sordid devil-worship?

War tears off the trappings of men and reveals the naked savage, and hunger gropes even deeper, till it unveils the snarling animal; throughout the Middle Ages god and man alike seemed to wage permanent and implacable war against every woman, and every woman went about from day to day starved of all recognition of her psychological needs and of the food which her emotions required. Nor did the great religious changes of the Reformation materially alter her position for the better; so deep-seated was the enmity between religion and women that the Reformers could not root it out of the world, for the simple reason that they could not root it out of their own hearts. Protestants persecuted witches with all the zeal of the Inquisition; Puritans despised womanliness as heartily as Tertullian, though with less literary fire. Martin Luther was perfectly certain that witches had intercourse with the Devil, and his enemies, the Catholics, preached sermons proving that he himself was the result of such intercourse. In both cases the belief, held as firmly as the belief that the crucified Christ rose from the dead, grew from the inflamed imaginations of woman-haters, of men who loathed the fact that they were constantly tempted away from what they believed right by daughters of Eve, the first and most fatal temptress of all.

Witchcraft may have been filthy, but was it not natural? And cannot we assume that the millions of women who never went to a witch's Sabbath, never officiated in a Black

Mass, never avenged themselves on men who despised them
so by charms to procure impotence, never had sexual intercourse with the man who personified the devil, had in them
tendencies and temptations of like nature but less strength?
If you want to understand one side of woman's nature, under the strain of those days, look at it magnified a hundred
times into the proportions of a common witch. Moreover,
the foul details of witchcraft are outbid in foulness by the
care and curiosity with which men, inquisitors, witch-
finders, and the rest, dwelt upon them, elaborated them,
expounded them. Nothing fascinates one sort of righteous
man so much as the vileness he can discover in the opposite
sex.

The Witch, the Nun, the Lady: not one of these was a
satisfactory solution to the problem of living; all of them
lived on, however, into modern times, changed in detail but
ever fundamentally the same. The period of witches had
scarcely begun, as we have said, when the Renaissance was
supposed to have set man's spirits free and it lasted until
Revolutionary Europe awoke from the older superstitions;
the Nun, secularized, and denied the hopes of nuptials with
Christ, lives among us as the product of prudery and mistaken virtue; often, indeed, she is a married woman who
finds even marriage weighted down with the old views of
the wickedness of sex, which lead now as ever to beliefs
in the essential wickedness of women. The Lady, alas, is
everywhere, more of a parasite than ever; more neurotic and

unsettled, less capable of hiding herself from the pains of ennui; her men have sheathed the sword and learnt salesmanship instead of the art of tourneys, they worship the god of business, rather than Mars, the god of war; but it is all the same to the Lady and her life is as empty as ever before. Let us watch the transition from the old to the new.

Chapter VI

MODERN TIMES: FROM WOMANLY WOMAN TO INTELLIGENT BEING

§ 1. *Effect of the Renaissance.* IT is none of our concern to justify or to fix the division between mediæval and modern times, but it is possible to explain how that division affects our subject matter. There was no break in the continuity of women's history, but new elements entered in and changed its course. What has gone before, the primitive taboo outlook, the Christian fear of woman's uncleanness and dangerousness, the Roman principle of law, the worship of fertility, the mediæval fruition into Lady, Nun and Witch, all these constitute the race memory, the tradition, the emotion of men to women, the conservative doctrine, which were now to be re-shaped and re-grouped by radical forces and new knowledge.

Everybody knows what great events are vaguely assumed to have caused by their massed influence the Renaissance, the re-birth of man, spiritually and intellectually. The discovery of America in 1492, enlarging the sphere of human imagination and teasing out the spirit of adventure; the capture of Constantinople by the Turks in 1453 and the consequent dissemination of fugitive knowledge from the libraries and studies of the Eastern capital; the Reformation, freeing men from religious inertia when in 1517 Luther nailed up his theses, which vitalized even where they destroyed; the decay of the great secular Empire, paving the way for the new loyalties of nationalism and dynasticism; the last break-down of feudalism and its adjuncts, paving the way for the new loyalties of capitalism and labour; the deposition of the earth from its usurped throne in the centre of the universe, resulting in the diminished grandeur of earth's chief parasite, man; the popular use of great inventions, such as the mariner's compass, of printing, of paper, of gunpowder; all these great events, crowded into what was virtually but a moment of time, altered in a very few years the sea, the sky and the earth, the universe about men, and with equal force, the universe within their minds and souls.

But what was the effect of all this upon women? The Renaissance, though it certainly did not emancipate women, any more than it destroyed the superstitions and tyrannies of past centuries, enhanced their position in more than one direction. In the first place, the horrible obsession which immortality, life in death, had become, gradually assumed more normal proportions; instead of cowering under the elongated shadow of the idea, men walked side by side with it as a companion, and enjoyed with its timely assistance a new opportunity to make the best of both worlds. People began to tire of its co-partner, death in life, and to tire also of the vale of tears; they offered prayers for fine smiling weather and expected them to be answered. When the sex-horror, which seems almost indissoluble from religious genius, thundered out of the mouths of Luther and Calvin and Knox, fewer people listened, and these listened half-heartedly. For there was sap in the trees and in men, and the spirit of the times desired colour and vivacity, and to share between the sexes the gift of the world, the flesh and even the devil. In these circumstances, women came into their own; religion, which had hitherto been largely at enmity with them, their happiness and their progress, became humanized. A tangible example of this is of course the recognition of the humanity of priests and the marriage of the clergy. An ounce of experience of wives and daughters qualified these to understand the needs of women far more than pounds of curiously detailed knowledge of secret sinning that was to be gained at confessionals and codified into manuals.

Then again a reviving love of this world brought with it an enhancement of respect for women's work: long the guardians of domestic comfort and economy, the new love of life gave them in every home a palace to decorate, rather than prison walls to whitewash. A sixteenth-century Englishwoman was more of a companion to her menfolk than ever before, or, until very recently, ever since. She was indeed a co-partner in the revival of learning and of the art of living.

It is to this especially that women in Elizabeth's reign owed their high status, and to comprehend this, we shall have to enquire briefly into their intellectual attainments: for, as Diotima told Socrates, the intellect and its cultivation bring a higher form of fertility and a nobler pregnancy into human life. In Greece this was women's loss; it denied them their one claim to esteem; in the Middle Ages it was their gain, but it alienated them from ordinary life, because men despised brains then as much as the ancient Athenians despised women. In the more modern period it was a greater gain than ever before, since men and women alike shared in the common love of ideas; the superior wedding of soul with soul became something in which both sexes could share.

In the history of women, the Renaissance means increased esteem and increased interests; just as in the history of Greek intellect men got a start of women and rigidly refused to lessen the distance, so in the new learning, women had a start over men and though they did not keep it, for a time at least they ran side by side. But we must not suppose that the Renaissance is the beginning of a period of uninterrupted improvement in the status of women. It is true that without that great period or series of events, women, and men too, might have gone on in a state of inertia forever, and that it started the motion which led to the later colossal developments; but a great interruption to progress very soon made itself felt. The Elizabethan period was followed by a gradual decline, until in about 1750, women in England had reached a new low level hardly in advance of their position in the twelfth century.

§ 2. *Women Under Eliza-beth.* WHAT were the attainments of women in Elizabeth's reign?

"To say how many gentlewomen and ladies there are," wrote Harrison in his Description of England, "that besides sound knowledge of the Greek and Latin tongues are thereto no less skilful in the Spanish, Italian and French, or in some one of them, it resteth not in me, sith I am persuaded that, as the noblemen and gentlemen do sur-mount in this behalf, so these come very little or nothing at all behind them for their parts; which industry God con-tinue, and accomplish that which otherwise is wanting!

"Besides these things, I could in like sort set down the ways and means whereby our ancient ladies of the court do shun and avoid idleness, some of them exercising their fingers with the needle, others in caulwork, divers in spin-ning silk, some in continual reading either of the Holy Scriptures, or histories of our own or foreign nations about us, and divers in writing volumes of their own, or translat-ing of other men's into our English or Latin tongue, whilst the youngest sort in the meantime apply their lutes, citherns, prick song and all kind of music, which they use only for recreation's sake when they have leisure and are free from attendance upon the queen's majesty or such as they belong unto. How many of the eldest sort also are skilful in surgery and distillation of waters, besides sundry other artificial practices pertaining to the ornature and commendations of their bodies, I might (if I listed to deal further in this be-half) easily declare; but I pass over such manner of dealing, lest I should seem to glaver and curry favour with some of them. Nevertheless, this I will generally say of them all, that as each of them are cunning in something whereby they keep themselves occupied in the Court, so there is in manner none of them but when they be at home can help to supply the ordinary want of the kitchen with a number of delicate dishes of their own devising, wherein the Portuguese is their chief counsellor."

Undoubtedly the energetic queen modified and heightened the esteem in which her sex was held: and in no way can we get a clearer foretaste of the succeeding degradation of women, which we shall shortly study, than by turning to Hannah More's summary of her character. "If we were to estimate Elizabeth," says that remarkable woman in her *Hints Towards Forming the Character of a Young Princess*, "as a private female, she would doubtless appear entitled to but little veneration. If as an instrument raised up by Divine Providence to carry through the most arduous enterprises in the most difficult emergencies, we can hardly rate her too highly. We owe her much as Englishmen. As Protestants, what do we not owe her? If we look at the woman, we shall see much to blame; if at the sovereign, we shall see almost everything to admire." This curious dichotomy between being a female and being a public character is the measure of the distance women fell in the intervening period, and it is still usual to call Elizabeth "unfeminine" because she showed a certain strength of will unusual in the average woman. Hannah More would strongly disapprove of her because she did not in the least conform to the ideal of a Female Character which was laboriously built up by all the writers, divines and influential leaders of opinion in the course of the next two centuries.

We find another pregnant contrast if we read first Ascham's approving statement that Elizabeth "readeth now at Windsor more Greek every day than some prebendaries of this church doth read Latin in a whole week,"—with Addison's words on women and education. "Women," says Addison, "while untainted by affectation have a natural cheerfulness of mind, tenderness and benignity of heart, which justly endears them to us, either to animate our joys or soothe our sorrows; but how are they changed, and how shocking do they become, when the rage of ambition or the pride of learning, agitates and swells those breasts, where only love, friendship, and tender care should dwell."

The difference between Ascham and Addison, between Harrison and Hannah More, is a striking one; almost as striking as the difference between Elizabeth and Queen Anne.

Moreover, it is possible to illustrate the difference in another way. If we turn to *England's Parnassus,* a sort of anthology or dictionary of poetic quotations, published in 1660, we are able to see roughly the attitude to women of the cultured classes; for we are at liberty to assume that the quotations chosen to exemplify "woman" are typical of the most popular way of approaching her. What do we find?

Out of thirty-six quotations under the heading "Woman" the following are the first three:

> Women be
> Framed with the same parts of the mind as we,
> Nay, nature triumphs in their beauties' birth,
> And women made the glory of the earth; . . .
>
> What art so deep, what science is so high,
> Unto the which women have not attained,
> Who list in stories old to look may try
> And find my speech herein nor false nor fain'd,
> And though of late they seem not to come nigh
> The praise their sex in former times have gain'd,
> Doubtless the fault is either in backbiters,
> Or want of skill or judgment in their writers.
>
> Among the many rare and special gifts,
> That in the female sex are found to sit,
> This one is chief, that they at meerest shifts,
> Give best advice and show most ready wit,
> But man except he chews and thinks and sifts,
> How every part may answer to their fit,
> By rash advice doth often over-shoot him,
> And doth accept the things that do not boote him.

The rest of the quotations are lovers' complaints of her inconstancy, her weakness, her unkindness, her cruelty; with one or two wise saws, which tell us that "women are kind by kind and coy for fashion," and that "in women's mouths no is no negative." But among them we come upon two or three which are of exactly the same stamp as the old taboo outlook of savages and early Christians.

Be not therefore too proud and full of scorn,
O womenkind, that men come of your seed,
The fragrant rose grows on the pricking thorn,
The Lily fair comes of a filthy weed,
In loathsome soil men sow the wholesome corn,
The basest mould the fairest flower doth breed,
Ungrateful, false, crafty you are, and cruel,
Born of our burning hell to be the fuel.

Discourteous women, Nature's fairest ill,
The woe of man, that first createst curse,
Base female sex, sprung from black Ate's loins,
Proud, disdainful, cruel and unjust. . . .
Born to be plagues unto the thoughts of men,
Brought for eternal pestilence to the world.

Base bullion for the stamp's sake we allow,
Even so for men's impression do we you,
By which alone our reverend fathers say,
Women receive perfection every way.

If we compare these three last quotations with the three first, we will see the dualism of men's outlook towards women simply illustrated. It is strange but true that in the sixteenth century the more liberal point of view persisted alongside of the other, while in the eighteenth century it hardly exists at all. Can we suggest any reason for it?

§ 3. *Character* In the first place, there was the character of
of Elizabeth. the Queen. An Addison in Elizabeth's day would have been guilty of more than an insult to the female sex, he would have been guilty of disloyalty, if not of trea-

son; moreover, he could hardly have written as he did with personal experience of the Gloriana who from the very throne of England gave the lie to his delineations, his censures and his smirking innuendoes.

Elizabeth is, as we have said, the negative of all that Addison knew as woman, and the reader will do well to bear in mind the following full-length portrait of her, left us by Sir John Melville, who was sent by Mary Queen of Scots in 1564 on a mission to her sister queen.

"The Queen my mistress had instructed me to leave matters of gravity sometimes, and cast in merry purposes, lest otherwise I should be wearying; she being well informed of the Queen's natural temper. Therefore in declaring my observations of the customs of Dutchland, Poland and Italy, the business of the women were not forgot, and what country weed I thought best becoming gentlewomen. The Queen said she had clothes of every sort, which every day thereafter, so long as I was there, she changed. One day she had the English weed, another the French, and another the Italian, and so forth.

"She asked me which of them became her best. I answered in my judgment the Italian dress, which answer I found pleased her well, for she delighted to shew her golden coloured hair, wearing a caul and bonnet as they do in Italy. Her hair was more reddish than yellow, curled in appearance naturally. She desired to know of me what colour of hair was reputed best, and which of them two was fairest. I answered, the fairest of them both was not their worst faults. But she was earnest with me to declare which of them I judged fairest. I said she was the fairest Queen of England and mine the fairest Queen of Scotland. Yet she appeared earnest. I answered they were both the fairest ladies in their countries; that her Majesty was whiter, but my Queen was very lovely.

"She inquired which of them was of highest stature? I said my Queen. Then, saith she, she is too high, for I myself am neither too high nor too low. Then she asked what kind of exercise she used? I answered that when I received my dispatch, the Queen was lately come from the Highlands, hunting. That when her more serious affairs permitted, she was taken up with reading of histories; that sometimes she recreated herself in playing upon the lute and virginals. She asked if she played well. I said reasonably, for a Queen.

"That same day after dinner, my Lord of Hunsdean drew me up to a quiet gallery, that I might hear some music, but he said that he durst not avow it, where I might hear the Queen play upon the virginals. After I had hearkened a while, I took up the tapistry that hung before the door of the chamber, and seeing her back was toward the door, I entered within the chamber, and stood a pretty space hearing her play excellently well, but she left off immediately, so soon as she turned her about and saw me. She appeared to be surprised to see me, and came forward, seeming to strike me with her hand, alledging she used not to play before men, but when she was solitary, to shun melancholy.

"She said my French was good, and asked if I could speak Italian which she spoke reasonably well. . . . Then she spake to me in German which was not good, and would know what kind of books I most delighted in, whether theology, history or love matters."

Such a woman was Queen Elizabeth, and we may be sure from the evidence of literature that women in her day, though they may not have resembled her in the type of their personalities, at least resembled her in having a personality of some sort or other. No Procrustes could have fitted Elizabeth on to the bed called The Female Character, nor many of her female subjects either. They had brains and they used them, and of this we have even better evidence than that of Harrison.

In Elizabeth's age indeed there began a new literature,

designed especially to be read by women first, and we may
be sure that a demand existed for such a literature, or Lyly
would never have dedicated his Euphues to women in words
such as these: "It resteth, Ladies, that you take the pains
to read it, but at such times as you spend in playing with
your dogs, and yet will not pinch you of that pastime, for I
am content that your dogs lie in your laps, so that Euphues
may be in your hands, that when you shall be weary in reading of the one, you may be ready to sport with the other.
. . . Euphues had rather lie shut in a lady's closet, than
open in a scholar's study." It is a curious fate that this book
so designed for feminine amusement now seems so dull that
none but students dream of reading it; yet, absurd as it is,
it began the long tradition of English novels. "There is no
possibility of error," writes Jusserand, "with Lyly com-
mences in England the literature of the drawing room, that
of which we speak at morning calls, productions which in
spite of vast and many changes, still occupy a favourite
place on the little boudoir tables."

Moreover, Elizabeth had a definite effect upon the public
opinion of her day in certain practical matters, as when she
stubbornly refused to strengthen the laws and the penalties
against witchcraft in spite of much clamour and pam-
phleteering. Superstition had to wait a few years for its satisfaction, until the accession to the English throne of a man
and a Scotchman.

In short, we may look back to the sixteenth century as
to a cheerful and satisfactory period of women's history,

but even then we must avoid exaggeration of the intellectual dignity enjoyed by them: it is a very different matter to be learned from being accepted as a reasonable being; and the first precedes the second. When we read that the ladies of the Court of Elizabeth were learned, we are not to suppose that they were treated as the intellectual equals of the gentlemen; but we can assume that the first step had been taken. Why did the journey thus begun not come within reasonable distance of its end until the nineteenth century? We must examine the new force which now began to militate against women's status after the brief hour of success we have sketched.

§ 4. *Puritanism and Licence.*   "TAKE from them their periwigs, their paintings, their jewels, their rowles, their bolsterings, and thou shalt soon perceive that a woman is the least part of herself. When they be once robbed of their robes, then will they appear so odious, so ugly, so monstrous, that thou wilt rather think them serpents than saints, and so like hags, that thou wilt fear rather to be enchanted than enamoured. Look in their closets and there shalt thou find an apothecary's shop of sweet confections, a surgeon's box of sundry salves, a pedlar's pack of new fangles. Besides all this their shadows, their spots, their lawns, their leefekyes, their ruffs, their rings, show them rather cardinal's courtesans than modest matrons. If everyone of those things severally be not of force to move thee, yet all of them jointly should mortify thee."

It might at first be thought that we have here a few sentences from Tertullian, or a statement by Odon of Cluny in his less disgusting moods; but in fact it is merely Euphues complaining in that work which, as we have seen, was dedicated to women themselves. It is yesterday's thunderbolt used by today's children in a game of marbles. It is Tertullian's sentiments used mockingly by a lover. And the feminine readers of Euphues could afford to laugh at such a passage although for centuries their predecessors had had their souls made to bleed by a like expression of less counterfeit sentiments. Today, if a girl talks about her legs in public someone may say laughingly: "I'm shocked at you"; we know that the words are not serious, though twenty-five years ago they would have been, and the girl would have been accused of lack of modesty; the phrase has become friendly, time has drawn its sting. So too with the blusterings of Euphues: they show that the history of women has advanced into a different stage from that which went before; a stage in which women were more emancipated—less dangers than companions.

But the change was not to last long, for Euphues and Elizabeth heralded a false dawn, and several black clouds were on the horizon. Within a very few years of the Queen's death there was published a pamphlet with the following title: "The Unloveliness of Love-locks: a summary discourse proving the wearing and nourishing of a lock or love-lock to be altogether unseemly, and unlawful unto Christians. In which there are likewise some passages collected out of the Fathers, Councils and sundry authors and historians against face-painting, the wearing of supposititious, powdered, frizzled, or extraordinary long hair, the inordinate affectation of corporal beauty, and women's mannish, unnatural, impudent and unchristian cutting of their hair."

If we compare these words with those quoted from Euphues we have, symbolically expressed, the nature of the causes which led to the degradation of women after their brief advance in the preceding period; for it is not a mere question of whether or not women should bob their hair, powder their noses, or look beautiful; it is the whole attitude towards life and the relations between the sexes, which exist behind these superficialities, that stands revealed in the two quotations. In the first we know that the speaker is in no sense serious, in the second he is undoubtedly so; Puritanism, the force which was now beginning to grow strong enough to colour or rather to uncolour social life, was convinced, like Tertullian, that a woman must either be a courtesan or "homely," that she must either be a temptation or a nonentity; and that attention to physical beauty was nothing more than an invitation to licence. We have seen more than once where such an assumption leads, we know from earlier examples that it leads to the general degradation of women. It is indeed bad for the general spiritual health of women that they should be regarded as potential or actual courtesans, but it is better for them to be courtesans than nothing at all. The inevitable effect of Puritanism as a militant enthusiasm was the further degradation of women, for it revived the attitude towards them which saw them chiefly as a snare and a delusion for males.

It was not at once, however, that the evil results of this attitude became universal, and while we must ascribe to

Puritanism part of the ensuing degradation of women, we must not forget that though all Puritans felt it wrong for women to be beautiful, some believed it right for them to be educated. The second cause of women's degradation was the rise elsewhere of a feeling that all women should be beautiful and none at all educated. This was the attitude of the court and grew steadily till we reach the licence and flippancy of Charles II and his circle, in which women were not merely a temptation but a temptation to which one must incessantly and gleefully succumb; a temptation, which could be thrown away or forgotten once it had served this useful and solitary purpose.

Between these two, Puritanism and Licentiousness, the position of women in society rapidly became worse; and if we are to judge between them the latter was the worse of the two. Orgiastic cults, in honour of the Great Mother of the Gods, marked at one period, as we have seen, the rise of women; but secularized orgies, devoid of reverence and honesty, turned women into the implements of masculine inconstancy of purpose. A religious prostitute in Phrygia in B. C. 1000 was in a higher state of development than a Christian mistress at the court of Charles. Puritanism, on the other hand, did produce a Lucy Hutchinson.

This lady married Colonel John Hutchinson and has left us her famous memoirs of his exploits during the Civil War period. In the following passage we have a picture of the Puritan woman at her best: "My father and mother fancying me then beautiful, and more than ordinarily apprehensive, applied all their cares, and spared no cost to improve me in my education, which procured me the admiration of those that flattered my parents. By the time I was four years old I read English perfectly, and having a great memory, I was carried to sermons, and while I was very young could remember and repeat them exactly, and being caressed, the love of praise tickled me, and made me attend more heedfully. When I was about seven years of age, I remember I had at one time eight tutors in several qualities, languages, music, dancing, writing, and needle-work; but my genius was quite averse to anything but my book, and that I was so eager of, that my mother thinking it prejudiced my health, would moderate me in it; yet this rather animated me than kept me back, and every moment I could steal from my play I would employ in any book I could find, when my own were locked up from me. After dinner and supper I still had an hour allowed me to play, and then I would steal into some hole or other to read. My father would have me learn Latin, and I was so apt that I outstript my brothers who were at school, although my father's chaplain that was my tutor was a pitiful dull fellow. My brothers, who had a great deal of wit, had some emulation at the progress I made in my learning, which very well pleased my father, though my mother would have been contented I had not so wholly addicted myself to that as to neglect my other qualities; as for music and dancing, I profited very little in them, and would never practise my lute or harpsichord but when my masters were with me; and for

my needle, I absolutely hated it; play among other children
I despised, and when I was forced to entertain others such
as came to visit me, I tired them with more grave instruction
than their mothers. . . . Very profitable serious discourses
being frequent at my father's table and in my mother's
drawing-room, I was very attentive to all, and gathered up
things that I would utter again to great admiration of many
that took my memory and imitation for wit. I was convinced
that the knowledge of God was the most excellent study,
and accordingly applied myself to it and to practise as I was
taught . . . but I thought, when I had done this on the
Lord's day, and every day performed my due tasks of reading and praying, that then I was free to anything that was
not sin, for I was not at that time convinced of the vanity of
conversation which was not scandalously wicked; I thought
it no sin to learn or hear witty songs and amorous sonnets or
poems, and twenty things of that kind, wherein I was so apt
that I became the confidante in all the loves that were man-
aged among my mother's young women, and there was none
of them but had many lovers, and some particular friends
beloved above the rest."

Lucy Hutchinson could claim a thorough knowledge of
French and Latin and some Greek and Hebrew also; and
she translated Lucretius into English verse, "in a room
where my children practised the several qualities they were
taught with their tutors, and I numbered the syllables of
my translation by the threads of the canvas I wrought in,
and set them down with a pen and ink that stood by me."

She was of course exceptional but she was an exception which could not have existed two generations later and she illustrates the good side of Puritanism and the happy side of women's status in this period. We are hardly likely to take her as an example: she was too precocious, her virtues a little narrow perhaps, but she compares very favourably with most university-educated women, and men too, today.

On the opposite side of the social world was the "pedantic but pretty" Duchess of Newcastle, who established a salon on the most approved French lines and filled ten volumes folio with the heterogeneous offspring of her fertile muse. "It pleased God," she said, "to command his servant Nature to indue me with a poetical and philosophical genius even from my very birth," and she made every use of her talents. She was no mere pedant, however, but had ideas of her own on everything, including dress; and as a dress reformer her goal was not merely the convenient but the beautiful, or at least the fantastic. Pepys tells us in his diary how he "met my Lady Newcastle going with her coaches and footmen all in velvet; herself with her velvet cap, her hair about her ears, many black patches about her mouth, without anything about her neck, and a black vest fitted to the body." In short the Duchess of Newcastle was a woman of character and her importance in our history is twofold: first because of the sentiment she expressed in these words. "I dare not examine the former times," she says, "for fear I should meet with such of my sex that have outdone all the glory I can aim at or hope to attain; for I confess that my ambition is restless and not ordinary; because it would have an extraordinary fame. And since all heroic actions, public employments, powerful governments and eloquent pleadings are denied our sex in this age or at least would be condemned for want of custom, is the cause I write so much."

The reader will readily note that the Duchess would have less excuse for turning to literature today than in her own time, but what is more significant is that in the ensuing century Hannah More, who certainly resembled Lucy Hutchinson more closely than the Duchess of Newcastle, did not even regret for herself or other women the disabilities and restrictions imposed upon her sex. To the Duchess it was a matter of sorrow that she and other women were impotent in the arena of public life; to Hannah More it was right and proper that this should be so. "What an accession would it bring to the public strength," she wrote in her *Strictures on the Modern System of Female Education,* which was called forth largely by fears lest the infidelity of France should overrun England also; "could we prevail on beauty, and rank, and talents, and virtue confederating their several powers, to exert themselves with a patriotism at once firm and feminine, for the general good! I am not sounding the alarm to female warriors, or exciting female politicians: I hardly know which of the two is the most disgusting and unnatural character." The Duchess of Newcastle may not have been without her faults, she may have driven in a chariot drawn by the blind cow of pedantry and the ass of eccentricity, but she had not lost all belief in a woman's right to act and argue, to take part in public life; she and women are seen in a higher status in her words of regret, than Hannah More and eighteenth-century women, who thought her aspirations "disgusting and unnatural."

The second point of general interest for us about the Duchess is that while the Puritans disapproved of her because she used her mind, the court laughed at her because, like Penelope, she remained chaste during the long absence of her husband; the world was still divided between those who did not think a woman should be emancipated, and those who thought that the outward sign of emancipation was adultery.

§ 5. *Under-work and Over-work.* To these two causes for women's retrogression after the Renaissance we may add two others, which did not begin to operate until rather later than the days of Lucy Hutchinson and the Duchess of Newcastle. "The ladies of that day," says Trevelyan, "were forced to give a large part of their lives to household duties, and had less to spare for society and culture. In the absence of country doctors, it was the women of the house who practised the quaint lore of the art of healing—in part medicine, in part charm and white magic. Almost all the food, drink and delicacies of the landlord's families came off the estate, and in small manors the brewing of the beer, the salting of the Martinmas beef and the daily cooking were the province of the wife and daughters; even in fine houses it was their business to preserve the garden fruit, and to sew for household use or ornament during long hours that would now be either devoted to more intellectual or more athletic pursuits, or else dissipated in conventionalities and distractions.

"While the daughters of the well-to-do were not yet divorced from the business of life, in the futile and languorous drawing-rooms to which Miss Austen's heroines were confined, on the other hand no professions or trades higher than manual were open to women, and scarcely any education was provided for them save that which each home could give. A very few clever women were classical scholars; a somewhat larger number were Puritan theologians, or students of English and even of Italian poetry."

One of these causes is revealed by this quotation; as the eighteenth century began to unroll there became more and more firmly established a wealthy leisured class with a different code from the wealthy, busy class which had hitherto existed. In consequence, the women who had found a certain happiness in domestic occupations found these gradually taken from them; the gentlewoman of the sixteenth and seventeenth centuries prided herself upon busy and skilful fingers; in the eighteenth century it became genteel to have idle hands resting upon one's lap and all activity reduced to a clacking tongue. The tyranny of leisure closed its chains about the wrists and hearts of an ever-growing section of womankind, who were useless by men's choice rather than their own and by social convention rather than natural necessity. We have constantly seen that work is needed for happiness; yet under the golden sun of prosperity women's work dried up like a river bed in time of drought, and the process continued almost unbroken until it reached the last absurdities of Victorian drawing-rooms. To puritanism and licence we have to add then parasitism as a growing cause of women's degradation and by adding a fourth cause, over-work, we round off the double antithesis. Under-work and over-work henceforth go hand in hand as shapers of women's history.

Even as early as the time of the Stuarts one half humanity degraded itself by thinking work degrading, the other half was degraded by poverty and toil. Long before 1640 even there was much industrial labour done by women and "although the state of things among the families of the continental peasantry was perhaps worse," says Trevelyan, "yet English women and children were overworked long before the era of the factory system."

It is at this point that we must consider a defect in this brief history which must have been apparent to the reader. It has been quite impossible to avoid the common fault of all histories, which is to concentrate upon the doings and aspirations of the minority of human beings to the neglect of the great mass, who work in silence and feel inarticulately. A great part of these pages has been concerned only with a small class where wealth and culture have accumulated, and too little has been said of the rest of humanity. In primitive societies the distinction did not exist, but as soon

had not the faintest idea of what she was speaking; their thoughts fled at once to the Female Character, solidified into a thousand poems, a thousand homilies, and a thousand wise saws. We may laugh at the savage, and deplore his methods of making rice and corn fruitful; but we should remember that there was far less reasonableness in the Female Character than there was in the Great Mother of the Gods; far less humanity, and far more injury to women.

It will be worth our while to dissect the anatomy of this myth with considerable care; for on the one hand it is the culmination of the experiences, the follies, the prejudices, and the desires of preceding ages; and, on the other, it is the real enemy against which the whole succeeding movement of feminism really fought. We will begin with a condensation of a very famous little book, an eighteenth-century "What a Young Girl Ought to Know," written by a Dr. Gregory of Edinburgh and entitled *A Father's Legacy to His Daughters*. Nothing could more clearly describe the attitude towards women of those days, for Dr. Gregory was by no means an extremist but in some ways quite a progressive and endowed on occasion with his share of distorted good sense.

A FATHER'S LEGACY TO HIS DAUGHTER

". . . You must expect that the advices which I shall give you will be imperfect, as there are many nameless delicacies, in female manners, of which none but a woman can judge. You will have one advantage by attending to what I am going to leave with you; you will hear, at least once in your lives, the genuine sentiments of a man who has no interest in flattering or deceiving you. . . .

"Though the duties of religion, strictly speaking, are equally bind-ing on both sexes, yet certain differences in their natural character and education, render some vices in your sex particularly odious. . . . Your superior delicacy, your modesty, and the usual severity of your education, preserve you, in a great measure, from any temptation to those vices to which we are most subjected. The natural softness and sensibility of your dispositions particularly fit you for the prac-tice of those duties where the heart is chiefly concerned. And this, along with the natural warmth of your imagination, renders you particularly susceptible of the feelings of devotion.

"There are many circumstances in your situation that peculiarly require the supports of religion to enable you to act in them with a spirit and propriety. Your whole life is often a life of suffering. You cannot plunge into business, or dissipate yourselves in pleasure and riot, as men too often do, when under the pressure of misfortunes. You must bear your sorrows in silence, unknown and unpitied. You must often put on a face of serenity and cheerfulness when your hearts are torn with anguish, or sinking in despair. Then your only resource is in the consolations of religion. It is chiefly owing to these that you bear domestic misfortunes better than we do.

"Women are greatly deceived when they think they recommend themselves to our sex by their indifference about religion. Even those men who are themselves unbelievers, dislike infidelity in you. Every man who knows human nature connects a religious taste in your sex with a softness and sensibility of heart. At least we always consider the want of it as a proof of that hard and masculine spirit which of all your faults we dislike most. Besides, men consider your religion as one of their principal securities for that female virtue in which they are most interested. If a gentleman pretends an attachment to any of you, and endeavours to shake your religious principles, be assured he is either a fool, or has designs on you which he dares not openly avow. . . .

"One of the chief beauties in a female character, is that modest reserve, that retiring delicacy, which avoids the public eye, and is disconcerted even at the gaze of admiration. . . . When a girl ceases to blush, she has lost the most powerful charm of beauty. That extreme sensibility which it indicates, may be a weakness and incumbrance in our sex, as I have too often felt, but in yours it is peculiarly engaging. Pedants, who think themselves philosophers, ask why a woman should blush when she is conscious of no crime? It is a sufficient answer, that nature has made you to blush when you are guilty of no fault, and has forced us to love you because you do so. . . .

"Wit is the most dangerous talent you can possess. It must be guarded with great discretion and good nature, otherwise it will create you many enemies. . . . Be even cautious in displaying your good sense. It will be thought you assume a superiority over the rest of the company. But if you happen to have any learning, keep it a profound secret, especially from the men, who generally look with a jealous and malignant eye on a woman of great parts, and a cultivated understanding. . . .

"Consider every species of indelicacy in conversation as shameful in itself, and as highly disgusting to us. All double entendre is of this sort. The dissoluteness of men's education allows them to be diverted with a kind of wit, which yet they have delicacy enough to be shocked at when it comes from your mouths, or even when you hear it without pain and contempt. Virgin purity is of that delicate nature that it cannot bear certain things without contamination. It is always in your power to avoid these . . . you will be reproached perhaps with prudery. . . . The men will complain of your reserve. They will assure you that a franker behaviour would make you more amiable. But, trust me, they are not sincere when they tell you so. I acknowledge that on some occasions it might render you more agreeable as companions, but it would make you less amiable as women: an important distinction which many of your sex are not aware of. . . .

"There is a species of refinement in luxury, just beginning to prevail among the gentlemen of this country, to which our ladies are yet as great strangers as any women upon earth; I hope, for the honour of their sex, they may ever continue so: I mean the luxury of eating. It is a despicable selfish vice in men, but in your sex it is beyond expression indelicate and disgusting. . . .

"By the present mode of female manners, the ladies seem to expect that they shall regain their ascendancy over us, by the fullest display of their personal charms, by being always in our eyes at public places, by conversing with us with the same unreserved freedom as we do with one another; in short, by resembling us as nearly as they possibly can. But a little time and experience will show the folly of this expectation and conduct.

"The power of a fine woman over the hearts of men, of men of the finest parts, is even beyond what she conceives. They are sensible of the pleasing illusion, but they cannot, nor do they wish to dissolve it. But if she is determined to dispel the charm, it certainly is in her power, she may soon reduce the angel to a very ordinary girl.

"There is a native dignity in ingenuous modesty, to be expected in your sex, which is your natural protection from the familiarities of the men, and which you should feel previous to the reflection that it is your interest to keep yourselves sacred from all personal freedoms.

"Let me now recommend to your attention that elegance, which is not so much a quality in itself, as the high polish of every other. . . . In a word it is the perfection of taste in life and manners; every virtue and every excellency in their most graceful and amiable forms. You may perhaps think that I want to throw every spark of nature out of your composition, and to make you entirely artificial. Far from it. I wish you to possess the most perfect simplicity of heart and manners. I think you may possess dignity without pride, affability without meanness, and simple elegance without affectation. Milton had my idea, when he says of Eve:

" 'Grace was in all her steps, Heaven in her eye,
        In every gesture dignity and love. . . .'

"But though good health be one of the greatest blessings of life, never make a boast of it, but enjoy it in grateful silence. We so naturally associate the idea of female softness and delicacy with a correspondent delicacy of constitution, that when a woman speaks of her great strength, her extraordinary appetite, her ability to bear excessive fatigue, we recoil at the description in a way she is little aware of.

"The intention of your being taught needlework, knitting and such like, is not on account of the intrinsic value of all you can do with your hands, which is trifling, but . . . to enable you to fill up, in a tolerably agreeable way, some of the many solitary hours you must necessarily pass at home. . . .

"Dress is an important article in female life. The love of dress is natural to you, and therefore it is proper and reasonable. Good sense will regulate your expense in it, and good taste will direct you to dress in such a way as to conceal your blemishes, and set off your beauties, if you have any, to the greatest advantage. But much delicacy and judgment are required in the application of this rule. A fine woman shews her charms to most advantage, when she seems most to conceal them. The finest bosom in nature is not so fine as what imagination forms. . . .

"I would have you dance with spirit, but never allow yourselves to be so far transported with mirth as to forget the delicacy of your sex. Many a girl in the gaiety and innocence of her heart is thought to discover a spirit she little dreams of.

"I know no entertainment that gives such pleasure to any person of sentiment or humour as the theatre. But I am sorry to say there are few English comedies a lady can see without a shock to delicacy. You will not readily suspect the comments gentlemen make on your behaviour on such occasions. . . . Sometimes a girl laughs with all the simplicity of unsuspecting innocence, for no other reason but being infected with other people's laughter: she is then believed to know more than she should do. If she does happen to understand an improper thing, she suffers a very complicated distress: she feels her modesty hurt in the most sensible manner, and at the same time is ashamed of appearing conscious of the injury. The only way to avoid these inconveniences is never to go to a play that is particularly offensive to delicacy. Tragedy subjects you to no such distress. Its sorrows will soften and ennoble your hearts. . . .

"Though a woman has no reason to be ashamed of an attachment to a man of merit, yet Nature, whose authority is superior to philosophy, has annexed a sense of shame to it. It is even long before a woman of delicacy dares avow to her own heart that she loves; and when all the subterfuges of ingenuity to conceal it from herself fail, she feels a violence done both to her pride and to her modesty. . . .

"It is a maxim laid down among you, and a very prudent one it is, that love is not to begin on your part, but is entirely to be the consequence of our attachment to you. Now, supposing a woman to have sense and taste, she will not find many men to whom she can possibly be supposed to bear any considerable share of esteem. Among these few it is a very great chance if any of them distinguishes her particularly. Love, at least with us, is exceedingly capricious, and will not always fix where reason says it should. But supposing one of them should become particularly attached to her, it is still extremely improbable that he should be the man in the world her heart most approved of. As, therefore, Nature has not given you that unlimited range in your choice which we enjoy, she has wisely and benevolently assigned to you a greater flexibility of taste on this subject. . . . A man of taste and delicacy marries a woman because he loves her more than any other. A woman of equal taste and delicacy marries him because she esteems him and because he gives her that preference. . . . If his attachment is agreeable to you, I leave you to do as nature, good sense and delicacy shall direct you. If you love him, let me advise you never to discover to him the full extent of your love, no not although you marry him. That sufficiently shews your preference which is all he is intitled to know. If he has delicacy he will ask for no stronger proof of your affection, for your sake; if he has sense he will not ask it for his own. This is an unpleasant truth, but it is my duty to let you know it. Violent love cannot subsist, at least cannot be expressed, for any time together, on both sides; otherwise the certain consequence, however concealed, is satiety and disgust. Nature in this case has laid the reserve on you."

No words could draw a more concise or a fairer picture of what the eighteenth century expected of a woman: nor was Dr. Gregory an exaggeration of the spirit of his age; in many ways he was exceedingly sensible; twice in his little book he warns his daughters of venereal disease, an admonishment which most Victorians regarded not only as unnecessary for girls, but wicked and indecent also; and there are other sparks of enlightenment in his pages. There is nothing to equal the grossness of Addison's outlook on women and education: that great essayist has been constantly praised as a woman's author and a portrayer of the fair sex, yet his views on the raw material of his art were hardly elevated.

"Women are not informed" (he writes) "for great cares themselves but to soothe and soften ours; their tenderness is the proper regard for the toils we undergo for their preservation; and the ease and cheerfulness of their conversation our desirable retreat from the labours of study and business. They are confined within the narrow limits of domestic offices, and when they strive beyond them they move eccentrically and, consequently, without grace.

"Agrippina, born with an understanding and dispositions which could, at best, have qualified her for the sordid helpmate of a pawnbroker or usurer, pretends to all the accomplishments that ever adorned man or woman, without the possession or even the true knowledge of any one of them. She would appear learned, and has just enough of all things, without comprehending anyone, to make her talk absurdly upon everything. . . . Mean tricks, shallow cunning, and breach of faith, constitute her mistaken system of politics. . . .

"Eudosia, the most frivolous woman in the world, condemns her own sex for being too trifling. She despises the agreeable levity and cheerfulness of a mixed company; she will be serious, that she will; and emphatically intimates, that she thinks reason and good sense very valuable things. She never mixes in the general conversation, but singles out some one man, whom she thinks worthy of her good sense, and in a half voice, or sotto voce, discusses her solid trifles in his ear, dwells particularly upon the most trifling circumstances of the main trifle . . . modestly confessing every now and then, by way of parenthesis, that possibly it may be thought presumption in a woman to talk at all upon these matters. . . . If Eudosia would content herself with her natural talents, play at cards, make tea and visits, talk to her dog often, and to her company but sometimes, she would not be ridiculous, but bear a very tolerable part in the polite world. . . .

"Should some lady of spirit, unjustly offended at these restrictions, ask what province I leave her sex? I answer, that I leave them what has not been peculiarly assigned by nature to ours. I leave them a mighty empire—Love. There they reign absolute, and by unquestioned right, while beauty supports their throne. . . . But then, those who are deposed by years or accidents, or those who by nature were never qualified to reign, should content themselves with the private care and economy of their families, and the diligent discharge of domestic duties. . . . I therefore require that those women who insist upon going beyond the bounds allotted to their sex, should previously declare themselves hermaphrodites, and be registered as such in their several parishes; till when I shall not suffer them to confound politics, perplex metaphysics, and darken mysteries."

But it is, of course, for women themselves that Addison is most solicitous: it is to safeguard them from the consequences to their own happiness of unwomanly attributes that he writes so passionately. "Man," he says, "when secluded from society, is not a more solitary being than the woman who leaves the duties of her own sex to invade the privileges of ours. She seems, in such circumstances, like one in banishment; she appears like a neutral being between the sexes; and though she may have the admiration of both, she finds the happiness of neither."

§ 7. *Rousseau* SIXTY years are covered by the period between
and Dr. For- Addison and Dr. Gregory's little posthumous
dyce.   work, and throughout the whole time women
were dominated by this degrading philosophy. Even when
the century began to veer towards revolutionary changes in
ideas and institutions, it was not women who first benefited;
the great name which was in so many ways the morning star
of the revolutionary epoch, Rousseau, had, as we have already seen, nothing to offer them. Indeed, nothing can show
more clearly the depth to which the myth of the Female
Character had penetrated into the human spirit than the
words in which the apostle of natural man described his
idea of natural woman. It is our object to emphasize and
to illustrate this myth, since all previous history is concen-
trated in it, and so before analysing Dr. Gregory's or Addison's conception we will turn directly to Rousseau.

"Whether I consider the peculiar destination of the sex, observe
their inclinations, or remark their duties, all things equally concur
to point out the peculiar method of education best adapted to them.
Woman and man were made for each other; but their mutual dependence is not the same. The men depend on the women only on account of their desires; the women on the men both on account of their
desires and their necessities: we could subsist better without them than
they without us. . . .

"For this reason, the education of the women should be always
relative to the men. To please, to be useful to us, to make us love
and esteem them, to educate us when young, and take care of us
when grown up, to advise, to console us, to render our lives easy
and agreeable: these are the duties of women at all times, and what
they should be taught in their infancy. So long as we fail to recur

to this principle we run wide of the mark, and all the precepts which are given them contribute neither to their happiness nor our own.

"In this union of the sexes, both pursue one common object, but not in the same manner. From their diversity in this particular, arises the first determinate difference between the moral relations of each. The one should be active and strong, the other passive and weak; it is necessary that the one should have both the power and the will, and that the other should make little resistance.

"This principle being established, it follows that the woman is expressly formed to please the man: if the obligation be reciprocal also, and the man ought to please in his turn, it is not so immediately necessary: his great merit is in his power, and he pleases merely because he is strong. This, I must confess, is not one of the refined maxims of love; it is, however, one of the laws of nature, prior to love itself.

"If woman be formed to please and be subjected to man, it is her place, doubtless, to render herself agreeable to him, instead of challenging his passion. The violence of his desires depends on her charms; it is by means of these that she should urge him to the exertion of those powers which nature hath given him. The most successful method of exciting them, is to render such exertion necessary by resistance; as in that case, self-love is added to desire, and the one triumphs in the victory which the other obliged to acquire. Hence arise the various modes of attack and defence between the sexes; the boldness of one sex and the timidity of the other; and, in a word, that bashfulness and modesty with which nature hath armed the weak, in order to subdue the strong. . . .

"Girls ought to be active and diligent; nor is that all; they should also be early subjected to restraint. This misfortune, if it really be one, is inseparable from their sex; nor do they ever throw it off but to suffer more cruel evils. They must be subject, all their lives, to the most constant and severe restraint, which is that of decorum: it is, therefore, necessary to accustom them early to such confinement, that it may not afterwards cost them too dear; and to the suppression of their caprices, that they may the more readily submit to the will of others. If, indeed, they be fond of being always at work, they should be sometimes compelled to lay it aside. Dissipation, levity, and inconstancy, are faults that readily spring up from their first propensities, when corrupted or perverted by too much indulgence. To prevent this abuse, we should teach them, above all things, to lay a due restraint upon themselves. The life of a modest woman is reduced, by our absurd institutions, to a perpetual conflict with herself: not but that it is just that this sex should partake of the sufferings which arise from those evils it hath caused us. . . .

"There results from this habitual restraint a tractableness which women have occasion for during their whole lives, as they constantly remain either under subjection to the men, or to the opinions of mankind; and are never permitted to set themselves above those opinions. The first and most important qualification in a woman is good-nature and sweetness of temper: formed to obey a being so imperfect as man, often full of vices, and always full of faults, she ought to learn betimes even to suffer injustice, and to bear the insults of a husband without complaint; it is not for his sake, but her own, that she should be of a mild disposition. The perverseness and ill-nature of the women only serve to aggravate their own misfortunes, and the misconduct of their husbands; they might plainly perceive that such are not the arms by which they gain the superiority.

"Daughters should be always submissive; their mothers, however, should not be inexorable. To make a young person tractable, she ought not to be made unhappy; to make her modest she ought not to be rendered stupid. On the contrary, I should not be displeased at her being permitted to use some art, not to elude punishment in case of disobedience, but to exempt herself from the necessity of obeying. It is not necessary to make her dependence burdensome, but only to let her feel it. Subtilty is a talent natural to the sex; and as I am persuaded all our natural inclinations are right and good in themselves, I am of opinion this should be cultivated as well as the others; it is requisite for us only to prevent its abuse. . . .

"A man speaks of what he knows, a woman of what pleases her; the one requires knowledge, the other taste; the principal object of a man's discourse should be what is useful, that of woman's what is agreeable. There ought to be nothing in common between their different conversation but truth.

"We ought not, therefore, to restrain the prattle of girls in the same manner as we should that of boys, with that severe question: To what purpose are you talking?—but by another, which is less difficult to answer: How will your discourse be received? In infancy, while they are as yet incapable to discern good from evil, they ought to observe it, as a law, never to say anything disagreeable to those whom they are speaking to: what will render the practice of this rule also the more difficult, is, that it must ever be subordinate to the former, of never speaking falsely or telling an untruth.

"It is easy to be conceived, that if male children be not in a capacity to form any true notions of religion, those ideas must be greatly above the conception of females: . . . As the conduct of a woman is subservient to the public opinion, her faith in matters of religion should, for that very reason, be subject to authority. Every daughter ought to be of the same religion as her mother, and every wife to be of the same religion as her husband: for though such religion should be false, that docility which induces the mother and daughter to submit to the order of nature, takes away, in the sight of God, the criminality of their error."

In fact, according to Rousseau, the ideal woman should be so educated in duplicity, in apparent innocence and actual concentration upon the one end of exciting a man's desires, as to resemble in all her attributes, what he describes as follows about her dress: "Her dress is extremely modest in appearance, and yet very coquettish in fact: she does not make a display of her charms, she conceals them; but in concealing them, she knows how to affect your imagination. Every one who sees her will say, There is a modest and discreet girl; but while you are near her, your eyes and affections wander all over her person, so that you cannot withdraw them; and you would conclude, that every part of her dress, simple as it seems, was only put in its proper order to be taken to pieces by the imagination."

Dr. Fordyce draws the perfect picture of a woman's part, if not so voluptuously, at least with equal clearness as Rousseau: he is astonished, he tells the young ladies in his sermons, at the folly of many women, who are still reproaching their husband for leaving them alone, for preferring this or that company to theirs, for treating them with this or the other mark of disregard and indifference; when, to speak the truth, they have themselves in a great measure to blame. Not that he would justify the men in anything wrong on their part. But had they, the ladies, behaved to them with more respectful observance, and a more equal tenderness, studying their humours, overlooking mistakes, submitting to their opinions in matters indifferent, passing by little instances of unevenness, caprice, or passion, giving soft answers to hasty words, complaining as seldom as possible, and making it their daily care to relieve their anxieties and prevent their wishes, to enliven the hour of dullness, and call up the idea of felicity; had they pursued this conduct, he doubted not but they would have maintained and even increased their esteem, so far as to have secured every degree of influence that could conduce to their husbands' virtue or their own mutual satisfaction; and their house might at that day have been the abode of domestic bliss. Mary Wollstonecraft in 1794 was the first woman who cared and dared to comment openly and in print on this by exclaiming "such a woman ought to be an angel—or she is an ass—for I discern not a trace of the human character, neither reason nor passion in this domestic drudge, whose being is absorbed in that of a tyrant's."

§ 8 *"The*
Female Char-
acter."

IN these elegant extracts from a learned doctor, who wrote a guide to what a young girl should know; from an essayist who is regarded especially as a connoisseur of the feminine heart; from the great preacher of naturalness and equality, we have a clear picture of the Female Character; of the conception of women, which had grown up as a result of many centuries of Christian civilization; and we will do well to analyse some of its elements.

First we note that a clear division is marked between the sexes, covering not merely physical distinctions, but every sort of mental and moral trait. Men can do one thing, women another; men are good when they do one thing, or at least not very culpable; women sin terribly in doing the very same thing. Some virtues are male, others female; some vices are allowed men, others, such as duplicity and cunning and lying, are permitted women, provided they contribute to the sum total of masculine content.

In this sexual division of labour and activity we find something very different from what the facts given in the first chapter, or the habits of savages, would lead us to expect. We are not told that women, as a sex, should not

work in coal mines, none of our authors would have protested against the fact mentioned above about female labour beneath the ground, and Hannah More would have
deprecated any such protest as Bolshevism—or Jacobinism,
as it was then called; but we are definitely told that no
woman should be too healthy. Dr. Gregory, a medical man
and Fellow of the Royal Society, goes so far as to suggest
that quite normally women are permanent invalids. Dr.
Fordyce, whose book of sermons was a rival guide to young
girls' behaviour, says, "Let it be observed that in your sex
manly exercises are never graceful; that in them a tone and
figure, as well as an air and deportment, of the masculine
kind, are always forbidding; and that men of sensibility
desire in every woman soft features, and a flowing voice, a
form not robust, and demeanour delicate and gentle." Dr.
Gregory goes so far as to say that Nature, about which he
ought to know much as a Natural Philosopher of merit, so
combines weak physique with feminine virtue, that robust
health makes men suspicious of a woman's morality.

Now is not this precisely the same outlook as the taboo
outlook of a savage, but translated into a sphere whence
the savage had the sense to exclude it? Physical weakness
in woman was not regarded as a desirable attribute in a
primitive community where every woman was useful, but to
the Gregorian point of view no woman ought to be useful
and so physical weakness was no drawback but a virtue, a
natural attribute. To the savage it was a natural attribute
of woman to make certain earthenware pots rather than

others, to sow the fields but not to reap them, to plaster the sides of houses but not to make the roofs; all of these are absurd enough doubtless, but they are not so absurd as making natural attributes out of illness and weakness.

Moreover, it is of interest to note that Dr. Fordyce is not original in telling his young ladies that men of sensibility desire in every woman soft features and a form not robust, that is, not muscular; though he was probably right enough in the diagnosis of the taste of his time. His men of sensibility were not at all to be distinguished from many African savages. Beneath Kilimanjaro men are just as sensible to plumpness as in Dr. Fordyce's London: for three months before her marriage every girl retires into seclusion and is shut up in a cage in her mother's hut. "During this period," we are told, "she may do no sort of work, but is given the most fattening food and is daily anointed. Much of the food must be supplied by the suitor, who sends milk, bananas, oxblood mixed with milk and butter; finally he must supply a fat sheep, the half of which he will send cooked for the bride, and the half raw for the parents. All these things are called: "things to supply the bride in the cage!"

Among the Banyankole of the same region, the preparation for pleasing men of sensibility begins about the age of ten, from which time the girl must lead a sedentary life, drinking large quantities of milk, and eating porridge. "By the end of a year of this confinement, the girl would lose all desire for any form of activity and even lose the power of walking, so that she could only waddle. The fatter she grew, the more beautiful she was considered, and her condition was a pronounced contrast to that of the men, who were athletic and well developed." To Rousseau such habits were doubtless part of the satisfactory nature of natural man; we are surprised, however, to find them imitated by the Christian Dr. Fordyce. He was the child of his age, and that age believed that women should be physically weak, and that strength was unnatural and probably even the cloak of a multitude of sins.

In the second place we note that women are to have defective brains: here we meet once more the *"imbecilitas"* of Roman law and also to a large extent the attitude of ancient Athens. Female brains, they felt, were a prelude to unchastity, they were at any rate an inconvenience to any man. Boswell disagreed with Dr. Johnson and thought that it would be an inconvenience to have an intelligent wife; for, thought the great lexicographer, it were a miserable thing when the conversation between man and wife could only be such as whether the mutton should be boiled or roasted, and probably a dispute at that; nevertheless a wife of a studious or argumentative turn would be very troublesome:—"for instance, if a woman should continually dwell upon the subject of the Aryan heresy." A deficiency of intellect was, then, even to the moderately sensible Dr. Johnson, an advantage in a woman, and we are therefore not surprised to find that he regarded it as a natural characteristic: when Boswell told him of a Quaker lady whom he had heard preach, he made the celebrated comment: "Sir, a woman's preaching is like a dog's walking on his hind legs. It is not done well; but you are surprised to find it done at all."

Dr. Johnson, of course, knew many clever women, but his circle was exceptional: we may be quite certain that in ordinary circles a young woman did best if she followed Dr. Gregory's advice and hid whatever knowledge and sense she happened to possess:—but to this particular matter we must return later.

In the third place we have a very clear belief that women's need of religion was founded on a basis very different from men's. There is no suggestion of her as priestess or teacher, no mysterious knowledge was hers to be got by men only from her lips: she must be religious because that way lies chastity. "Religion is the opium of women," is really what Dr. Gregory's remarks imply, and so definitely is the exercise of religion to be regarded as evidence of chastity, that is as of the thing which makes men desire a woman, that Dr. Fordyce goes the whole way and recommends it as an aphrodisiac or love potion. "Never," he tells the young ladies in one of his sermons, "never, perhaps, does a fine woman strike more deeply, than when, composed in pious recollection, and possessed with the noblest considerations, she assumes, without knowing it, superior dignity and new graces; so that the beauties of holiness seem to radiate about her, and the bystanders are almost induced to fancy her worshipping amongst her kindred angels." In short, religion for women has hardly changed since the ceremony of "frightening the woman" which we noticed among the Australian savages; men felt they could not trust the morals of their wives or daughters unless they were cowed by the conventional religion of society. Since a young man was allowed to sow his wild oats here on earth, he need not sow prayers and reap their harvest so meticulously.

A further point which is very clear from our material on the Female Character was that chastity and modesty were to be used merely as tools for the capture of men, as a bait which appealed to their sensuality. Rousseau thought of a woman's ideal setting as a seraglio, and Dr. Fordyce apparently saw no other object in woman's existence, no other object in female education than the fascination of men by the debasement and debilitating of mind and body. But, in order to achieve success, a woman had to imitate an acrobat and ride round the arena of society with one foot on one horse and the other on another: the one an innocent and indeed ridiculous chastity of mind and body, the other a sly, lascivious duplicity, the whole trick fit only for a whore who has to keep one eye on a possible customer and the other on a woman policeman.

Chastity is an excellent thing, even though, as we saw, many savages do not regard it as a positive virtue, but in itself it is not a panacea for all evil; it used to be at least a Christian grace, but to the age of which we are speaking it was little but an adjunct to the laws of property. Dr. Johnson was quite clear about the chief reasons why women must be chaste and, said he, illegitimate children must be penalized from birth, "because the chastity of women being of the utmost importance, *as all property depends upon it,* they who forfeit it should not have any possibility of being restored to good character." Adultery, he was clear, was a heinous crime for "confusion of progeny constitutes the essence of the crime; and therefore a woman who breaks her marriage vows is much more criminal than a man who does it. A man to be sure is criminal in the sight of God: but he does not do his wife a very material injury, if he does not insult her; if, for instance, from mere wantonness of appetite, he steals privately to her chambermaid. Sir, a wife ought not greatly to resent this. I would not receive home a daughter who had run away from her husband on that account." It is equally illuminating to note what Dr. Johnson thought the treatment should be for a woman who had married beneath her. "Were I a man of rank," he told Mrs. Thrale, "I would not let a daughter starve who had made a mean marriage, but, having voluntarily degraded herself from the station which she was originally entitled to hold, I would support her only in that which she herself had chosen, and would not put her on a level with my other daughters. You are to consider, madam, that it is our duty to maintain the subordination of civilized society; and when there is a gross and shameful deviation from rank, it should be punished so as to deter others from the same perversion."

In short, the Female Character is to be based on Chastity; this is the *sine qua non* of all women; it must be noted, too, that they do not say "You will find that life is happiest if it is so arranged that it is pure," or "There are certain things of so great a value that women cannot give them away with impunity upon the whim of the moment," or "There are other things in life which may be lost by too great a concentration upon physical things," or "One must consider the feelings of other people and often refrain from pleasures which would cost too much." Chastity is an end in itself, a virtue instead of a negation, and this for thoroughly barbaric reasons. Dr. Johnson gives us one, chastity in women is essential because on it depends all the law of property, for this sacred thing property, all sorts of barbarities are to be practised, illegitimate children degraded, seduced girls cast out, all to safeguard property. In consequence of this the woman is definitely regarded as more blameworthy than the man. Dr. Johnson says so in so many words, he would not receive home his daughter if she ran away from her husband because of his adulteries with the servants in her own house, nor would he receive back a daughter who had been seduced. In this we can only call Dr. Johnson a barbarian; not a savage because in savage communities a higher perception of humanity is found, as among the Lango of Africa, where the seduced girl is liable to no punishment and is not held guilty of an offence, though compensation has to be paid by the man to the girl's guardian. Should the girl give birth to a child as the result, the amount of compensation is increased, but the child stays with the girl. Should the man wish to marry her, the compensation paid is calculated in the dowry, and the child then goes with the girl to its father. Should the girl die in child-birth the compensation must be brought up to the amount payable for manslaughter. Now which is the more ethical, the Lango savage or the Great Lexicographer, who said "Don't cant in defence of savages"?

It is worth while remarking here what terrible harm has come to women by the association of chastity and property in this sense; for as it is hard for a rich man to enter heaven, it is as hard for a rich woman to be happy on earth. Seeing that her much property must be guarded by an inordinate series of defences around her chastity, she has invariably been curtailed beyond reason in her liberties, and had her pleasures, her movements, and her habits stunted and de-formed. She has seen her poorer sisters maintain a freedom necessary to useful work, while she has had to accept an imprisonment without hard labour to safeguard what was probably never in danger. In no country in the world has the lot of a woman with unearned income been so healthy, nor yet so happy, as that of one who has to justify her exist-ence by providing her daily bread by the sweat of her brow —but to this we shall return later.

It becomes quite clear that not ethics but economics rules the behaviour of eighteenth-century women; they are the slaves of reasons of state, of social conventions based upon no code of morals worthy of the name: they are indeed slaves; tethered goats allowed only enough rope to hang themselves; they suffer from all the superstition of all the irrational centuries whose weight they bore. And, as we have seen, they were worse off than the Duchess of Newcastle who at least knew her lot in life to be unjustly curtailed; these slaves, as Rousseau saw of men, though not of women, had tasted the last poison of slavery and ceased to regret even the chains which bound them. Let us look a little at one of them who has left a name.

§ 9. *Hannah More.* THIS was the age of the Blue-stocking Clubs, so-called because a Mr. Benjamin Stillingfleet, author of tracts relating to Natural History, and a man of notably grave dress including always a pair of blue stockings, was an habitué of one such gathering of intelligent women and men. "Such was the excellence of his conversation," says Boswell, "that his absence was felt as so great a loss, that it used to be said, 'we can do nothing without the blue-stockings,' and thus by degrees the title was established."

Among the Blue-stockings were Mrs. Hannah More, Miss Monckton, Mrs. Montague, Mrs. Elizabeth Carter, Fanny Burney, Mrs. Thrale, and many others; but, of them all, Hannah More is the most important to our understanding of our subject.

Hannah More is one of the greatest woman writers of English prose, and withal a very arresting personality. As a writer she has more facility of style than felicity of judgment; nevertheless, when Mr. Augustine Birrell buried her complete works in his back garden, he was himself the loser by his petulance. She has, moreover, the immense virtue in our eyes of being at once the product and the mirror of her period, and in her innumerable works there is ample evidence to be discovered of the public opinion of her time. She herself was suspected by some, if not of radicalism, at least of an unwomanly activity of mind; when she speaks we do not hear the mumblings of some provincial tyrant of a dame-school, but the clear, outspoken affirmations of a mind which was admired by Dr. Johnson and David Garrick, by Burke and Reynolds and Wilberforce. Her sentiments did not therefore lag behind the practice of the age in enlightenment or reasonableness.

We have seen herein that she did not call women to worship Bellona or Pallas Athene, but she introduces them to the nature of a far more powerful goddess, Propriety. "Propriety is to a woman what the great Roman critic says action is to an orator; it is the first, the second, the third requisite. A woman may be knowing, active, witty, and amusing, but without propriety she cannot be amiable. Propriety is the centre in which all the lines of duty and agreeableness meet."

Among the greatest enemies of the true worship of Propriety, according to this her arch priestess, are the novelists, and first among these is Rousseau, "the first popular dispenser of this complicated drug, in which the deleterious infusion was strong, and the effort proportionately fatal. . . . He does not paint an innocent woman ruined, repenting, and restored, but, with a far more mischievous refinement, he annihilates the value of chastity, and, with pernicious subtlety, attempts to make his heroine appear almost more amiable without it. He exhibits a virtuous woman, the victim not of temptation, but of reason—not of vice but of sentiment—not of passion, but of conviction; and strikes at the very root of honour, by elevating a crime into a principle."

It is instructive to place beside Hannah More's criticism of Rousseau, the praise of another woman, Madame de Staël: "Though Rousseau has endeavoured to prevent women from interfering in public affairs, and acting a brilliant part in the theatre of politics, yet, in speaking of them, how much has he done it to their satisfaction! If he wished to deprive them of some rights foreign to their sex, how has he for ever restored them all those to which it has a claim! And in attempting to diminish their influence over the deliberations of men, how sacredly has he established the empire they have over their happiness! In aiding them to descend from a usurped throne, he has firmly seated them upon that to which they were destined by nature; and though he be full of indignation against them when they endeavour to resemble men, yet when they come before him with all the charm, weakness, virtues, and errors of their sex, his respect for their persons amounts almost to adoration."

The degradation of women which called forth Mary Wollstonecraft's *Vindication* was neglected as much in Madame de Staël as in Hannah More, and just as the first is attacked fiercely in the *Vindication,* so, from another angle, Hannah More attacks Mary Wollstonecraft. To

Hannah More religion and chastity were the essential bases of female character to an extent which well-nigh made them secondary sexual characters in themselves; to Rousseau and Madame de Staël, weakness and "sensibility" and duplicity were to an equal degree female virtues: to Mary Wollstonecraft both doctrines were deplorable; woman must live to serve and know herself as well as God and Man, and the ways of God must be as justified to her as to her husband. She therefore called for knowledge, and in such a way as to lead quite definitely to the putting of orthodoxy of religion, morals and politics in a second place, if necessary.

Hannah More saw the consequences: "Not only novels and romances have been made the vehicles of vice and infidelity, but the same allurement has been held out to the women of our country, which was employed by the first philosophist to the first sinner—knowledge. Listen to the precepts of the new enlighteners, and you need no longer remain in that situation in which providence has placed you! Follow their example, and you shall be permitted to indulge in all those gratifications which custom, not religion, has tolerated in the male sex!" Although she herself devoted a life-time to the cause of education, she could not see anything in what Mary Wollstonecraft called education except seduction, and Mary herself was nothing more than a woman who "asserts in a work intituled *The Wrongs of Women,* that adultery is justifiable and that the restrictions placed upon it by the laws of England constitute one of the *wrongs of women.*" Hannah More goes on to describe

Mary and her other rebel sympathizers in excellent English: "this most destructive class in the whole wide range of modern corrupters, who affect the most desperate work of the passions, without so much as pretending to urge their violence in extenuation of the guilt of indulging them. They solicit the very indulgence with a sort of cold-blooded speculation, and invite the reader to the most unbounded gratifications, with all the saturnine coolness of a geometrical calculation. . . . The system is a dire infusion, compounded of bold impiety, brutish sensuality, and exquisite folly, which, creeping fatally about the breast, checks the moral circulation, and totally stops the pulse of goodness by the extinction of the vital principle: thus not only cloaking the system of actual virtue, but drying up the very fountain of future remorse and remote independence."

When we turn from this to the pages of the *Vindication*, we ask ourselves what fixed ideas on life in general contributed to blind and pervert so excellent a woman as Hannah More to the true nature of women's position and to the value of their first great champion. And since we may expect also to find in these fixed ideas the rivets of the chains which were binding women in the eighteenth century and from which women have not yet become entirely free, let us recapitulate some of Hannah More's fixed ideas in her own excellent and forceful words.

"Is it not a fundamental error to consider children as innocent beings, whose little weaknesses may perhaps want some correction, rather than as beings who bring into the world a corrupt nature and evil dispositions, which it should be the great end of education to rectify? This appears to be such a foundation truth, that if I were asked what quality is most important in an instructor of youth, I should not hesitate to reply, 'such a strong impression of the corruption of our nature, as should ensure a disposition to counteract it: together with such a deep view and thorough knowledge of the human heart, as should be necessary for developing and controlling its most secret and complicated workings.' "

"Most *men* are commonly destined to some profession, and their minds are consequently turned each to its respective object. Would it not be strange if they were called out to exercise their profession, or to set up their trade, with only a little general knowledge of the trades and professions of all other men, and without any previous definite application to their own peculiar calling? The profession of ladies, to which the bent of *their* instruction should be turned, is that of daughters, wives, mothers, and mistresses of families. They should therefore be trained with a view to these several conditions, and be furnished with a stock of ideas, and principles, and qualifications, and habits, ready to be applied and appropriated, as occasion may demand, to each of these respective situations. For though the arts which rarely embellish life must claim admiration; yet when a man of sense comes to marry, it is a companion whom he wants, and not an artist."

"Among other subjects which engross a good share of worldly conversation, one of the most attracting is beauty. Many ladies have often a random way of talking rapturously on the general importance and the fascinating power of beauty, who are yet prudent enough to be very unwilling to let their own daughters find out they are handsome. Perhaps the contrary course might be safer. . . . The less solicitous themselves, to conceal from her a secret which, with all your watchfulness, she will be sure to find out without your telling; but rather seek to lower the general value of beauty in their estimation."

"Who can forbear observing and regretting in a variety of instances, that not only sons, but daughters, have adopted something of that spirit of independence, and disdain of control, which characterizes the times? The *rights of man* have been discussed, till we are somewhat wearied with the discussion. To these have been opposed, as the next stage in the progress of illumination, and with more presumption than prudence, the *rights of woman.* It follows—that the world will next have—grave descants on the *rights of youth,* the *rights of children* —the *rights of babes!*"

"Girls should be led to distrust their own judgment; they should learn not to murmur at expostulation; they should be accustomed to expect and to endure opposition. It is a lesson with which the world will not fail to furnish them; and they will not practise it the worse for having learnt it the sooner. It is of the last importance to their happiness, even in this life, that they should early acquire a submissive temper and a forbearing spirit. They must even endure to be thought wrong sometimes, when they cannot but feel they are right. And while they should be anxiously aspiring to do well, they must not expect always to obtain the praise of having done so. But while a gentle demeanour is inculcated, let them not be instructed to practise gentleness merely on the low ground of its being decorous, and feminine, and pleasing, and calculated to attract human favour: but let them be carefully taught to cultivate it on the high principles of obedience to Christ."

Hannah More then stands revealed to us in her own words as a most interesting and important character, for of her it can be said that all the preceding thousands of years of woman's history have spent their accumulated force to achieve Hannah More: she is the end-product of the complicated growth with which we have occupied ourselves. And in seeing this we see the key to the whole process of the centuries.

Let the reader consider at once the primitive savage

woman and the woman Hannah More would have been
without her accidental abilities, the woman, that is, she
desires all her less gifted sisters to imitate. Is it not clear
that the seventeen centuries of Christianity, of Roman law,
of Greek culture, of Roman practical civilization, of accumulating wealth and expanding knowledge, have left
women far poorer in social value, social work, social virtue, than they were before all the complicated process called
civilization had begun? If the writer has succeeded in his
portrayal of his subject matter, it will be clear that there
has been no progress, but rather retrogression, in so far as
these are judged by a woman's claim to individuality, to
interests, to intelligence. This history of women from the
dim beginnings until the end of the eighteenth century
shows no absolute progess whatever: at times there are mod-
ifications, even ameliorations of their social status, but as a
whole women did not benefit except at second hand, by all
the progress, material and otherwise, the world had experienced. For women the Middle Ages, if not ancient history, lasted far longer than they did for society as a whole,
and for them the date which corresponds in importance to
that of the discovery of America, the capture of Constantinople, or the Reformation, is 1774: and the event is the
publication of the *Vindication of the Rights of Women.*

But with that event and the movement of emancipation to
which it led we are not concerned here: Hannah More was
our goal, just as she was the goal, apparently, of that in-
scrutable purpose which molded the female animal into

the Female Character in the course of the unnumbered centuries at which we have been glancing. It is our boast today that the Female Character has dissolved into the rational being who calls herself the modern woman: and without disturbing that comfortable belief let us pass over a century or so and read by way of Epilogue what seems to be written in the not far distant future.

Chapter VII

§ 1. THE history of women is, as we have said herein, the history of human ideas about the nature and differences of the two sexes; and as we have followed it, these ideas have consistently been based upon the same mistaken notions about biology. The primitive savage, the primitive Christian, the feudal knight, the seventeenth-century Puritan, the eighteenth-century essayist, the Victorian drawing-room tea-drinker; all alike thought and acted about women as they did because the same superstitions about biology and the same misinterpretation of feelings were common to all. The dawn came when people began to suggest that women were quite as reasonable by nature as men, and that wrong education was responsible for any difference between them in this respect. After that came political emancipation and economic emancipation, until today we can say that the first is complete and the second almost as far advanced as it is for individuals of the male sex.

But there still remained another sort of emancipation, the emotional, which had not until quite recently been so much as begun.

The historian who looks at the future as well as the past

is confronted by a greater difficulty in his readers than in his subject matter; for most people are so used to making of the future dreams to suit their own desires that they assume that everybody who attempts to prophesy is prophesying what he hopes will happen, or what he believes ought morally to happen; and they therefore believe that the historian is *advocating* rather than foretelling. For this reason, since any just picture of the future is bound to contain many elements which are distasteful to us, the historian of the future risks unpopularity in every word he utters. In what we are about to say, let the reader remember that moral judgments cannot enter: it is no use arguing about the facts as to whether they are good or bad; we can only consider that they are, or that in all probability they will be. The past we condone, the future we condemn; and of nothing is this truer than of the history of women. Bearing all this in mind and remembering that the historian tries to see things as they are and not as he wants them to be, what can we say of the future history of women?

The future today is foreshadowed in two geographical areas, America and Russia; in both these countries the present is nebulous, unformed, in fact, the embryo of a child yet to be born. It is largely to these places that we must look if we are to find indications of the women of tomorrow. There are strange similarities between them.

In the first place, both in America and in Russia the abolition of the family goes on apace, and in America this abolition has gone so far that there has actually been inau-

gurated a "mother's day" in which is celebrated the existence of that relationship. On Mother's Day the telegraph
companies offer the public suggestions for messages to be
telegraphed to mothers by their sons; and the literary genius
they employ to think out these things achieves this choice
morsel: "Though I am far away, mother dear, I am thinking of you always." In the old days a son could think of
that without assistance, but then in the old days the sons
would not have been away from their mothers habitually
and for long periods, at long distances. The very nature
of modern industry and of town life are such that the family
relationship is bound to be destroyed as far as its essentials
are concerned, and the only reason why America is more advanced in this matter than, let us say, England, is because
American industry and capitalism have gone further in
modifying life than English. Those in America or England who talk about the terrible Bolshevism of abolishing
the family have only to go as far as Spain to see that industrialism, by destroying peasant industry, which is family
industry, has also destroyed the old-fashioned family quite
as thoroughly as any experimental marriage law in peasant
Russia.

What are the factors which are bringing about the dissolution of the family in modern industrial states?

1. The father used to be the sole breadwinner, hence,
economically at least, his wife and his children were his
slaves. In theory he let them do what they liked of course,
but actually this meant that they were in the position of the

daughters of the character in *The Witch of Edmonton,* who said that they "Shall choose for themselves by my consent." Any father could say to a son or a daughter, "You must do what you like, but of course, if it is not what I like, don't expect any money from me."

In industrialized communities, every member of the family can become self-supporting and independent, if he desires it, and the father is no longer a benevolent despot or a potential tyrant.

2. On the other hand, we must offset against this fact the fact that in the old days a father could by his own efforts make enough for his wife and younger children to live on. Nowadays in millions of families, the budget could not be balanced without the forced labour of women and children. To some, economic independence has meant the right to become a lady dentist or a lady shopkeeper, instead of wasting time at home, and these forget that for countless women the change has not worked out so well.

The change from the status of father as breadwinner to the new conditions must undermine the family relationships and the efficiency of the family as a unit, because it makes life harder for women, however it increases their dignity, and it leaves no time for the arts and crafts of domestic economy, since the wife is earning money instead of spending it economically.

3. From the last tendency there follows a tendency to degrade and diminish the shell in which the family lives; that is, their home. Compare a Spanish farmstead and a

New York apartment. The first has a very large room, in which all the family spend most of their waking hours when they are not working in the fields; they eat here, they talk here, they work here, they sit round an enormous hearth in winter. Round this big room are small ones in which they sleep, and underneath are the farm animals, overhead the garnered crops. In New York the cafeteria has taken away one function of the large room and its others have become obsolete; nothing but the bedrooms remain. Instead of all interests centring on the hearth, all interests diverge from it; the apartment is a dormitory, a cleaning place and sometimes an inefficient sandwich shop. That will not be true of most of the Americans who read this book, but it will be true of most Americans who live in the cities, and still more true fifty years hence.

In short, since women work outside the home, they do not work within; they cannot have servants, for these also can work outside; the children go to school, to camp, to college, and when they are sleeping at home, most of their amusements are away—cinemas, baseball matches, dances, motoring. Of course the abolition of the family goes on apace.

4. Before the growth of capitalism, the unit of production was the family. In Spain today you can see whole families engaged in making some article, shoes, ropes, mattresses, baskets, pottery, under one roof and that their own. Hence the family maintains its actual solidarity and remains in existence permanently.

In America and England industrialism sends the father

to one factory, the wife to another and the children to different cities and states in search of opportunity. Obviously family ties are weakened, obviously the family as an institution ceases to mean what once it meant. Not only is there physical distance among its members, but emotional distance also; each has its own interests, each is self-supporting emotionally as well as economically.

Now these are facts about which there can be no dispute, and moreover their effects are cumulative and increasing; it is no use shaking one's head about the institution of the family; it is just as little use advocating its abolition; the thing is happening without advocacy or denunciation. Either the family must be sacrificed to industrial capitalism or industrial capitalism must be sacrificed to the family, and though a historian may have his own wishes, he is bound to admit that of these two, the first seems the more probable. In America, the country most like the future of the whole capitalist world, we see indications that the future history of women will take place in circumstances where the family institution bears no resemblance whatever to what we retain in our minds and hearts.

Let us now turn to Russia. Here we have the advantage of being able to quote no less an authority than Trotsky, who has written in his book, *Problems of Life,* a great deal that is interesting historically and practically. "To institute the political equality of men and women in the Soviet State," says he, "was one problem and the simplest. A much more difficult one was the next—that of instituting the in-

dustrial equality of men and women workers in the factories, the mills and the trade unions, and to do it in such a
way that the men should not put the women to disadvantage.
But to achieve the actual equality of men and women within
the family is an infinitely more arduous problem. All our
domestic habits must be revolutionized before that can happen." Trotsky goes on to deprecate the anarchistic break-
down of marriage and morals which has taken place in revolutionary Russia, but we are less interested in this than in
what is to be built up again in place of what has been destroyed. "Gigantic events," he says, "have descended on the
family in its old shape, the war and the revolution. And
following them came creeping slowly the underground mole
—critical thought, the conscious study and valuation of
family relations and the forms of life. . . . We need more
socialistic economic forms. Only under such conditions can
we free the family from the functions and cares that now op-
press and disintegrate it. Washing must be done by a public
laundry, catering by a public restaurant, sewing by a public workshop. Children must be educated by good public
teachers who have a real vocation for the work. Then the
bond between husband and wife would be freed from everything external and accidental, and the one would cease to
absorb the life of the other. Genuine equality would at last
be established. The bond will depend on mutual attachment.
And on that account, particularly, it will acquire inner
stability, not the same, of course, for everyone, but com-
pulsory for no one."

In short, Trotsky, who is surely most likely of contemporary men to think and dare deep into the future, sees as the ultimate revolutionary family precisely what capitalist America sees as an actuality today, a family with communal washing, communal eating and communal clothing, a public school system and a complete emancipation of the wife from domesticity. If America and Russia agree upon this, we are entitled to say, there lies the future of woman, in that type of family. We are approaching a time when we shall not argue for or against the phrase "a woman's place is her home," for we shall not have the least idea what such a phrase ever meant.

We have said that women's political emancipation has been completed, but of course this is not altogether true. Political emancipation does not mean the having of a vote, but the having as well the power of learning how to use it. Nobody can deny that a woman hedged about with domesticity has less opportunity of learning how to be a political being than her husband who moves about in the world; and since it has been decided by the more advanced portions of humanity that a woman must be a man's political equal, we may be quite sure that domesticity will go the way of the purdah, the harem and the seraglio.

"But," people will say, "what of the human relationships? Marriage as an economic relationship is doomed to radical change, but still there will be mothers and children, husbands and wives." That is a statement both patently true and deeply deceptive. It is quite impossible to say what will happen in the future to human relationships, but we know from experience that when economic institutions change, emotional relationships change also. We know also that a very great deal of what has been said in the past about emotions has been dictated by purely selfish economic thought: men having forced women into an unfavourable position have convinced themselves and women also that this position is the best for them. In so far then as what Trotsky calls outside compulsion will cease to bind the relationships of the future, we may hope that those relationships will be based more and more upon inner compulsions, but to that we shall return later when we have examined certain other factors in the future.

Women in the future will then be free of the economic institution which was regarded by the last generation whether in our father's or in our own day as the only form of marriage which is permissible; capitalism and communism both seem to demand this by reason of their very nature. The historian must state this, though the man or woman may regret or applaud it. If the reader regrets it, he must remember that while Trotsky's idea of marriage and even the modern marriage in capitalistic states seem shocking to us, the average Spanish peasant is shocked by a young Englishman or a young American who does not consult his father in every detail of his daily life as a business man. The Spanish peasant is as often as not one of ten or more children and his family "complex" may be illustrated by an actual example. D. has had twenty sons and daughters all by the same mother, and of them fourteen are alive, and at the moment they range from nine years to thirty. One son is disowned for having run counter to the rather strict moral code of his milieu—your peasant is no libertine like his cousin of the towns;—three sons are of mature age and for each of them D. has a business. That is, D. is interested in wine, electricity and timber, and each of the three manages one of these under the direction of his father. The eldest son, S., a well-educated man of thirty, a first-rate amateur violinist who reads French and a little English and paints moderately well in oils and has incidentally a cultured wife, asks D.'s advice on every point and his permission to leave the village for a week-end; he lives in the adjoining house and shares the family garage. Since three businesses are the limit of D.'s capacity, the next two sons are both destined for the church, one as a priest and one as a monk. All the daughters live at home except two who are married and two who are nuns. Last year one of the older sons was due to be conscripted, but as so often in modern Spain, the D.'s are all anti-Government in their sympathies and this son has gone into voluntary exile in France. This has enabled D. to shut down one of his three businesses, and once or twice a year the whole family goes to visit the exile. On the last occasion he, whom we shall call F., was found to have developed a certain French freedom in his relations with his women customers, and in the presence of his family he went so far as to touch a girl in a cheery greeting. The eldest brother S. rebuked him for behaving so in front of his father and mother and bade him keep his new habits until their backs were turned.

Now consider this family's outlook upon what we are already used to seeing in America and England; to them our habits are as reprehensible as Trotsky's ideas are to us, because they represent our sixteenth century and Trotsky perhaps represents our twenty-first. Our family bears little or no resemblance to theirs; we do not have twenty children or even ten, and on the other hand, we do not lose six by death; but though to us the moral lies in the last fact, to them we are shocking and gross and immoral to plan for a small number of children. Our sons leave the parental roof as soon as they go into business, and the Spanish peasant is horrified at the consequent lack of paternal influence; all our sons in his eyes are exiled to a dangerous France across the borders which are drawn in a close ring about the family home. In D.'s house there are also one or two stray aunts and other unattached relatives, an integral part of the family community, and, as we have said, the grown-up sons live next door after marriage, the grown-up daughters remain at home always waiting. Trotsky can find no innovations as deep as these—he stops short at communal laundries; it is we who have disintegrated the family community.

It is a curious thing, however, that nearly everyone believes that the family of today is the family of a hundred years ago, or even the family of the Old Testament. We are more influenced by what we read than by what we experience. We talk of its being against human nature for such things as families to change, and we assume that the man who says that they can and will change is inhuman and depraved. Yet let us remember, if we wish to understand the future history of women, that no institution is permanent, and that no argument is less likely to be sound than one based on the unchangingness of human nature.

1. We would call it contrary to human nature to expect our wives to tolerate the addition of a second wife to the household; yet polygamy has often been practised with the consent and support of women.

2. We would call it contrary to human nature to expect a man to leave his wife with her relatives and to visit her occasionally there, always being treated as a stranger and an outsider when he did so; yet such a marriage arrangement has often existed.

3. We would call it contrary to human nature to expect a mother to deliver up her children to a State Medical Board and to abide happily by their sentence of death or life, to have her maternal feelings crushed and her marital affairs supervised; yet Sparta succeeded in doing this for several hundred years.

4. We would call it contrary to human nature to expect several men to share one woman as their common wife; yet such a scheme works happily in Tibet and elsewhere to this day.

5. We would call it contrary to human nature for a whole community to practise the adoption of one another's children to such an extent that scarcely anyone has his own

children and nearly everyone someone else's; yet this is a fact in the Andaman Islands today.

In short, we have no reason to expect that the future will respect our ideas of what family relationships should be, seeing that these ideas are but a passing phase in the universal kaleidoscope of human nature. Men and women, parents and children, will always be tied together by bonds of emotion, but the forms which the expression of these emotions take at any time are conditioned by social convention and social necessity. Since the position and future of women depends very largely upon the character of the family group, we must ask ourselves honestly what industrial capitalism or its Russian alternative, Communism, is likely to do to that group; then we shall know something definite about our future history, seeing that an ounce of economic necessity is worth a ton of exemplary or cautionary tales.

§ 2. WE have constantly seen throughout this history of women that the right to work is absolutely essential to the happiness of women and that this right to work has been frequently denied to whole groups. Some people may find this second statement rather hard to believe at first sight, especially as in America and throughout most of the highly industrialized world this right is not only admitted, but the virtue has been made a necessity. Yet there has been for a very long time a leisured class to whom work was neither a necessity, nor a possibility, the leisured class with white soft

hands to whom work was degrading, the class of Jane
Austen's drawing-rooms still to be found in no small number in Mayfair, and its equivalents all over the world. Let
us read a paragraph where the consequence of this has been
put with extreme force and not a little heat:

"On the one hand women are reduced to the lowest stage of degradation, but on the other they have dominion. 'Ah you wish us to
be merely objects of sensuality! Very well! As objects of sensuality
we will enslave you,' say women. Woman's emancipation does not lie
in obtaining the vote or being made a judge but in obtaining sexual
equality with men: having the right to have a man or refrain from
having him at her wish, and to choose a man, and not be chosen. You
say that is abominable? Very well! Then do not let men have such
rights. At present women are deprived of these rights, which men
possess. And to make up for that, she acts on men's sensuality, and
through his sensuality subdues him in such a way that he retains only
the formal right of choice, while in reality she chooses. And having
once mastered that weapon, she abuses it, and obtains a terrible power
over men."

"But where is this special power?" asked I.

"Where is her power! Everywhere and in everything! Go past the
shops in any large town. The amount of labour there stored is beyond
compute—uncounted millions; but see whether in nine-tenths of those
shops there is anything for men's use? All the luxury of life is wanted
and kept up by women. Count up all the factories. An immense part
of them produce useless ornaments, vehicles, furniture and trifles, for
women. Millions of people, generations of toilers, perish, working like
galley-slaves in the factories, only to satisfy her caprice. Women, like
queens, hold nine-tenths of the human race in slavery and hard-
labour. And all because women have been degraded and deprived
of their equal right! So they revenge themselves by acting on our
sensuality, and snaring us in their net. Yes, it all comes to that."

These words were written by Tolstoi at a time when increasing deposits of calcium salts had intellectualized rather than cooled his passions; but when we have allowed for all Tolstoi's faults and the tortuous extravagance of his Russian soul, there is a most important challenge contained in the residue; and the great distaste which some of his ideas must arouse in us, is no excuse for not examining it.

We have seen the growth, especially during the eighteenth century, of that myth The Female Character; stripped of its frills its sole object was to please men and to avoid anything which might "harden" the woman, any work intellectual or manual which might weight down with mundane contacts the ethereal nothingness of her complacent character. This is in short parasitism. Tolstoi saw quite clearly that a Jane Austen drawing-room involved the enslavement of a large portion of the human race; he saw through the incredible fallacy that waste is good for trade, that luxury trades are creators of labour, and that therefore the luxurious parasitical female who does nothing but look attractive is a benefactor to the workers because they get paid for her extravagances. He saw that the art of being attractive absorbs more labour than the building of a trans-continental railway and that the needs of a society woman are far greater than those of a first-rate engineer. It is therefore no exaggeration to say that women in their task of being attractive enslave the world, for they force it to work at what they require.

Now if we return to America what do we find happening among the women of that wealthy but not necessarily happy land? We want to know the answer to this since we can perhaps catch a glimpse of the future through its keyhole. What is the relation of women to work in America today? We find the following interesting groups:

I. A group of women who work to help balance the family budget and who have exchanged domestic slavery for economic slavery.

II. A group of women who work partly to balance the family budget, and partly to make possible an increased standard of living. These are more fortunate than the first group and can claim to have gained not perhaps economic independence, but certainly the power of economic cooperation.

III. A group of women who remain domesticated in the old sense of the word and offer little new light to our problems of the future.

IV. A group of women who are complete parasites: that is, who do no productive labour, at all, however busy they may be with activities useful or otherwise.

Of these four groups the second and the fourth are most typical of American life today, that is, though they are probably a minority of the population, they provide the significant form of women's life in their community. The first group, that of most working women, cannot honestly be claimed as a product of emancipation, although a certain type of feminist continually does so: like child-labour it is the product of the industrial revolution: the working women are become machines, like their husbands, owing to no kind of ethical progress but owing to economic pressure. If we look away from America to its antithesis, what do we find in Russian communism that is indicative of the future of this class? It is to be stereotyped and exalted by "instituting the industrial equality of men and women in the factories, the mills, and the trade unions, in such a way that the men should not put the women to disadvantage." If we consult Buharin, whose A.B.C. of Communism is the guide to practical and theoretical matters in Russia and elsewhere wherever Russia is to be imitated, we find two and a half pages devoted to the equality and freedom of both sexes. It is clear from these that women are to be freed from domesticity in the way we have already seen in Trotsky's words, in order to compete or to cooperate on equal terms with men in the labour market. In short under communism sex distinction will disappear in industry, women who were forced into industry by the rapacity of industrialism, will be helped to remain there as a natural right. Our first group will remain in the future and its problems cease to be part of the history of women and merge into the general history of humanity.

The third group is to be found chiefly outside the great centres of population, where life is still linked up with peasant culture, less changed by the forces of industrialism.

As these last become more and more powerful, less women will be able to remain domesticated, for just as peasant industry cannot compete in the same community with factory industry, so the family where the unit of breadwinning is the father, cannot compete for long in the same community with families where the unit of breadwinning is the family as a whole. The last domesticated women will be those who live on farms and contribute work, though not wages, as their share of the family income by producing eggs, milk, butter, bacon and the rest. Even here the status of women must decline, for country life cannot compete with town life in its emotional attractions and the more active women will flee from country domesticity to the anti-domestic atmosphere of the crowded places. Thus, just as the women in the first group will remain as they are, but will have their positions secured, so the women in the third group will become fewer and duller; and for the same reason, because domesticity stands in the way of industrialism. Men have long ago had to realize that women prefer the tyranny of the factory to the tyranny of the home, and they regard the first as the lesser of two drudgeries and that no amount of sentiment can prevent the march of economic events.

But it is the other two groups which we shall find most instructive, seeing that their problems and significance are new. Let us first consider the women who work partly to balance the family budget and partly to make possible an increased standard of living.

What is the motive force behind their desire to work?

Quite clearly it is the quest for emotional freedom, in particular for a freer sex life. The average worker in office or shop aims at a state of existence in which she can see more of men and can see men more intimately: make her spend her earning within the old family circle or make her contribute the whole of her earnings to the family budget and she will soon cease to glory in economic emancipation. These tendencies are bound to increase and nobody but a few sentimentalists will be able to keep their eyes closed to them much longer; quite soon the logic of events and the inexorable hand of death will scatter from the world the heads which are as yet busily shaking at the immorality of the younger generation, and the vacant minds which still attribute these symptoms to the decline of religion, the movies, prohibition, the cheap motor car, when the real cause is economic emancipation. The old feminists expected that this emancipation would destroy the dual standard of morality by making it unnecessary for women to wait about to catch their man. Men therefore, they thought, would have to behave themselves better in order to gain favour; but they reckoned without their daughters, who have done away with the dual standard well enough, but not by demanding Galahads so much as by themselves becoming Aspasias.

Moreover the final drama in this emotional emancipation is being enacted in our time. After all, though men have been enemies of women, though they invented the Female Character, they have had a ready ally in Nature itself. By decreeing that the result of a free emotional life should be negligible and momentary for a man, but permanent and devastating for a woman, nature made all talk of equality between the sexes laughable. The opposition to the making public of that knowledge which saves women from the penalty of undesired motherhood is the last and bitterest battle waged by man to keep woman in subjection. Men know that so long as women are under the sentence which nature decreed for them, all talk about emotional freedom is innocuous; and since men have a terror beyond all others of what would happen to their vested interests should this last security fail them, we see a battle of the sexes and one sex with its back to the wall fighting the thing which will devastate the whole structure of the Female Character.

The historian who glances at the future may regret that the family is disappearing, that women are demanding what men have always taken, that the control of maternity is setting women for the first time on a level with men; but he cannot pretend that it is otherwise.

And there is another certainty upon the horizon. It is implicit in the nature of the fourth class of women, those who are economically complete parasites. We have seen what happens to parasites, how their nature degenerates and becomes despicable and we know also that what is biologically true is as true socially. Parasites whether as a class or as a sex suffer a change and a change for the worse. And yet, if we look into the future of the parasitical class of modern American women, we are forced to see a different probability for their future. In ancient Greece the parasitical class of male citizens, doing no productive labour, and shifting the responsibility for making the earth yield her increase on to slaves, built up a culture which has dominated later history. In modern America the group of parasite women have turned the scales; their men are willing slaves, who do the work of the world and provide their wives with the means for cultured idleness: what will come of this?

In the first place American men subjected to the discipline of present business methods must become, as a group, less and less interested in life, and more and more absorbed in making a living. They will become more mechanical and less imaginative, more absorbed in things and less in people. Already they have reached the stage where another interest excels their interest in women, and in this they resemble the knights of chivalry, whom we saw preferring horses and war to women, for they prefer cars and commerce to them. Just as war bored women with men in feudal days, so business is boring them with men in modern America; and just as troubadours came into vogue as a relief from knights in armour, so writers, lecturers and poets have their vogue today as a relief from men in offices.

Finding themselves therefore amply provided with the means to do what they like and finding also that their own sex is better educated, more alive emotionally and imaginatively than the other, what will American women do? They will continue the process of deintellectualizing men until these become convenient robots, they will patronize and dominate the arts and literature and reorganize social institutions to suit themselves. They will discover new human relationships and a new attitude of individual towards individual; and at a no distant date instead of the phrase "a woman's place is her home," we shall hear repeated interminably and idiotically the words "a man's place is his office." Finally there will be discovered and elaborated a strange concept, the Male Character, and the male human animal will find himself hidden and forgotten beneath an artificial creation embodying all the traits which render him most convenient to his wife. Nothing can stop this process unless a means can be found to prevent any woman being educated and to render birth-control a forgotten aberration of ancient history; for once both sexes use their reasons equally, and have no unequal penalty awaiting the exercise of their emotions, then women cannot fail to dominate. Theirs is the stronger sex once nature and art cease their cruel combination against them, because it possesses a greater singleness of purpose and a greater fund of imagination, for those are the two properties which all men must forfeit under the institutions and necessities of our industrial civilizations. Seeing that, as Chaucer said, women seem to desire domination, and seeing that few men are happy until they get someone else to take over from them their will and their liberty of action; perhaps the world will be happier in the new régime. But all this is of only partial value as speculation on the future; for men and women are purely relative terms, and long before the tendencies of our times work to their logical conclusions, men and women, as we know them, will have ceased to exist; and human nature will have forgotten the "he and she." According to our own personal feelings we may regret that we shall not live to see that time, or congratulate ourselves on living at a time which antedates it.

THE END